THE NEW TEEN TITANS

VOLUME
ONE

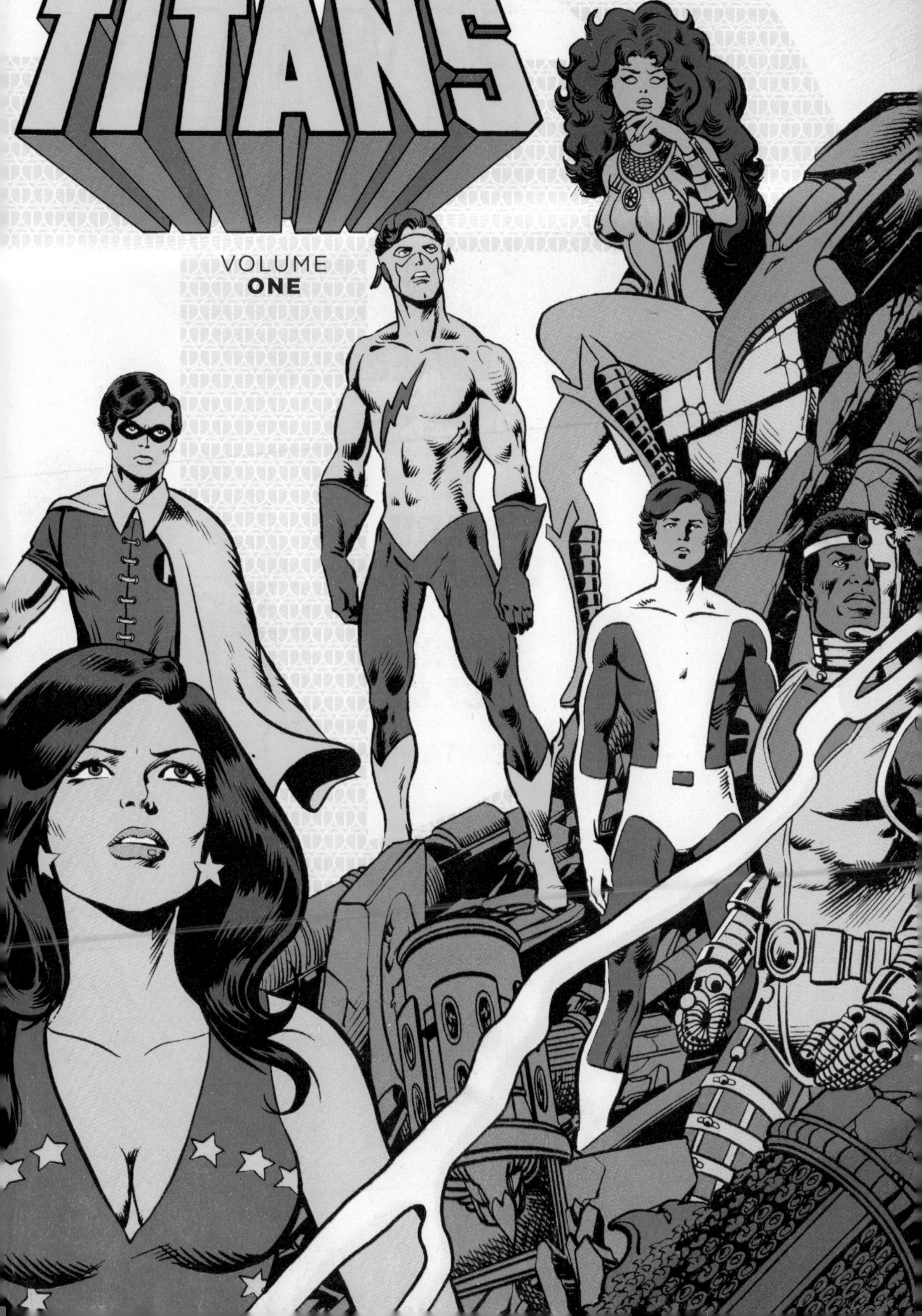

THE NEW TEEN TITANS

VOLUME ONE

WRITTEN BY
MARV WOLFMAN

ART BY
GEORGE PÉREZ
and
ROMEO **TANGHAL**

WITH
DICK **GIORDANO**
FRANK **CHIARAMONTE**
CURT **SWAN**
PABLO **MARCOS**

COVER ART BY
GEORGE **PÉREZ** and DICK **GIORDANO**

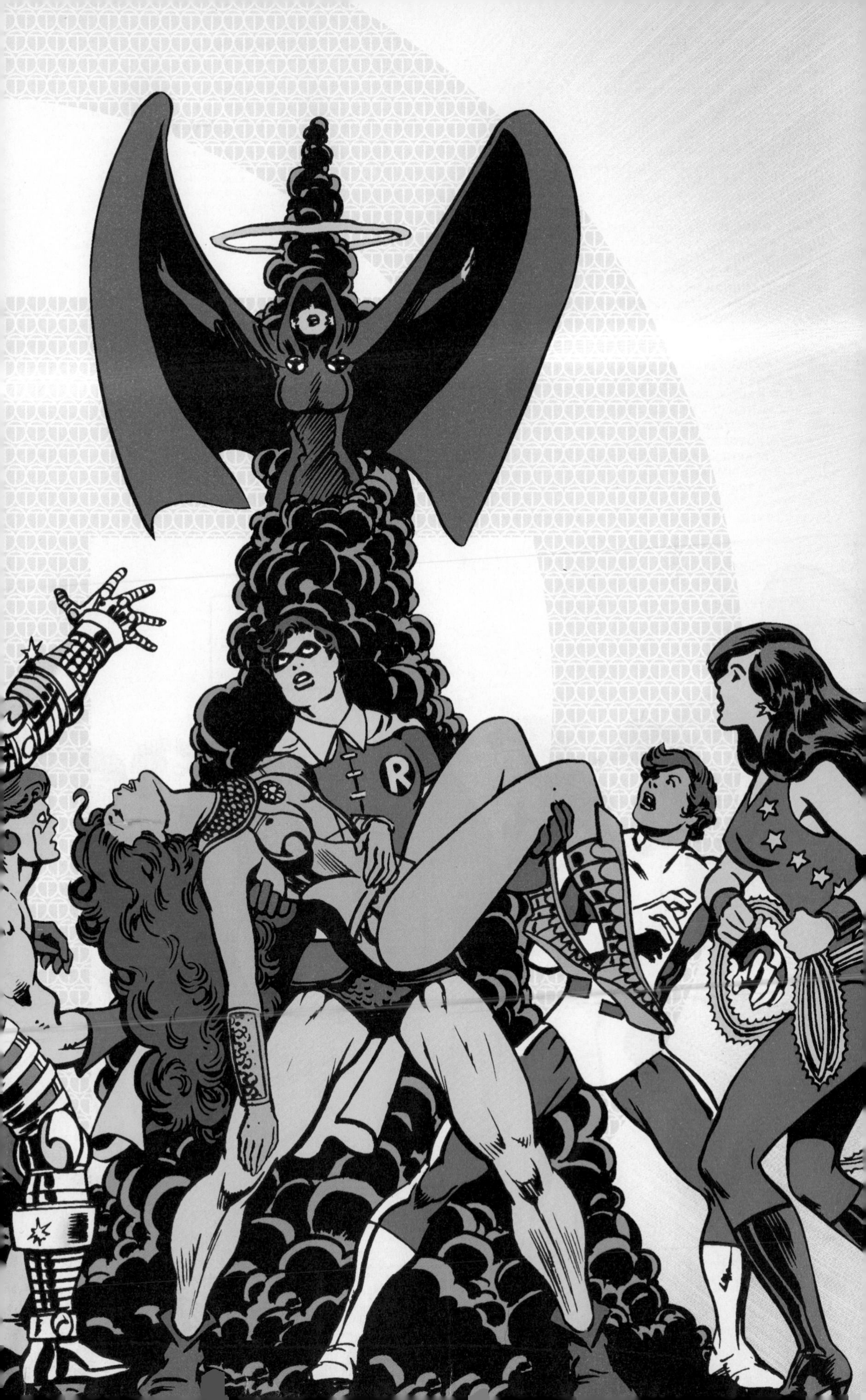

LEN **WEIN** Editor – Original Series
JEB **WOODARD** Group Editor – Collected Editions
SCOTT **NYBAKKEN** Editor – Collected Edition
STEVE **COOK** Design Director – Books
CURTIS **KING JR.** Publication Design

BOB **HARRAS** Senior VP – Editor-in-Chief, DC Comics

DIANE **NELSON** President
DAN **DIDIO** and JIM **LEE** Co-Publishers
GEOFF **JOHNS** Chief Creative Officer
AMIT **DESAI** Senior VP – Marketing & Global Franchise
Management
NAIRI **GARDINER** Senior VP – Finance
SAM **ADES** VP – Digital Marketing
BOBBIE **CHASE** VP – Talent Development
MARK **CHIARELLO** Senior VP – Art, Design & Collected Editions
JOHN **CUNNINGHAM** VP – Content Strategy
ANNE **DEPIES** VP – Strategy Planning & Reporting
LAWRENCE **GANEM** VP – Editorial Administration & Talent
Relations
ALISON **GILL** Senior VP – Manufacturing & Operations
HANK **KANALZ** Senior VP – Editorial Strategy & Administration
JAY **KOGAN** VP – Legal Affairs
DEREK **MADDALENA** Senior VP – Sales & Business Development
JACK **MAHAN** VP – Business Affairs
NICK **NAPOLITANO** VP – Manufacturing Administration
CAROL **ROEDER** VP – Marketing
EDDIE **SCANNELL** VP – Mass Account & Digital Sales
COURTNEY **SIMMONS** Senior VP – Publicity & Communications
JIM (SKI) **SOKOLOWSKI** Senior VP – Comic Book Specialty &
Newsstand Sales
SANDY **YI** Senior VP – Global Franchise Management

Cover color and interior color
reconstruction by TOM **MCCRAW**
THE NEW TEEN TITANS VOLUME ONE
Published by DC Comics. Copyright © 2014 DC Comics.
All Rights Reserved. Introduction Copyright © 1999 DC Comics. All
Rights Reserved. Originally published in single magazine form in
DC COMICS PRESENTS 26, THE NEW TEEN TITANS 1-8, THE NEW
TEEN TITANS ANNUAL 1 and TALES OF THE NEW TEEN TITANS 1-4.
Copyright © 1980, 1981, 1982 DC Comics.
All Rights Reserved. All characters, their distinctive likenesses and
related elements featured in this publication are trademarks of
DC Comics. The stories, characters and incidents featured in this
publication are entirely fictional. DC Comics does not read or accept
unsolicited submissions of ideas, stories or artwork.

DC Comics, 2900 W. Alameda Avenue, Burbank, CA 91505
Printed by RR Donnelley, Owensville, MO, USA. 2/19/16. Third Printing.
ISBN: 978-1-4012-5143-7

Library of Congress Cataloging-in-Publication Data

Wolfman, Marv.
  The new Teen Titans. Volume one / written by Marv Wolfman ; art by George
Pérez and Romeo Tanghal.
     pages cm
  Contents: Introduction -- Where nightmares begin! from DC Comics presents
#26 (October 1980) -- The birth of the Titans! from the New Teen Titans #1
(November 1980) -- Today...the Terminator! from the The New Teen Titans #2
(December 1980) -- The fearsome five from the New Teen Titans #3 (January
1981) -- Against all friends! from the New Teen Titans #4 (February 1981) --
Trigon Lives! from the New Teen Titans #5 (March 1981) -- Last kill! from the New
Teen Titans #6 (April 1981) -- Assault on Titans' tower from the New Teen Titans
#7 (May 1981) -- A day in the lives from the New Teen Titans #8 (June 1981) --
Teen heartthrobs.

ISBN 978-1-4012-5143-7 (paperback)

1. Graphic novels. I. Pérez, George, 1954- II. Tanghal, Romeo. III. Title.

741.5'973--dc23

2015297016

All stories by MARV WOLFMAN,
all cover art and story pencils by GEORGE PÉREZ,
and all story inks by ROMEO TANGHAL, except where noted.

INTRODUCTION

In the Batman story that appeared in the April, 1940 issue of DETECTIVE COMICS, National Comics (now DC Comics) introduced Robin, the Boy Wonder, the first of what would be a long line of super-hero sidekicks. The common wisdom at the time was that a young sidekick would appeal more to comic book readers than the adult parental-figure hero because readers would be better able to identify with someone their own age.

Garbage!

As a kid reader I hated kid sidekicks. How on Earth could I, a slightly overweight, non-sports enthusiast comic book reader identify with some super-hero kid doing triple-flips on a high beam all the while spouting quick witticisms? I was the sidekick's age; I knew I could never be him. On the other hand, the adult hero was something I could, in my most insane fan delusion, aspire to become.

Also, if truth be told, I hated the way kid heroes were drawn, which was short. Very short. Munchkin short. The DC kids: Robin, Kid Flash, Aqualad, Speedy, etc. all seemed to rise up to slightly above waist-high on the hero. So, as adults they'd be what? Four foot two? Yeah, I'd be really afraid of them.

Furthermore, the kids didn't act like me or my friends. They used outdated slang that no self-

respecting real kid used. Heck, most of my friends barely used slang at all. The sidekicks were also respectful of all elders. Let's not even begin to go there. Sometimes I wondered if Robin had to ask Batman's permission to go to the little hero's room.

I felt, I truly believed, that if I ever got the chance to write teenage characters I'd at least try to make them appear as close to what I felt like as a teen as I could. They would be real people first and super-heroes second. They would also be completely responsible for themselves. Why should super-heroes with powers and abilities far beyond those of mortal men have to answer to adult mentors? Not on my watch.

In the very late 1960s, shortly after we became semi-professional comic book writers, Len Wein, my best friend and fellow writer, and I got the chance to write an issue of DC's sidekick comic, THE TEEN TITANS. Though our ideas at the time outstripped our talent, we were determined to make these teen heroes act the same way we and our friends acted.

During the 1970s, I moved to Marvel Comics where I wrote and edited on a number of titles, including *Tomb of Dracula*, *The Man Called Nova*, *The Fantastic Four* and *Spider-Man*. I also was assigned Marvel Two-In-One, a team-up comic featuring the Fantastic Four's Thing character and some other Marvel hero.

Now, if I didn't like teen heroes, I absolutely hated writing team-up books. My forte, I believed, was developing characters, not writing one-shot adventures, and team-up books were all about solo stories. In 1980, when I decided to make the switch from Marvel to DC, I asked DC not to assign me to any team-up titles.

So naturally my first two DC assignments were THE BRAVE AND THE BOLD and WORLD'S FINEST, both single-story team-up books.

I knew the only way to get off these assignments was to come up with new titles to write. Because I had enjoyed working on the Titans, I asked if there would be interest in reviving the long-deceased series. The answer

was no. The Powers That Be believed readers were so turned off by what had gone on during the previous incarnations of the title that they would never buy a new version.

Not the kind who ever took no for an answer, I began to come up with some new ideas. Rather than just redo the book, we would create a few new characters even as we juiced up some of our favorite old Titans.

I'm often asked how we came up with the New Titans. The answer is both simple and very complex. It is my belief that the best characters have strong, traumatic origins that you can constantly revisit and find new wrinkles to play with. Superman's origin echoed the biblical story of Moses. Doomed to die, an infant was sent by his parents on a journey to another land where he grew up to become a great hero. Batman watched as his parents died. Spider-Man let a burglar kill his favorite uncle and from that day on, his guilt motivated him to combat crime. These heroes were born of tragedy, and the trauma that created them continued to motivate them throughout their adventures. Psychologically speaking, we are what we were.

The New Titans would be created in the same way, and their origins would control their later actions. Starfire was an alien princess whose weak-willed father, Myand'r (meander) sold her into slavery in order to save his planet from destruction. Raven's mother was an Earth woman raped by an interdimensional demon. In order to save Vic Stone's life, his father had to turn his son into a living cyborg.

Are you sensing another pattern? The Titans' origins all stemmed from parent/child differences. The theme for the Titans began and remained young versus old. Son and daughter versus father and mother. These universal conflicts, understood by all teens as they grow up and separate from their parents, could be revisited time and time again. I believe that they gave the Titans a depth of character that had not, up to that time, been often seen in comics.

There was more. I believed that the Titans themselves needed to be emotionally at odds with each other even while they needed to be friends. To facilitate this I set up two theoretical triangles: one for the male characters, one for the females. For example, put Wonder Girl at the top of the women's triangle. Donna Troy came from an Amazon race who believed not only in peace but were also warriors. On one corner of the triangle put Raven, whose interdimensional society were extreme pacifists who would never fight, not even to save their lives. On the other corner put in Starfire, who comes from a pure warrior culture. Three sides of the same coin, so to speak, with enough in common that they could be friends, but with enough differences to keep them at odds. This fundamental conflict, one hoped, would create good stories.

Also take a look at them emotionally: Raven was shy and introverted and found it difficult to confide in others. Starfire was outgoing and pure lusty emotion. Wonder Girl, once again, was directly in the middle.

The same kind of triangle was created for the guys. Robin, later Nightwing, was the level-headed and capable leader who, because he was kept on a tight leash by Batman, often felt inadequate for the task at hand. He also had a need to prove himself to Batman. Because everyone in his life had died on him, Changeling believed he had very little to offer anyone and covered it up with an outward bravado. Cyborg was a logical scientist type who rejected that approach to become an angry young man. Nightwing's logical approach to life and anger toward his "parent" was shared by Cyborg while his feelings of inadequacy were shared by Changeling. Cyborg and Changeling had also been physically altered by their parents, and that helped bring them together.

The characters were created so that they would play off each other, but they were still only words on paper. They needed to have real life breathed into them. That happened when George Pérez came onto the scene.

I'd known George at Marvel and liked him. We'd fought early on when I was an editor and he was a newbie artist, but as time went on, we became friends. George specialized in drawing group comics: *The Avengers, The Fantastic Four*, et cetera. The more characters the merrier. George was also one of the very best storytellers among the younger artists. He would be the perfect artist to bring the Titans to life.

Like Starfire and Raven, George and I are similar but opposites. George is outgoing and gregarious while I'm rather quiet and introverted. Still, like our characters, we somehow clicked. I saw George up at Marvel one day and asked if he'd be interested in working on the new Titans comic. George was looking for something new to draw and figured that the Titans would only last a few issues, but it could be fun to draw.

You see, in 1980 DC was having a tough time selling comics. Most new books were cancelled after only six issues, so it wasn't that farfetched to believe the Titans would be a fun ride for a few months before once again going off into comic-book limbo.

Armed with George as artist and Len Wein as editor, Len and I met with the Powers That Be and verbally pitched the new Titans idea. We talked about how this would be like no other Titans comic. It would be powerful. It would be fun. Who knows, it might even sell. We must have given a great pitch, because we not only got the Titans comic but were asked to do a 16-page story that would be inserted free into another title (DC COMICS PRESENTS #26).

George got started designing the characters. To say his designs were absolutely spot-on perfect would be to diminish his accomplishment. He made Kory, Vic, Raven and the original old Titans — Robin, Kid Flash, Wonder Girl and Beast Boy (modified to Changeling) — into real people. I've said it before and I'll keep saying it: There is no better artist partner in comics than George. Ask anyone who has worked with him.

Before the first issue came out, when only the ads for the comic were starting to appear, we received a ton of mail complaining about these new Titans. Who were these characters? Get them out of the book! Bring back Gnaark, the caveman Titan. After issue one came out, the very same readers wrote back swearing allegiance to the NEW Titans. George and I were ecstatic. THE NEW TEEN TITANS #1 sold through the roof. They liked us. They really liked us. But we still didn't think the book would last.

Issue one sold well. Issue two didn't sell as well. Three sold even poorer. Four worse. Five was in the dumper. Six... well, with six we beat out the sales of issue number one and we never stopped climbing.

Note: To those of you who cancel comics with their second or third issue before they have a chance to find their audience, think about this.

The Titans became a surprise hit. George stayed on the book for almost five years, then he returned a few years later for another short run. I remained as writer for over sixteen years, which must be a record of some sort. But, at last, I ran out of stories I needed to tell, and sales started to decline, so I asked DC to let me off the book. We agreed to cancel THE NEW TEEN TITANS with my last issue.

I am very proud that I've been able to co-create so many characters that have resonated with so many readers, and I hope that George and my Titans will be around for many generations of readers to come. It's almost 19 years later as I write this, and although there are more than a few of the nearly 250 Titans stories I wrote that I wish had never been printed, I still deeply love these characters. Here's hoping you feel the same.

— **MARV WOLFMAN**
November 7, 1998

SPECIAL TEEN TITANS PREVIEW

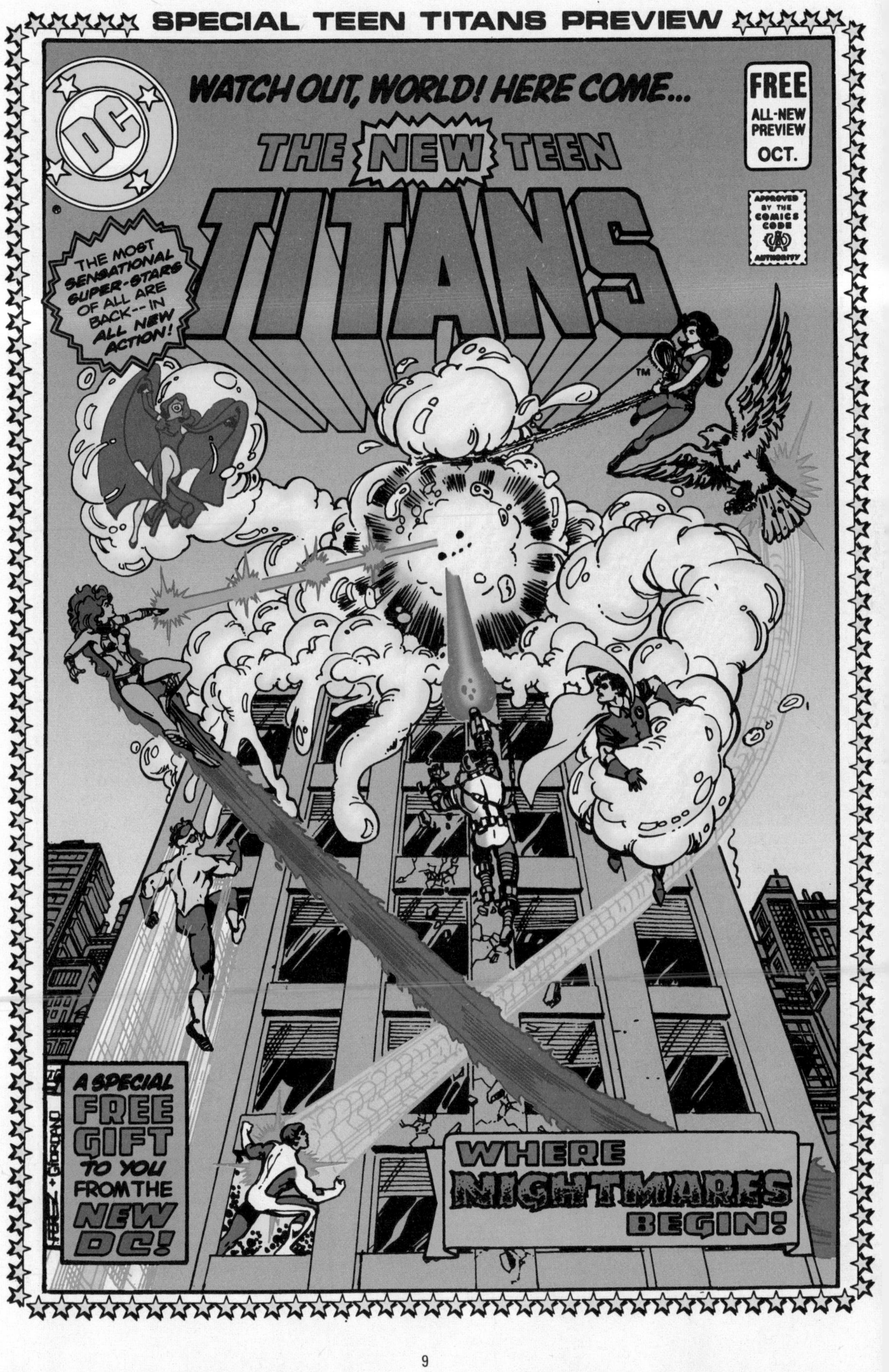

WATCH OUT, WORLD! HERE COME...
THE NEW TEEN TITANS
FREE ALL-NEW PREVIEW OCT.
APPROVED BY THE COMICS CODE AUTHORITY
THE MOST SENSATIONAL SUPER-STARS OF ALL ARE BACK--IN ALL NEW ACTION!
A SPECIAL FREE GIFT TO YOU FROM THE NEW DC!
WHERE NIGHTMARES BEGIN!

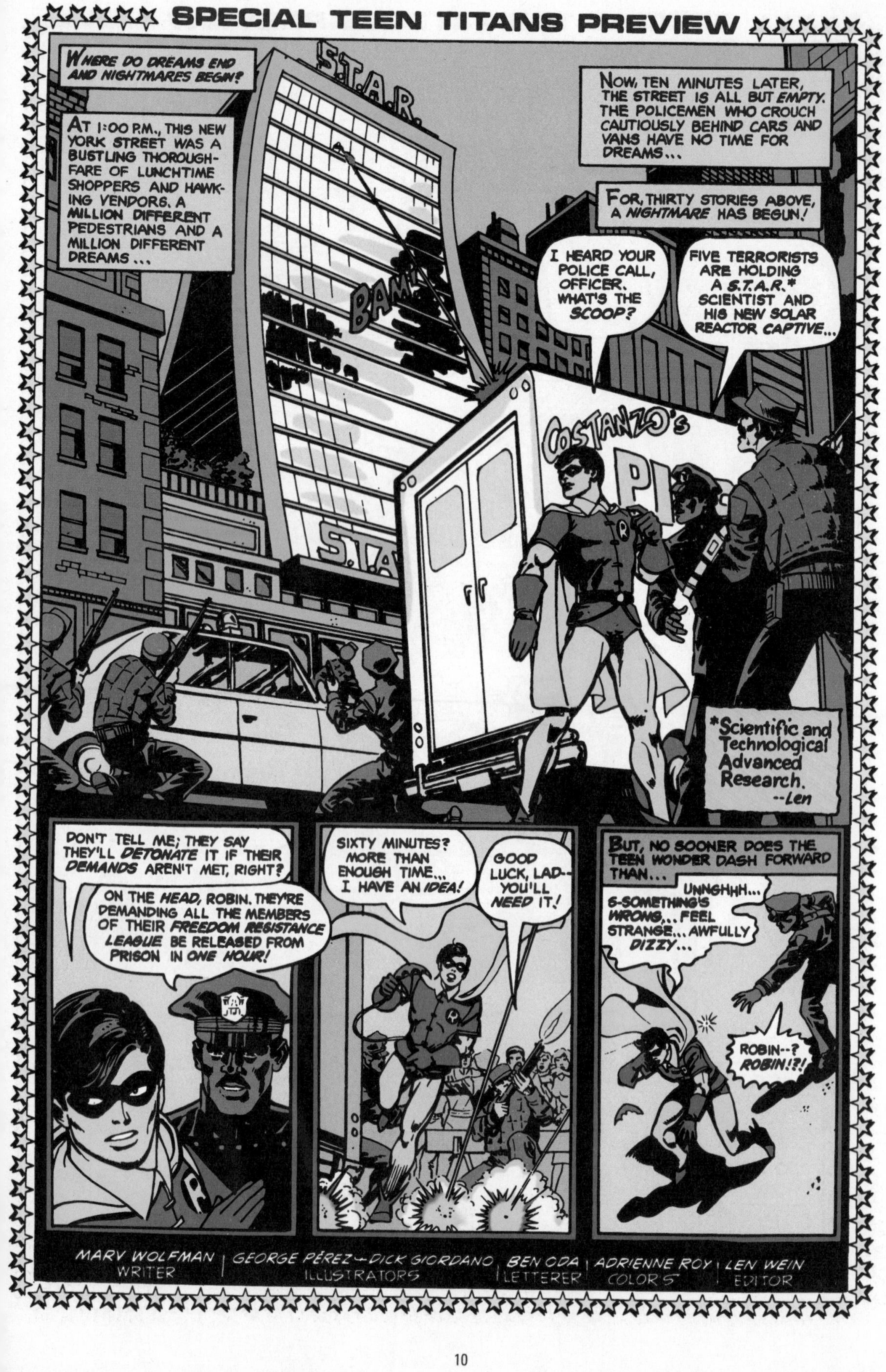
SPECIAL TEEN TITANS PREVIEW
WHERE DO DREAMS END AND NIGHTMARES BEGIN?
AT 1:00 P.M., THIS NEW YORK STREET WAS A BUSTLING THOROUGHFARE OF LUNCHTIME SHOPPERS AND HAWKING VENDORS, A MILLION DIFFERENT PEDESTRIANS AND A MILLION DIFFERENT DREAMS...
S.T.A.R.
BAM!
NOW, TEN MINUTES LATER, THE STREET IS ALL BUT EMPTY. THE POLICEMEN WHO CROUCH CAUTIOUSLY BEHIND CARS AND VANS HAVE NO TIME FOR DREAMS...
FOR, THIRTY STORIES ABOVE, A NIGHTMARE HAS BEGUN!
I HEARD YOUR POLICE CALL, OFFICER. WHAT'S THE SCOOP?
FIVE TERRORISTS ARE HOLDING A S.T.A.R.* SCIENTIST AND HIS NEW SOLAR REACTOR CAPTIVE...
COSTANZO'S
*Scientific and Technological Advanced Research. --Len
DON'T TELL ME; THEY SAY THEY'LL DETONATE IT IF THEIR DEMANDS AREN'T MET, RIGHT?
ON THE HEAD, ROBIN. THEY'RE DEMANDING ALL THE MEMBERS OF THEIR FREEDOM RESISTANCE LEAGUE BE RELEASED FROM PRISON IN ONE HOUR!
SIXTY MINUTES? MORE THAN ENOUGH TIME... I HAVE AN IDEA!
GOOD LUCK, LAD-- YOU'LL NEED IT!
BUT, NO SOONER DOES THE TEEN WONDER DASH FORWARD THAN...
UNNGHHH... S-SOMETHING'S WRONG... FEEL STRANGE... AWFULLY DIZZY...
ROBIN--? ROBIN!?!
MARV WOLFMAN WRITER
GEORGE PÉREZ—DICK GIORDANO ILLUSTRATORS
BEN ODA LETTERER
ADRIENNE ROY COLORS
LEN WEIN EDITOR

ROBIN--? DIDN'T YOU *HEAR* ME? ARE YOU ALL RIGHT?

HUH? THAT *VOICE*--?!?

YOU?

WONDER *GIRL?* WHERE DID *YOU* COME FROM?

STOP FOOLING AROUND, ROB, WE'LL BE LATE FOR THE *TITANS* MEETING.

TITANS? WHAT ARE YOU *TALKING* ABOUT? WHAT ABOUT THE TERROR-- HUH?

EVERYTHING'S *GONE*-- WHERE DID *S.T.A.R. LABS* DISAPPEAR TO?

YOU SURE YOU'RE *OKAY?* YOU LOOKED SORT OF *DIZZY* THERE FOR A SECOND.

AND THE DAY YOU DON'T RECOGNIZE *TITANS' TOWER*...

TITANS! WHAT? I--I'VE NEVER BEEN HERE BEFORE IN MY LIFE!

YOU SHOULD BE SO *LUCKY,* ROBBIE!

SAY, WHO'S THE JERK WHO CALLED THIS LITTLE *SHINDIG* TOGETHER ANYWAY?

I HAD THE CUTEST *STEWARDESS* READY AND RARIN' TO GO--

--THEN THE STUPID *TITANS* ALARM HADDA GO AND *RUIN* EVERYTHING!

I TELL YA, ROBBIE--THERE'S JUST NO *JUSTICE* IN THIS WORLD!

2

I'M ALMOST AFRAID TO *ASK*--BUT IS THAT *YOU*, BEAST BOY?

YOU SHOULD'VE CALLED YOURSELF *THE JERK!* IT FITS YOU *BETTER.!*

WHAT'S *WITH* YOU, *BATBOY?* YOUR *SHORTS* TOO TIGHT OR SOMETHING?

ROBBIE'S PLAYING *GAMES,* CYBORG. HE'S PRETENDING HE DOESN'T *REMEMBER* US.

IN *YOUR* CASE, THAT'S PROBABLY JUST *WISH FULFILLMENT!*

BEAST BOY? YOU BURN OUT YOUR *BRAINS?* YOU KNOW I'M NOW CALLED *THE CHANGELING!*

WH-WHO ARE YOU?

DON'T LET THEM *BOTHER* YOU, ROBIN. I STILL *LOVE* YOU!

THIS PLANET WOULD STILL SEEM *STRANGE* TO ME IF IT WEREN'T FOR YOU!

A *GOLDEN GIRL!* WHO--?

YOU DON'T *REMEMBER STARFIRE?* MAN, YOU *DEFINITELY* GOT A LOOSE SCREW!

STARFIRE? CYBORG? A *NEW* TITANS? *NONE* OF THIS MAKES *SENSE.*

THE TITANS *DISBANDED* MONTHS AGO! THE ONLY ONES HERE I *KNOW* ARE *WONDER GIRL* AND *BEAST BOY!*

LOOK, IT'S *CHANGELING!* DO I HAFTA PAINT IT ON MY *FOREHEAD?*

BEAST BOY WAS *NOWHERE! CHANGELING* HAS GOT *STYLE!* RHYTHM! *PIZZAZZ!*

KRIK!

HOPE I'M NOT *TOO LATE,* GUYS. I WAS IN THE MIDDLE OF A SCHOOL TEST!

KID FLASH? THANK *GOODNESS!* SOMEONE *ELSE* I *KNOW!*

MAYBE *YOU* CAN TELL ME WHAT'S GOING ON.

WHAT DO YOU MEAN, ROBIN?

ROBBIE'S GONE *BANANAS,* FLASHER.

S-SOMETHING MUST BE *WRONG* WITH ME...

IT'S AS IF I'VE *BLACKED OUT* PART OF MY *LIFE!*

③

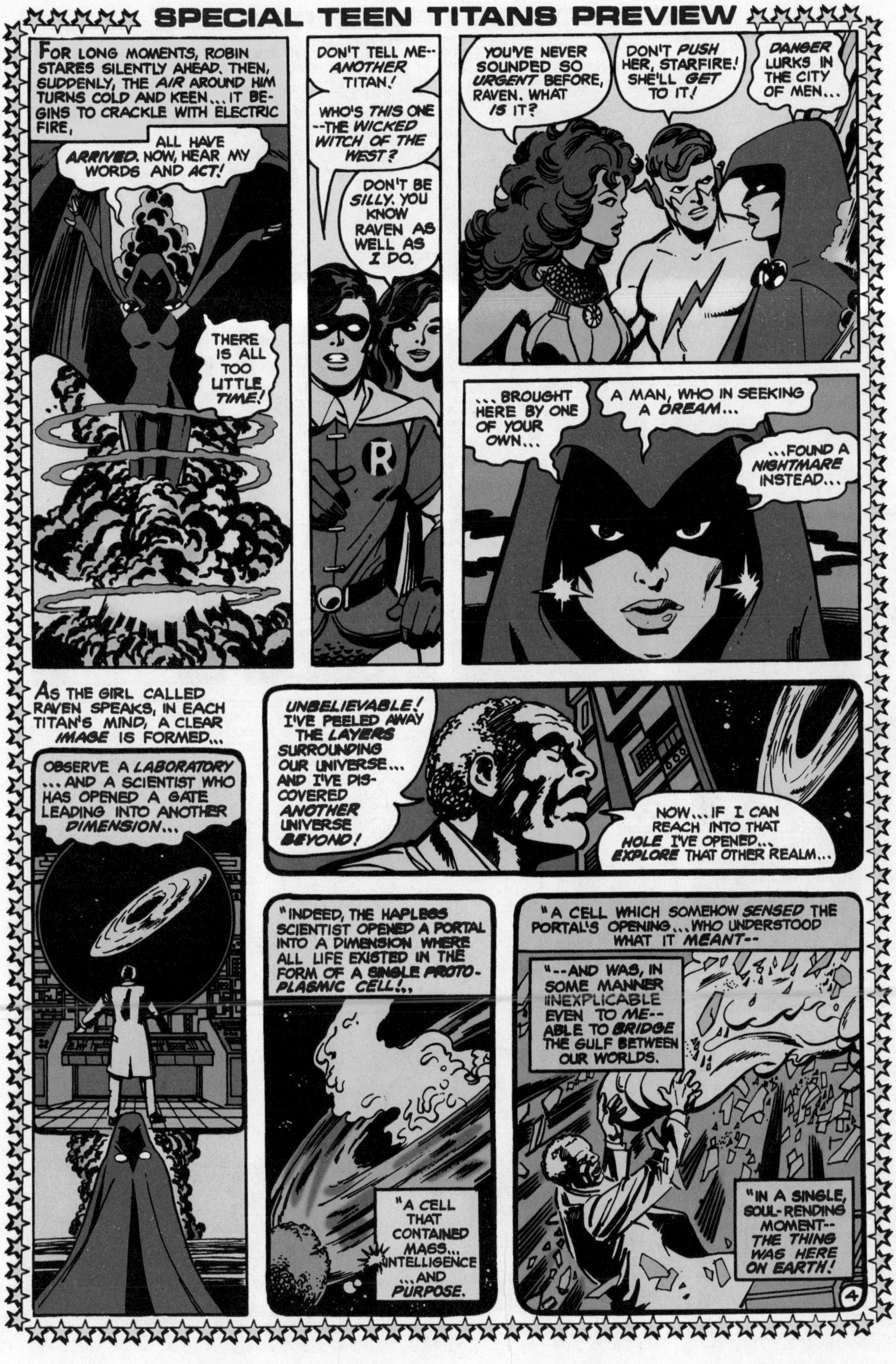
SPECIAL TEEN TITANS PREVIEW
FOR LONG MOMENTS, ROBIN STARES SILENTLY AHEAD. THEN, SUDDENLY, THE AIR AROUND HIM TURNS COLD AND KEEN... IT BEGINS TO CRACKLE WITH ELECTRIC FIRE.
ALL HAVE ARRIVED. NOW, HEAR MY WORDS AND ACT!
THERE IS ALL TOO LITTLE TIME!
DON'T TELL ME-- ANOTHER TITAN!
WHO'S THIS ONE --THE WICKED WITCH OF THE WEST?
DON'T BE SILLY. YOU KNOW RAVEN AS WELL AS I DO.
YOU'VE NEVER SOUNDED SO URGENT BEFORE, RAVEN. WHAT IS IT?
DON'T PUSH HER, STARFIRE! SHE'LL GET TO IT!
DANGER LURKS IN THE CITY OF MEN...
... BROUGHT HERE BY ONE OF YOUR OWN...
A MAN, WHO IN SEEKING A DREAM...
...FOUND A NIGHTMARE INSTEAD...
AS THE GIRL CALLED RAVEN SPEAKS, IN EACH TITAN'S MIND, A CLEAR IMAGE IS FORMED...
OBSERVE A LABORATORY ... AND A SCIENTIST WHO HAS OPENED A GATE LEADING INTO ANOTHER DIMENSION...
UNBELIEVABLE! I'VE PEELED AWAY THE LAYERS SURROUNDING OUR UNIVERSE... AND I'VE DISCOVERED ANOTHER UNIVERSE BEYOND!
NOW... IF I CAN REACH INTO THAT HOLE I'VE OPENED... EXPLORE THAT OTHER REALM...
"INDEED, THE HAPLESS SCIENTIST OPENED A PORTAL INTO A DIMENSION WHERE ALL LIFE EXISTED IN THE FORM OF A SINGLE PROTOPLASMIC CELL!...
"A CELL THAT CONTAINED MASS... INTELLIGENCE ...AND PURPOSE.
"A CELL WHICH SOMEHOW SENSED THE PORTAL'S OPENING... WHO UNDERSTOOD WHAT IT MEANT--
"--AND WAS, IN SOME MANNER INEXPLICABLE EVEN TO ME-- ABLE TO BRIDGE THE GULF BETWEEN OUR WORLDS.
"IN A SINGLE, SOUL-RENDING MOMENT-- THE THING WAS HERE ON EARTH!
4

IT MUST BE *RETURNED* TO ITS DIMENSION IMMEDIATELY!

FOR, IN ORDER TO *SURVIVE* HERE ON EARTH, IT IS ALTERING OUR *ATMOSPHERE* --FROM OXYGEN TO METHANE!

METHANE? THAT'LL KILL *EVERYONE!*

CAN WE *STOP* IT?

PROBABLY *NOT!* BUT WHAT'S OUR *ALTERNATIVE?*

LET'S *GO!*

NOT BEFORE I GIVE THE TITANS' *RALLYING CRY!*

I'VE BEEN *THREATENING* TO COME UP WITH ONE-- NOW I *WILL!*

UP, UP AND -- *NAH!* SUPES WOULD HAVE OUR *HIDES!*

HOWZABOUT-- *TITANS ASSEMBLE.!?!*

NOPE! THAT'S BEEN *USED!*

FORGET IT! I'LL COME UP WITH ONE SOME *OTHER* TIME!

IN THE MEANTIME-- *TITANS*--LET 'ER *RIP!*

HURRY! THERE IS STILL *TIME!*

AND WE CANNOT AFFORD ANOTHER MOMENT'S *DELAY!*

DON'T WORRY, ROBIN. I'LL *CARRY* YOU AS ALWAYS!

I STILL DON'T *UNDER-STAND...*

BUT, IF THERE'S *TROUBLE*-- NOTHING IS GOING TO STOP ME FROM *HELPING!!*

*S*IX TEENAGERS RACE FROM THEIR ISLAND HEADQUARTERS IN THE MIDDLE OF NEW YORK'S EAST RIVER--

5

--AND, LESS THAN TWO MINUTES LATER, FIND THEM-SELVES CAUGHT IN THE THROES OF A *NIGHTMARE* COME TO LIFE...

GREAT HERA! IT'S LIKE NOTHING I'VE EVER SEEN BEFORE.

HOLY HANKIES! RAVEN WAS *RIGHT*!

IF THAT ISN'T A *YEECHOID* FROM OUTER SPACE, I'M *JIMMY CARTER*!

AIN'T NOTHIN' WE CAN DO AGAINST SOMETHING LIKE *THAT*!

THEN, WHAT ARE YOU *WAITING* FOR, STARFIRE-- GO TO IT!

NOT *TRUE*, CYBORG--ONE OF MY *STARBOLTS* SHOULD BE QUITE EFFECTIVE!

NO ONE ATTACKS UNTIL I HAVE INVESTIGATED!

RAVEN--? YOU'RE GOING TO USE YOUR *ASTRAL FORM*--?

CORRECT, MY *ALIEN* FRIEND-- MY *SOUL SELF* SHALL SEEK OUT OUR FOE'S WEAKNESSES.

NOW-- STAND BACK AND BE SILENT!

RAVEN'S LITHE BODY IS *STILL* AS AN EBONY AURA RISES FROM HER VERY *SOUL*...

LIKE A DARK BIRD OF PREY, HER ASTRAL IMAGE SOARS SKYWARD, *CONTROLLED* BY RAVEN'S GRIM THOUGHTS...

IT CIRCLES THE PROTOPLASMIC CELL WHICH SUDDENLY *REACTS* TO ITS PRESENCE--

--BY UNLEASHING AN ALL-ENCOMPASSING *TENDRIL* THAT GRABS THE SOUL IMAGE AND HOLDS IT *FIRM*!

RAVEN? RAVEN!?! MY GOD-- IT'S *GOT* HER!

6

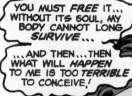

AND, THIRTY STORIES BELOW, A VELVETEEN-CLAD WOMAN SLUMPS WEAKLY TO THE GROUND...

WHAT *IS* IT, RAVEN? ARE YOU *ALL RIGHT?*

YOU MUST *FREE* IT... WITHOUT ITS SOUL, MY BODY CANNOT LONG *SURVIVE*...

...AND THEN...THEN WHAT WILL *HAPPEN* TO ME IS TOO *TERRIBLE* TO CONCEIVE!

...MY SOUL *CAPTURED*... CANNOT *ESCAPE*... HURRY...

I DON'T KNOW *HOW* BUT, SO HELP ME, RAVEN--

--ONE WAY OR ANOTHER I WILL *SAVE* YOU...

...OR *DIE* IN THE TRYING!

INCREDIBLE! IT'S ABSORBING MY STARBOLTS! THAT'S NEVER *HAPPENED* BEFORE!

MAYBE *YOU* CAN'T STOP IT, STARRY--BUT I STILL GOT MY OWN *BAGS OF TRICKS!*

AN' ONE OF 'EM SHOULD KNOCK THAT JELLO-REJECT RIGHT BACK WHERE IT *CAME FROM!*

ONE TITAN HOVERS ON THE VERGE OF DEATH. *FOUR OTHERS* CLOSE IN TO ATTACK, BUT, WHAT OF *ROBIN...?*

ONE MOMENT I'M GOING AFTER *TERRORISTS,* THE NEXT I'M TAKING ON A SPECIAL EFFECT FROM *THE EMPIRE STRIKES BACK!*

WHEN THIS IS *OVER* WITH, I WANT *ANSWERS*--

--AND I'LL *GET* THEM EVEN IF I HAVE TO TAKE ALL THOSE OTHER TITANS *APART!*

HUH? SUDDENLY... MY HEAD... *POUNDING...* GETTING *DIZZY...*

EVERYTHING GOING... *BLACK...*

HUH? WHAT HAPPENED? WHERE AM--?

ROBIN?

YOU WERE STUMBLING... RIGHT INTO THE PATH OF A *BULLET.* I HAD TO KNOCK YOU DOWN!

...KNOCK ME DOWN... I'M BACK IN *NEW YORK?*

SWEET HEAVEN... WHAT *HAPPENED* TO ME?

7

THERE'RE NO TEEN TITANS... NO CYBORG, OR RAVEN, OR STARFIRE...

IT MUST ALL HAVE BEEN SOME SORT OF BAD DREAM! BUT IT'S OVER NOW...

...I'M BACK TO REALITY, FACING THOSE TERRORISTS--

--AND USING MY NEW ROCKET GRAPPLER...

"...SHOULD GET ME UP TO THE S.T.A.R. LABS' ROOF!"

I FEEL BETTER ALREADY. JUST KNOWING I'M GOING UP AGAINST REAL FLESH-AND-BLOOD THUGS RATHER THAN SOME INTERSTELLAR BLOB!

STILL, I WISH I KNEW WHY I BLACKED OUT LIKE THAT! THERE'S NOTHING PHYSICALLY WRONG WITH ME--

--THOUGH I WONDER IF MY RECENT PROBLEMS WITH BRUCE MIGHT HAVE SOMETHING TO DO WITH IT!

EVER SINCE I DROPPED OUT OF COLLEGE, THERE'S BEEN A STORM BREWING BETWEEN US!

HE STILL THINKS OF ME AS HIS KID PARTNER AND NOT SOMEONE OLD ENOUGH TO GO OUT ON HIS OWN.

WELL, I CAN PROVE I'M READY... AND I WILL IF-- EH?

OH, NO--EVERYTHING STARTING TO SPIN...

...GETTING DIZZY, JUST LIKE BEFORE... JUST LIKE...

KRASH!

BUT HOW? HOW?

IT'S THE PROTOPLASM-- LASHING OUT AT ME!

OH, MY LORD!

8

C'MON, GANG-- *MOVE IT!* THAT BLOB IS STILL HOLDING *RAVEN!*

WE'VE GOT TO *SAVE* HER BEFORE IT'S *TOO LATE!*

WE ALL KNOW HOW YOU *FEEL,* KID FLASH-- BUT THAT THING JUST *SHAKES OFF* WHATEVER WE THROW AT IT!

NOT EVEN MY *GOLDEN LASSO* CAN HOLD IT! IT JUST OOZES RIGHT *THROUGH!*

SUDDENLY...

GREAT HERA! ELECTRICITY COURSING UP THROUGH THE *LASSO--!*

STOP IT, STARFIRE! IT'S SHOOTING *YOUR* BEAMS BACK AT *ME!*

ZKRAKK!

WELL, LOOKS LIKE IT'S UP TO *ME* TO SAVE THE DAY!

IF I'M NOT BACK IN THIRTY MINUTES, WOULD SOMEBODY PLEASE SEND OUT A *SEARCH PARTY?*

BEAST BOY... I MEAN, *CHANGELING*-- HE'S TURNED HIMSELF INTO A *BEAR!*

BUT, NO SOONER DOES THE SHAPE-SHIFTING TEEN *ENTER* THE PROTOPLASMIC BLOB THAN...

WHATEVER THAT THING IS-- IT'S FORCING HIM BACK INTO HIS *GAR LOGAN* FORM!

GET *BACK,* ALL'A YOU! I GOT THE ANSWER RIGHT *HERE!*

SOON'S I PLUG THESE *TRANSPONDERS* INTO MY ROBOT-SHELL--

--I'M GONNA *SHOW* THIS HUNK 'A GUNK WHAT IT'S LIKE TO FACE A GUY WHO'S HALF *MAN,* HALF *ROBOT*--

9

--AN' MAD AS ALL GET OUT!

YOU *WOUNDED* IT, CYBORG--! BUT *HOW?*

SKREAKKK!

TAPPED MY INTERNAL *POWER SUPPLY,* ROBBIE--SHOT A *ZILLION* DECIBELS OF WHITE SOUND RIGHT *THROUGH* IT!

ONLY I *CAN'T* KEEP IT UP MUCH *LONGER!* WE GOTTA DO SOMETHIN' TO FINISH IT OFF-- AN' *FAST!*

MEANWHILE, OUTSIDE...

CYBORG *WEAKENED* IT--IT'S UP TO US TO *COMPLETE* THE JOB! WE'VE GOT TO FREE *RAVEN!*

KID FLASH-- *DON'T!* DON'T YOU SEE IT STARTING TO *QUIVER?*

IT'S ABOUT TO--

SHWAMM

IT'S *ATTACKING* US--THROWING OFF ENDLESS WAVES OF ENERGY...

--TOO MUCH TO *ABSORB* INTO MY *OWN* SYSTEM!

BUT, AN INSTANT LATER...

HUH? WHERE DID IT *GO?*

WHO *CARES* WHERE IT WENT? RAVEN'S JUST *LYING* THERE... *UNCONSCIOUS!*

STARFIRE, I WISH I *KNEW!*

SHE MAY BE *DEAD...OR WORSE--!*

IF HER SOUL DOESN'T *RETURN* TO HER IN TIME...GOD ONLY KNOWS WHAT WILL HAPPEN TO HER *BODY!*

BUT ALL AT ONCE, *DARKNESS* SEEMS TO DRAPE THE MYSTERIOUS YOUNG WOMAN WHOSE *POWER* IS AS MUCH AN *ENIGMA* AS RAVEN IS HERSELF...

10

THEN, SUDDENLY SHE *RISES*, AND IN A VOICE AS CHILLING AS A DRIVING ARCTIC WIND...

WHY DO YOU *STAND* HERE? THE CREATURE HAS *ESCAPED* --

--AND WE MUST *FIND* IT WITHOUT DELAY!

RAVEN? RAVEN!

RAVEN'S *DISAPPEARED* AGAIN... AND KID FLASH LOOKS LIKE HE JUST *SWALLOWED* HIS LAST PIECE OF *GUM*!

BUT STILL, RAVEN IS *RIGHT*-- WE'VE GOT TO *FIND* THAT THING--AND I THINK I KNOW *WHERE*!

FLASHER'S A *JERK*! THAT WITCH IS EVEN *LESS* HUMAN THAN I AM!

YOU SURE YOU KNOW WHERE WE'RE *GOING*?

POSITIVE! WE *WOUNDED* THAT CREATURE! I'M BETTING HE'LL RETURN TO THE *LABORATORY* WHERE HE FIRST *APPEARED*!

S.T.A.R.? I HAD A *HUNCH* I WOULDN'T LIKE THIS!

SECONDS LATER, INSIDE THE *S.T.A.R.* LABS...

OBOY! YOU'RE NOT GOING TO *BELIEVE* THIS!

IT'S LIKE A *HURRICANE* TORE THROUGH THIS LAB! WHAT A *MESS*!

YOU'VE NEVER SEEN MY *ROOM* ON A *FRIDAY NIGHT*, HUH?

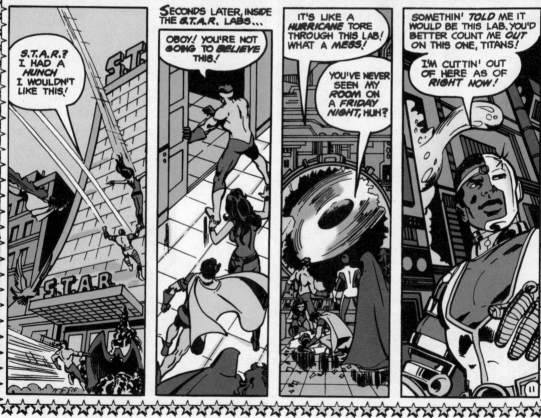

SOMETHIN' *TOLD* ME IT WOULD BE THIS LAB. YOU'D BETTER COUNT ME *OUT* ON THIS ONE, TITANS!

I'M CUTTIN' OUT OF HERE AS OF *RIGHT NOW*!

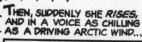

BUT, BEFORE THE OTHER TITANS CAN *RESPOND* TO CYBORG'S *STARTLING* STATEMENT...

UNGGHHH!

KRAK!

NO-- IT'S GOT *CYBORG!*

SUDDENLY, LIKE A WELL-OILED MACHINE, THE TITANS BLAST INTO ACTION...

CYBORG MUST HAVE *HURT* IT! MY STARBOLTS ARE MAKING IT CRY OUT IN *PAIN!*

SKREEEK!

ARGHH! IF THIS THING'S *WEAK,* I'D HATE TO SEE IT WHEN IT'S *WELL!*

SOMEONE! *ANYONE!* HELP ME!

THAT'S IT, GAR-- CHANGE INTO A *SNAKE--* SQUIRM OUT OF ITS *GRASP!*

B1OK!

FOOSH!

R-ROBIN...

Y-YOU CANNOT *DEFEAT* THE CREATURE THIS WAY ...I *BROUGHT* IT HERE. I *KNOW* HOW TO STOP IT!

THIS IS A *SEALED* LABORATORY... CREATURE MUST *RETURN* WHERE IT *CAME* FROM...

I *READ* YOU, PROFESSOR! WE'LL TAKE IT FROM *HERE!*

CLEAR OUT-- *FAST!*

WE'VE GOT TO PUMP THE *AIR* OUT OF THIS ROOM--*NOW!*

YOU GO--I'LL STAY *BEHIND!*

I DON'T NEED *OXYGEN* TO BREATHE-- AND YOU'LL NEED SOMEONE TO *FORCE* THIS THING BACK THROUGH THE *HOLE!*

BUT--?

TRUST ME, ROBIN--YOU KNOW I'M THE *ONLY* ONE OF US WHO CAN *DO* THIS!

NOW *MOVE* IT, TITANS--GO!!

IF EVERYONE IS OUT HERE-- WE CAN *SEAL* THE ROOM...

...DRAW OUT THE *OXYGEN...* AND THUS *PREVENT* THE CREATURE FROM CONVERTING IT INTO *METHANE!*

12

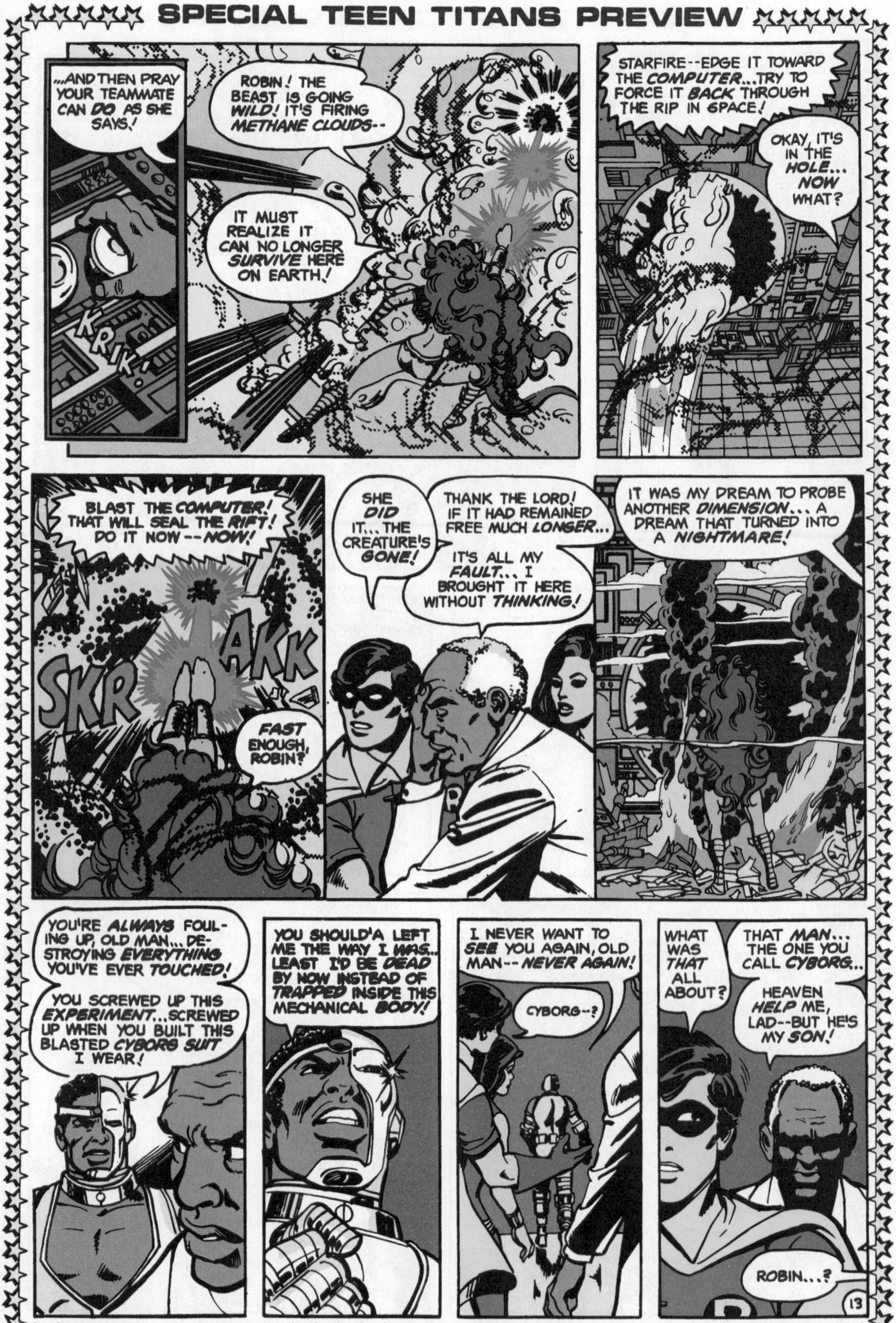
SPECIAL TEEN TITANS PREVIEW
...AND THEN PRAY YOUR TEAMMATE CAN DO AS SHE SAYS!
ROBIN! THE BEAST IS GOING WILD! IT'S FIRING METHANE CLOUDS--
IT MUST REALIZE IT CAN NO LONGER SURVIVE HERE ON EARTH!
KRIK!
STARFIRE--EDGE IT TOWARD THE COMPUTER...TRY TO FORCE IT BACK THROUGH THE RIP IN SPACE!
OKAY, IT'S IN THE HOLE... NOW WHAT?
BLAST THE COMPUTER! THAT WILL SEAL THE RIFT! DO IT NOW--NOW!
SKRAKK
FAST ENOUGH, ROBIN?
SHE DID IT... THE CREATURE'S GONE!
THANK THE LORD! IF IT HAD REMAINED FREE MUCH LONGER...
IT'S ALL MY FAULT... I BROUGHT IT HERE WITHOUT THINKING!
IT WAS MY DREAM TO PROBE ANOTHER DIMENSION... A DREAM THAT TURNED INTO A NIGHTMARE!
YOU'RE ALWAYS FOULING UP, OLD MAN... DESTROYING EVERYTHING YOU'VE EVER TOUCHED!
YOU SCREWED UP THIS EXPERIMENT...SCREWED UP WHEN YOU BUILT THIS BLASTED CYBORG SUIT I WEAR!
YOU SHOULD'A LEFT ME THE WAY I WAS... LEAST I'D BE DEAD BY NOW INSTEAD OF TRAPPED INSIDE THIS MECHANICAL BODY!
I NEVER WANT TO SEE YOU AGAIN, OLD MAN--NEVER AGAIN!
CYBORG--?
WHAT WAS THAT ALL ABOUT?
THAT MAN... THE ONE YOU CALL CYBORG...
HEAVEN HELP ME, LAD--BUT HE'S MY SON!
ROBIN...?
13

YOU *DID* IT, ROBIN!

HUH? NO! NOT *AGAIN!*

YOU KEPT MUTTERING SOMETHING ABOUT *PUMPING OUT THE AIR...*

AND NO SOONER DID WE *START--*

--THAN THOSE TERRORISTS WERE *PLEADING* WITH US TO LET THEM *SURRENDER!*

YOU SAVED THE *CITY...* WITHOUT OUR HAVING TO INJURE A SINGLE *PERSON!*

AND YOU SAVED *ME,* LAD...

YOU? BUT...

I'M *PROFESSOR STONE...* I INVENTED THE *SOLAR REACTOR* THEY WERE THREATENING TO *DYNAMITE!*

IT WAS MY DREAM TO MAKE THAT REACTOR THE NEW *POWER SOURCE* TO HELP HUMANITY--

--BUT THOSE VICIOUS MEN-- THEY *TOOK* MY DREAM... *CORRUPTED* IT...TURNED IT INTO A HORRIBLE ...TERRIBLE... *NIGHTMARE!*

SHORTLY...

I--I DON'T UNDERSTAND... *WAS* I HAVING NIGHTMARES?

BUT, IF I *WAS*-- HOW COULD THAT *SCIENTIST*-- A MAN I'VE *NEVER MET* BEFORE-- HAVE BEEN IN MY DREAMS? HOW?

I'VE GOT TO *SLEEP* ON THIS ONE--BUT I'M AFRAID THAT WHEN I *WAKE* UP...

...I'LL BE MORE IN THE *DARK* THAN I WAS *BEFORE!*

NO, ROBIN... VERY SOON ALL THAT YOU HAVE SEEN WILL MAKE *SENSE* TO YOU.

FOR THIS WAS NO *DREAM* THAT YOU HAVE EXPERIENCED... THE *NEW TEEN TITANS* ARE NO FIGMENT OF YOUR IMAGINATION!

INDEED, ROBIN-- THEY *EXIST,* THEY ARE YOUR *FUTURE*--

--A FUTURE THAT *LOOMS* EVER AND EVER *CLOSER!*

WE ASKED-- "WHERE DO *DREAMS* END AND *NIGHT-MARES* BEGIN?"

PERHAPS A *BETTER* QUESTION WOULD BE-- WHERE DO *NIGHTMARES* END AND *REALITY* BEGIN?

QUITE OBVIOUSLY--
THE BEGINNING!

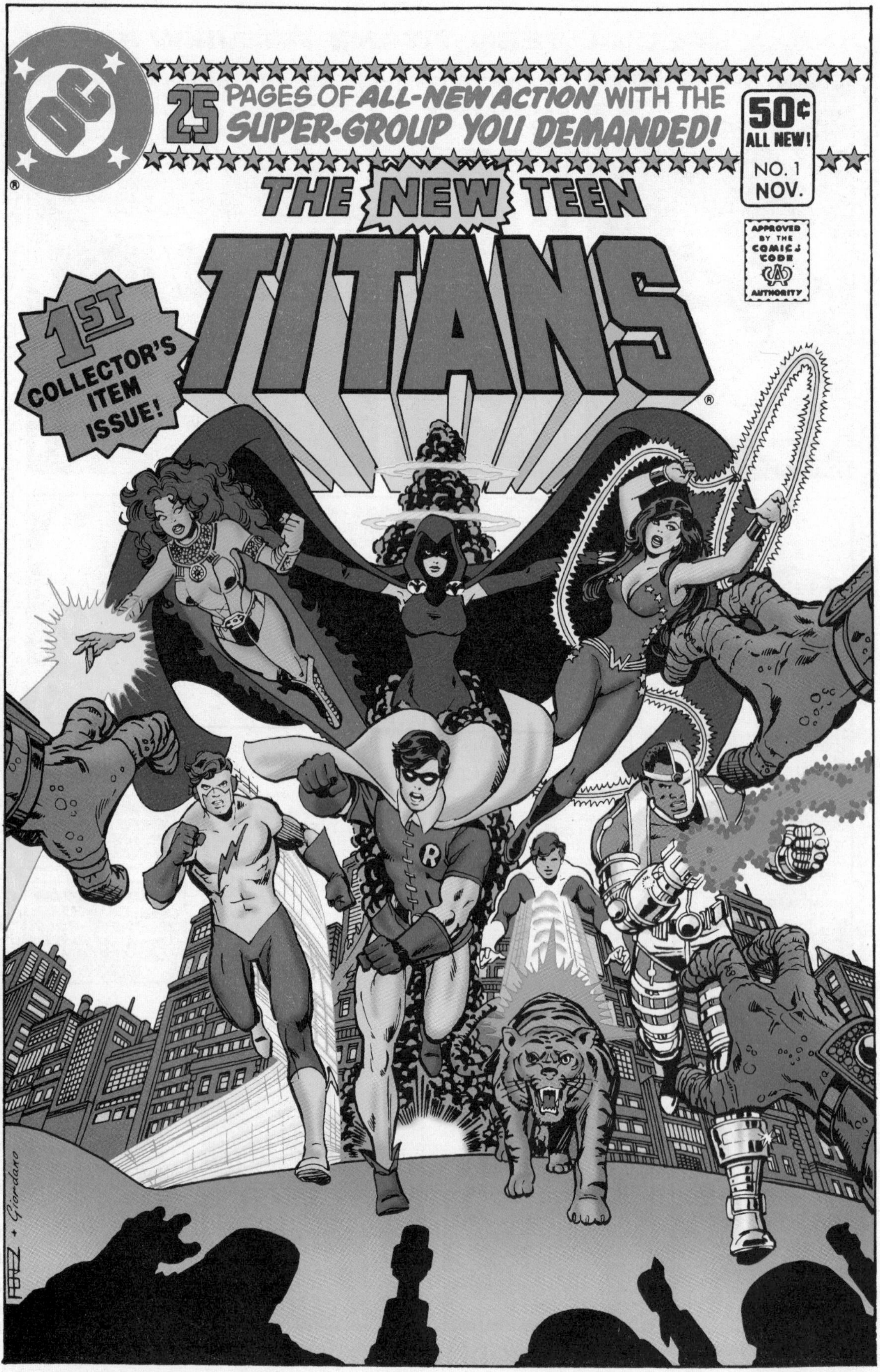
DC
25 PAGES OF ALL-NEW ACTION WITH THE
SUPER-GROUP YOU DEMANDED!
50¢
ALL NEW!
NO. 1
NOV.
THE NEW TEEN
TITANS
APPROVED BY THE COMICS CODE AUTHORITY
1ST COLLECTOR'S ITEM ISSUE!
PEREZ + Giordano

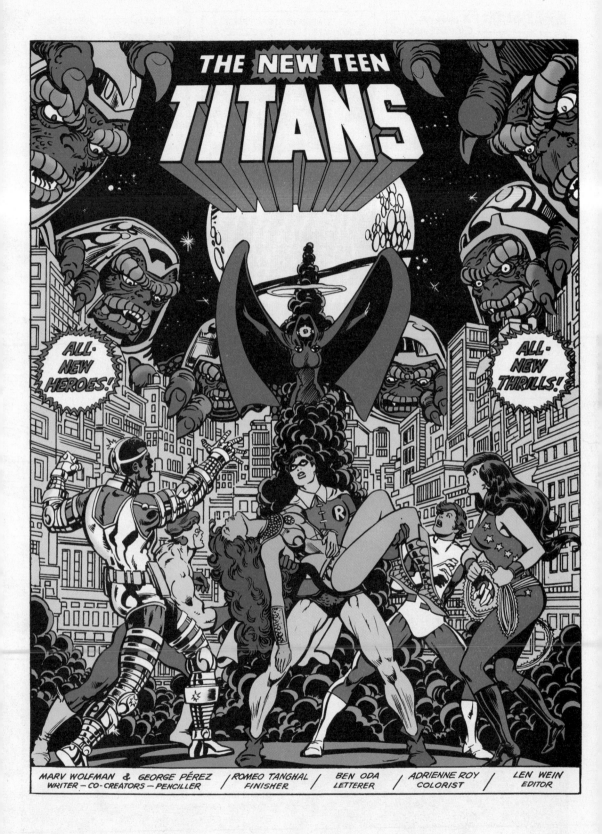

THE NEW TEEN TITANS

ALL-NEW HEROES!

ALL-NEW THRILLS!

MARV WOLFMAN & GEORGE PÉREZ
WRITER – CO-CREATORS – PENCILLER

ROMEO TANGHAL
FINISHER

BEN ODA
LETTERER

ADRIENNE ROY
COLORIST

LEN WEIN
EDITOR

EPILOGUE: A DARKLY-LIT CHAMBER ABOARD THE *SLAVE-SHIP Q'ST'R*...

〈OUT OF MY WAY, SLAVER!〉

〈I DON'T NEED *INTERFERENCE* NOW -- WHEN I'M SO CLOSE TO *ESCAPING!*〉

〈KORIAND'R..?〉 〈PRINCESS KORIAND'R TO YOU, GORDANIAN!〉

THE LITHE, GOLDEN GIRL FITS *COMFORTABLY* INTO THE *STAR-SLIDER*, HER SLIM HANDS EXPERTLY DARTING ACROSS THE COMPUTER CONSOLE...

FOR AN INSTANT THERE IS *NO RESPONSE*, THEN THE LOWER POD DOORS *OPEN*...

...THE SHIP SHUDDERS, QUIVERS, THEN DESCENDS AND LURCHES *FORWARD*...

‹TRAINED BY THE WARLORDS OF OKAARA, OR HAD YOU FORGOTTEN?›

SKREEEK!

KROK!

‹THE HANGAR DECK--›

‹--AND NO GUARD-DRONES?›

‹TROGAAR MUST BE SLIPPING IN HIS OLD AGE!›

‹A SHAME. I WAS HOPING MY STARBOLTS WOULD ELIMINATE A FEW MORE SLAVERS--›

‹--BUT I'LL HAVE TIME ENOUGH FOR THAT SOME OTHER DAY!›

‹THEY'VE LOCKED ON TO MY COORDINATES!›

‹NOW ONLY SOME LUCK AND X'HAL'S GOOD WISHES WILL GET ME THROUGH THIS MADNESS ALIVE!›

‹THANK X'HAL FOR MY PRECEPTOR'S TRAINING! OTHERWISE TROGAAR'S SHARPSHOOTERS WOULD HAVE CHALKED UP ANOTHER *KILL* BY NOW.!›

‹HMMM, THEY'RE CLOSING IN *FAST!* STILL, A SPACE-SLIDER SHOULD BE ABLE TO *OUTMANEUVER* ANY GORDANIAN *WARSHIP!*›

‹IF I CAN SLIP BEHIND HNYXX'S *MOON,* I SHOULD BE *LONG GONE* BEFORE THEY CAN BEGIN TO *ALTER* THEIR COURSE.›

NO!

‹TROGAAR MUST BE *DESPERATE* TO RECAPTURE ME! HE *DESTROYED* THE MOON RATHER THAN DETOUR AROUND IT!›

‹IT MUST BE *WORTH* MORE THAN I THOUGHT FOR HIM TO *DISINTEGRATE* A FORTRESS-MOON BELONGING TO THE *CITADEL!*›

‹WHICH IS GOOD TO KNOW.›

‹TROGAAR WANTS ME *ALIVE...* THAT MEANS THOSE *OTHER* SHOTS WERE MEANT AS *WARNINGS!*›

‹THEN THERE'S TIME TO ALIGN THE SHIP'S COMPUTERS FOR *PHASING ACTION!*›

‹I'M A BIT *NERVOUS.* NEVER HAD TO PREPARE FOR SPACE-SLIDING MYSELF --›

‹--BUT SINCE I DON'T SEEM TO HAVE ANY *CHOICE* --›

‹--LET'S GO DO IT!›

AND, IN LESS THAN A TWINKLING OF SOME FARAWAY STAR, PRINCESS KORIAND'R IS *GONE*...

4

THE *WAYNE FOUNDATION* IN MIDTOWN GOTHAM CITY...

N-N-NO--!

...THE *PROTOPLASM* ...LASHING OUT AT ME!

...THAT *BLOB* ...HOLDING *RAVEN!*

...GOT TO *SAVE* HER BEFORE IT'S *TOO LATE!*

B-BUT THAT THING JUST *SHAKES* OFF WHATEVER WE THROW AT IT!

...NOT AGAIN ...NO NEW TITANS... NO ...NO MORE... *NOOOOO--!*

OH, SWEET HEAVEN...THAT *NIGHTMARE* ...AGAIN.

EVERY NIGHT FOR A *WEEK,* THAT SAME HORRIBLE *DREAM...*

ALWAYS A NEW TITANS...FIGHTING THAT SAME AWFUL *MENACE...*

FOR PITY'S SAKE -- WHAT'S *HAPPENING* TO ME?

WHAT YOU HAVE *EXPERIENCED,* RICHARD GRAYSON, ARE HARDLY *NIGHTMARES!*

INDEED, THEY ARE MERELY *PREMONITIONS* OF *THINGS TO COME!*

YOU?

YOU'RE ONE OF THE GIRLS IN MY *DREAMS* ...THAT *WITCH* THEY CALL *RAVEN!*

HARDLY A *WITCH.* I AM YOUR *FRIEND...* AND I AM YOUR *FUTURE.*

THERE ARE *UNKNOWN* FORCES AT WORK... FORCES WHICH DEMAND THAT A *NEW TEEN TITANS* BE FORMED!

I INVADED YOUR *DREAMS* ONLY SO THAT YOU MAY COME TO *KNOW* ME...

...AND TO KNOW THAT WHEN, AT LAST, I *APPEARED* BEFORE YOU IT WAS TO SEEK YOUR *AID!*

5

I DON'T UNDERSTAND...

YET, YOU WILL STILL *BELIEVE* ME, RICHARD. YOU WILL *TRUST* ME.

AND YOU WILL *DO* AS I REQUEST.

TAKE THIS, SPEAK TO YOUR *FRIEND.* CONVINCE HIM TO *JOIN* OUR NEW TITANS.

SPEAK TO *WHO*? YOU JUST PICKED UP THE TELE--

HUH? *WALLY? WALLY WEST?* IS THAT *YOU*?

YOU OUGHTTA *KNOW,* ROBIN. IT'S *YOUR* DIME. WHAT'S UP?

I--I'M NOT *SURE*... BUT IT'S ABOUT THE *TEEN TITANS*...

SAY NO MORE, ROBIN... AND COUNT ME *OUT.* I'VE *QUIT* THE SUPER-HERO BIZ.

I HEARD *YOU* LEFT COLLEGE, BUT I'M STILL GOING... *FULL TIME!*

OKAY, WALLY. THANKS, *ANYWAY.*

YOU *HEARD* THE MAN. IT'S *NO GO.*

YOU DID ALL I *EXPECTED,* ROBIN. *I* WILL HANDLE *KID FLASH* NOW.

BUT *YOU* MUST FIND *WONDER GIRL.*

HEY! *WAITASEC!* I DON'T KNOW *WHERE* SHE--

NUTS! SHE DISAPPEARED!.

...JUST LIKE IN MY... *NIGHTMARE.*

FOR A LONG WHILE ROBIN SITS THINKING IN IN HIS ROOM, THEN, FINALLY...

SOMETHING *WRONG,* DICK? YOU'RE IN *COSTUME.* NEED ANY *HELP?*

HELP? NOT AT ALL, BRUCE.

THIS IS *ONE* THING I CAN HANDLE BY *MYSELF!*

6

BRUCE HAS BEEN *MAD* EVER SINCE I DROPPED OUT OF *COLLEGE*. HE STILL THINKS OF ME AS A *KID*.

WELL, THAT'S *HIS* HANG-UP. I *KNOW* WHAT I'M DOING.

MAYBE THIS NEW TITANS COMING UP RIGHT NOW IS A *GOOD IDEA*... I CAN *USE* A PLACE WHERE I CAN *PROVE MYSELF*--

EH--? THAT BLACK SHAPE... LIKE *RAVEN*. I--I REMEMBER THAT FROM MY NIGHTMARE.

SHE CALLED IT HER *SOUL-SELF*... AN *ASTRAL PROJECTION* OF SOME SORT...

IT'S *LEADING* ME SOME-WHERE... PROBABLY TO *WONDER GIRL*.

SHE STANDS *STARING* FOR A VERY LONG TIME --

--TRYING TO RECALL A *MEMORY* WHICH AT BEST WAS ALWAYS *VAGUE*...

UNTIL, AT LAST, SHE SUMMONS HER *COURAGE* -- AND CLEARS THE PATH BEFORE HER...

THIS OLD PLACE HASN'T BEEN *CLEANED* IN ALL THESE YEARS.

FIGURES! I GUESS THE OWNERS *ABANDONED* IT AFTER THE FIRE.

STILL, THIS IS WHERE *SHE* FOUND ME,

ALONE, FRIGHTENED, A CRYING BABE TOO SCARED TO *MOVE* WHILE THE *FLAMES* DANCED ALL AROUND ME...

...AND TOO *YOUNG* TO UNDERSTAND *WHY* THOSE TWO PEOPLE NEAR ME WOULDN'T *MOVE* AS THE FIRE DREW *CLOSER*...

7

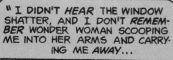

"I DIDN'T *HEAR* THE WINDOW SHATTER, AND I DON'T *REMEMBER* WONDER WOMAN SCOOPING ME INTO HER ARMS AND CARRYING ME *AWAY*...

"BUT I *DO* REMEMBER THAT THE *LANDLADY* SAID THE ROOM I WAS FOUND IN WASN'T EVEN *RENTED.*

"I WAS A *NOBODY,* UNTIL I WAS BROUGHT TO *PARADISE ISLAND* AND RAISED BY *HIPPOLYTA,* QUEEN OF THE *AMAZONS.*

"I WAS TRAINED AS AN AMAZON, GIVEN THEIR POWER, AND SOON I BECAME *WONDER GIRL*...

...AND I'M STILL WONDERING WHO I *REALLY* AM, WHO MY *PARENTS* WERE, WHO -- *EH?*

SOMEONE *BEHIND* ME!

INSTANTLY SHE SPINS, AS A SAVAGE *SNARL* CROSSES HER LIPS...

WONDER GIRL -- *HEY!*

ROBIN!?!

WHAT IN THE WORLD ARE *YOU* DOING HERE? CERTAINLY YOU CAN AFFORD A ROOM IN A *BETTER* PART OF TOWN!

CAN I *DROP DOWN* NOW, OR ARE YOU GOING TO *ATTACK* ME AGAIN?

DON'T BE *SILLY,* ROB. EH, ROB--

DID YOU BRING A *DOG* WITH YOU?

A DOG WITH *GREEN SKIN?*

NAH! I TOOK *MYSELF* OUT FOR A WALK.

R-ROBIN? WHAT'S *GOING ON?*

CAN'T YOU *GUESS,* BEAUTIFUL? IT'S THE ONE AND ONLY *CHANGELING,* LIVE AND IN PERSON!

BEAST BOY!?!

8

IF YOU TWO ARE PLAYING SOME KIND OF *JOKE* ON ME...

NOT *ME*, BEAUTIFUL. HECK, COMING HERE WASN'T EVEN *MY* IDEA.

AT LEAST I DON'T *THINK* IT WAS.

BY THE WAY, CALL ME *CHANGELING!* "BEAST BOY" WAS FOR THE *BIRDS.* ER...NO *OFFENSE*, ROBIN!

WONDER GIRL, I THINK I CAN *EXPLAIN* ALL THIS...

...BUT SOMETHING TELLS ME YOU'RE *NOT* GONNA BELIEVE IT. IT STARTED WITH THIS GIRL NAMED *RAVEN*...

RAVEN?

BUT, AS THE TEEN WONDER BEGINS HIS *EXPLANATION* OF SORTS...

ROBIN! WONDER GIRL! BEAST BOY! YOU'RE ALL *HERE* JUST LIKE RAVEN *SAID*.

KID FLASH?

I DON'T *UNDERSTAND.* I THOUGHT YOU WEREN'T *INTERESTED* IN THE TITANS ANYMORE.

I AM *NOW.* YOU BRIEF THE *OTHERS?*

THERE'S A *NEW* TEEN TITANS?

WHY *NOT?* THEY DON'T *LET* KID SUPER-HEROES INTO THE *Y.M.C.A.!*

WHERE *ELSE* ARE WE GONNA HANG OUT?

AFTER A HURRIED *EXPLANATION* IS MADE...

I TOLD RAVEN I'M *IN*.

THEN I GUESS, SO AM *I.* CHANGELING?

SURE, WHAT HAVE I GOT TO *LOSE*--?

--THAT IS, BESIDES MY *LIFE!*

FOUR TEENAGERS RACE FROM MIDTOWN MANHATTAN. EACH HAS REJOINED THE TITANS FOR A REASON OF HIS OWN...

...A REASON THAT, FOR *SOME*, MUST REMAIN *PRIVATE*, AT LEAST FOR *NOW*...

⑨

NEWARK CITY COLLEGE, NEW JERSEY...

REALLY WANNA SEE WHY I'M *TICKED OFF,* COACH?

LOOKIT, GOT 'ER SET AT *TWENTY-FIVE FEET!*

TWENTY-FIVE *FEET,* COACH. AN' I DON'T EVEN NEED A FLAMIN' *POLE!*

BELIEVE IT, MAN, TWENTY-FIVE FEET, STRAIGHT UP TO *HEAVEN*-- AN' I RAISE LESS SWEAT THAN *YOU* DO GOBBLIN' UP SOME *PEPPERONI PIZZA!*

WANT ME TO JUMP *THIRTY* FEET, COACH? HOW ABOUT *FORTY?* MAYBE A *HUNDRED* WILL CHANGE YOUR MIND?

PLEASE, VICTOR, DON'T *DO* THIS TO YOURSELF, YOU DON'T *BELONG* HERE ANYMORE!

HEY, MAN, I WORKED MY *TAIL* OFF FOR THIS. I SWEATED AN' TRAINED AN' THEN SWEATED SOME *MORE.*

I WAS *OLYMPIC MATERIAL,* COACH-- THE BEST ALL-AROUND ATHLETE YOU EVER HAD.

VICTOR, THAT WAS *BEFORE...*

BLAST IT, COACH-- I *KNOW* IT! BUT KNOWIN' IT DOESN'T MAKE IT ANY *BETTER!*

COACH

I *HATE* WHAT I'VE BECOME-- 'CAUSE IT *ROBBED* ME OF THE ONLY THING I EVER REALLY *WANTED!*

SPLANG!

I HATE BEIN' *HALF A MAN!*

10

ALL I EVER CARED ABOUT WAS *SPORTS.* YOU GOTTA LET ME ON THE *TEAM.* YOU *GOTTA...*

I'M *SORRY,* VICTOR. I TRULY AM *SORRY.*

COACH

SURE, YOU'RE *ALL* SORRY. *YOU,* 'CAUSE I'M A *ONE-MAN TEAM* ALL BY MY LONESOME...

MY *FATHER,* 'CAUSE HE TURNED ME INTO THIS... *FREAK.*

YOU SAID I DON'T *BELONG* HERE ANY-MORE, THEN WHERE IN BLAZES *DO* I BELONG?

WITH *ME,* VICTOR STONE, WITH OTHERS OF YOUR KIND.

HUH? WHAT ARE YOU *TALKIN'* ABOUT, LADY?

AN' HOW'D YOU GET *IN* HERE WITH-OUT ME *SEEIN'* YOU?

I KNOW ALL *ABOUT* YOU, VICTOR...

AND I CAN *HELP* YOU.

LADY, I AIN'T LIKE *NOTHIN'* YOU'VE EVER *SEEN* BEFORE.

LADY, I'M A *FREAK...* HALF MAN, HALF MACHINE... SOMETHING MY BIG-SHOT SCIENTIST FATHER CALLS--

--*CYBORG!*

HALF MY *FLESH* IS GONE, PATCHED UP WITH *PLASTICS.*

AN' MY *BONES,* THEY AREN'T *CALCIUM* -- NOW THEY'RE *UNSHATTERABLE MOLYBDENUM STEEL!*

35

HEY, WHO'S THE *STAR WARS* REJECT?

SO *THIS* IS WHAT YOU MEANT...

OTHERS JUST LIKE *ME*, HUH?

RAVEN, IS HE ANOTHER NEW *TITAN*?

HI, MY NAME'S--

I READ THE *PAPERS*, MISTER.

OKAY, LADY--I *BUY* IT. A FREAK *AMONG* FREAKS, RIGHT?

OH, BROTHER--

--WE'VE GOT OURSELVES A *WINNER!*

MUZZLE THE GREEN JERK AND I'M *IN!*

RAVEN, I THINK--

WAIT! I AM RECEIVING THE PSYCHIC WAVES OF OUR *FINAL* TITAN...

SHE HAS ARRIVED ON *EARTH*...

BUT HER *PURSUERS* ARE CLOSE BEHIND...

WE MUST *HURRY*, MY FRIENDS, WE MUST *FIND* OUR FINAL MEMBER BEFORE SHE IS *SLAIN*.

"SHE"? IS IT TOO LATE TO PRAY THAT SHE'S *STACKED*?

YOU HAVEN'T *CHANGED*, GAR, YOU'RE *STILL* AN INSUFFERABLE *CHAUVINIST!*

BETTER *BELIEVE* IT, BEAUTIFUL, AND AN *OINK* RIGHT BACK AT'CHA!

YOU SAY WE'RE *NEEDED*?

INDEED, VICTOR STONE-- AT THE *UNITED NATIONS PLAZA!*

12

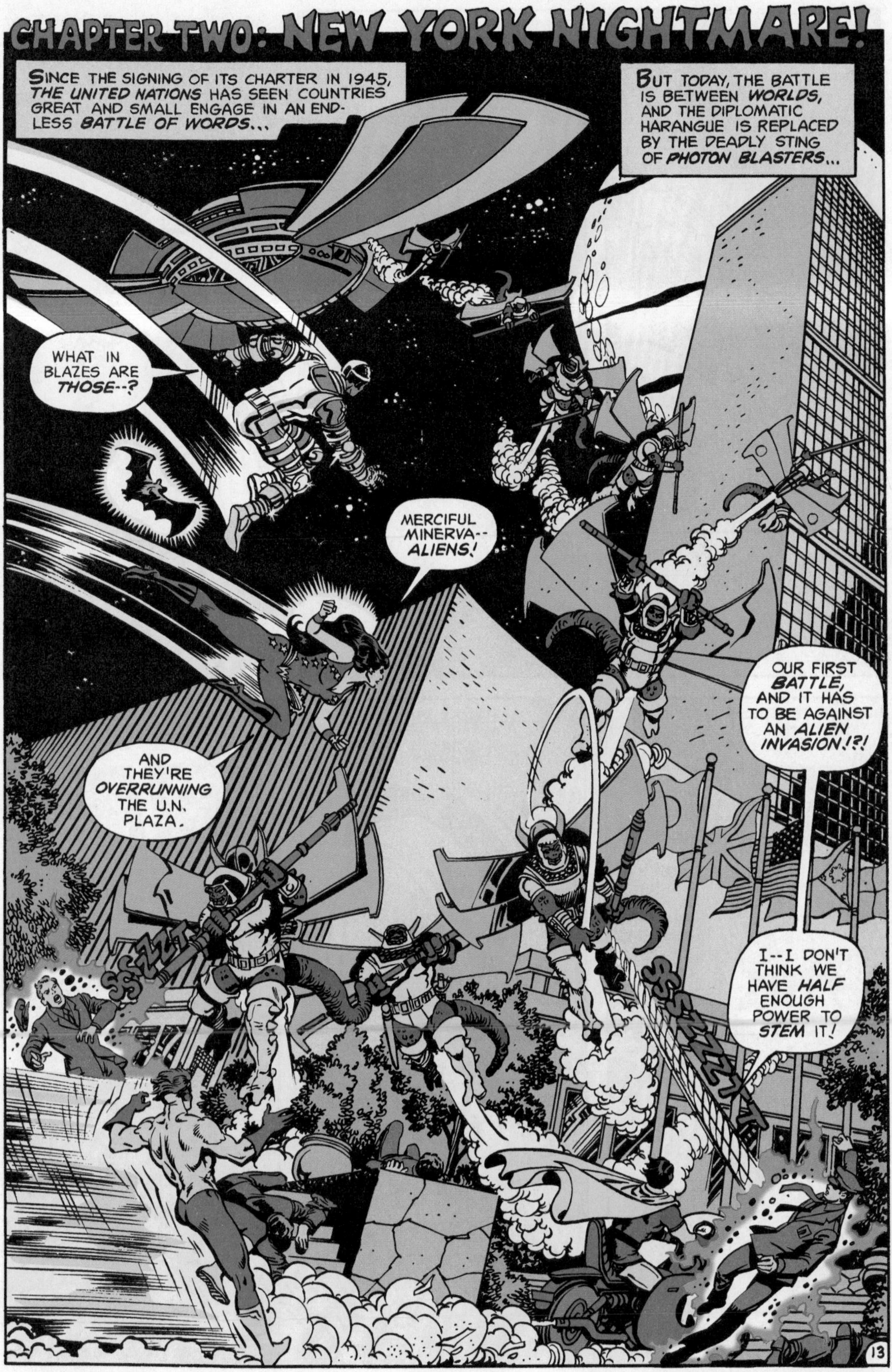
CHAPTER TWO: NEW YORK NIGHTMARE!
SINCE THE SIGNING OF ITS CHARTER IN 1945, THE UNITED NATIONS HAS SEEN COUNTRIES GREAT AND SMALL ENGAGE IN AN ENDLESS BATTLE OF WORDS...
BUT TODAY, THE BATTLE IS BETWEEN WORLDS, AND THE DIPLOMATIC HARANGUE IS REPLACED BY THE DEADLY STING OF PHOTON BLASTERS...
WHAT IN BLAZES ARE THOSE--?
MERCIFUL MINERVA--ALIENS!
AND THEY'RE OVERRUNNING THE U.N. PLAZA.
OUR FIRST BATTLE, AND IT HAS TO BE AGAINST AN ALIEN INVASION!?!
I--I DON'T THINK WE HAVE HALF ENOUGH POWER TO STEM IT!
SSZZZT
SSZZZT
13

WHY ARE YOU PUTTING US *DOWN*, ROB--?

CLOSE UP THESE BOZOS DON'T SEEM SO *TOUGH!*

SK'RAK

THEY WEREN'T *EXPECTING* US! BUT NOW THEY'VE HAD TIME TO--CYBORG!?!

AGGHHH! THAT STICK'A THEIRS--SHOOTIN' *ENERGY* RIGHT *THROUGH* ME!

KRAKAKRAK KRAK

As HIS ONE VISIBLE EYE NARROWS IN GRIM DETERMINATION, CYBORG'S *SOLAR-POWERED HAND* CLAIMS THE ALIEN POWER STAFF AS *HIS*...

C'MON, FROG--LEMME SHOW YOU WHERE YOU CAN *STICK THIS!*

KRAKK A SKREEEEK!

WHOEVER THESE ALIENS ARE, THEY'RE NOT ONLY *STRONG*, THEY'RE *ORGANIZED!*

BUT I LEARNED ABOUT *SIMILAR* BATTLE TACTICS ON *PARADISE ISLAND*--

--AND I WAS *TAUGHT* HOW TO TURN MY ATTACKER'S POWER *AGAINST* HIM!

HERA BE PRAISED! IT *WORKED!*

WHOOMP!

'ROBBIE! BOUNCE YOUR BUTT *THIS* WAY! I NEED *HELP!*

NO CAN *DO*, BEAST BOY-- I'VE GOT MY *OWN* PROBLEMS!

YEAH, LIKE REMEMBERIN' MY NEW *NAME!* IT'S *CHANGELING!*

(14)

BUT, NO SOONER HAS THE BATTLE *BEGUN*...

THUCK!

WHOO

...THAN, ABRUPTLY...

SPTOK

KROK

...IT IS *ENDED*.

WE WON? BUT *HOW*?

UP THERE, ROB--*LOOK*!

THUD

RAVEN! HER *ASTRAL IMAGE* IS HEADING FOR THE *SECRETARIAT BUILDING*!

SHE GOT US *INTO* THIS, BUT WHERE *WAS* SHE DURING OUR *FIGHT*?

SHE MUST HAVE BEEN *BUSY*, RAVEN WOULDN'T *DESERT* US!

I HAVE YET TO *LOCATE* OUR FINAL *MEMBER*...

I SENSE HER *PRESENCE*...SHE MUST BE *NEAR*!

STILL, BEFORE I CAN BEGIN TO SEARCH *ANEW*, I MUST REGAIN MY *STRENGTH*...

MY SOUL MUST ONCE MORE BECOME *PART* OF ME!

TO HAVE BODY AND SOUL *SEPARATE* FOR MORE THAN *FIVE* OF YOUR MINUTES WOULD SUBJECT ME TO *HORRORS* TOO TERRIBLE TO SPEAK OF!

15

THE EAST VILLAGE IS BLANKETED IN GRAY AND GRIME, AND THE STENCH OF CHEAP LIQUOR STAINS THE AIR. YET, NOT *EVERYWHERE* IS THERE SUCH A FORLORN BLEAKNESS...

SHE *FELL* OUT'A THE *SKY*, CAROL. BELIEVE ME!

I *WANNA*, GRANT. I MEAN, A GOLDEN GIRL'S GOTTA COME FROM *SOMEWHERE!*

BUT WHY DID YOU BRING HER *HERE?* AN' WHY *NOW?*

ESPECIALLY NOW?

YOU STILL WANT TO *LEAVE* ME, CAROL?

C'MON, IT'S *OVER.* BEEN OVER FOR *MONTHS.*

'SIDES, FROM THE WAY YOU'RE GAWKIN' OVER YOUR GOLDEN *GIRLFRIEND,* YOU ALREADY GOT YOUR *REPLACEMENT!*

BUT I DON'T WANT TO *REPLACE* YOU, CAROL. I *LOVE* YOU.

TROUBLE IS, YOU *ALSO* LOVED MICHELE AND JESSICA AND GOD KNOWS WHO *ELSE.*

JUST REMEMBER, I WASN'T FOOLIN' 'ROUND, GRANT.

BESIDES, LATELY YOU'VE *CHANGED...* THOSE NEW *FRIENDS* OF YOURS...

YEAH? WHAT *ABOUT* 'EM? THEY'RE GONNA *HELP* ME... HELP ME MAKE A *FORTUNE.*

BUT DOIN' *WHAT,* GRANT? I DON'T WANNA BE MIXED UP WITH--

16

40

LIKE THE MOMENT BEFORE AN ELECTRICAL STORM, THE AIR IN GRANT WILSON'S APARTMENT BECOMES CRISP... KEEN...
I'VE FOUND HER AT LAST ...AND IN TIME!
THERE IS STILL HOPE FOR HER SAFETY.
C-CAROL--?
W-WHO'S SHE, GRANT?
ANOTHER OF YOUR PLAYMATES?
SHE IS ILL, WEAK FROM HER ORDEAL.
BUT, THANK THE ALL, SHE LIVES.
BE CALM, MY FRIEND. WE SHALL SEE YOU ARE TAKEN CARE OF!
RAVEN LIFTS A SLENDER HAND TOWARD THE ALIEN GIRL, TO DRAW AWAY THE PAIN, REMOVE THE HURT, BUT...
IF THESE ARE YOUR FRIENDS, GRANT, I'M CUTTIN' OUTTA HERE RIGHT NOW!
HE IS SILENT AS HE STEPS FORWARD, CROWDING THE CRAMPED STUDIO APARTMENT. BEFORE HIM STAND THE HUMANS... AND KORIAND'R! THEREFORE, THE HUMANS MUST BE REMOVED...
KRAKABOOOM!!
HIS POWER IS TERRIBLE!
NOT EVEN I CAN FIGHT HIM!
IN A CRUEL MOMENT, IT IS OVER...
...AND THE WAR-DRONE ALLOWS A GRIM SMILE TO CROSS HIS CRUEL FACE...
17

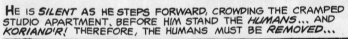

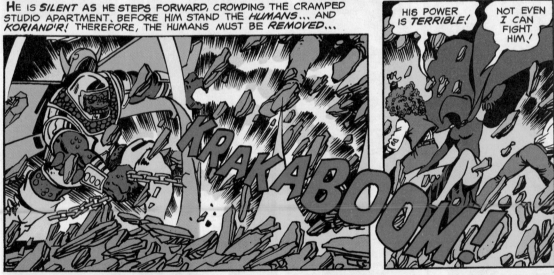

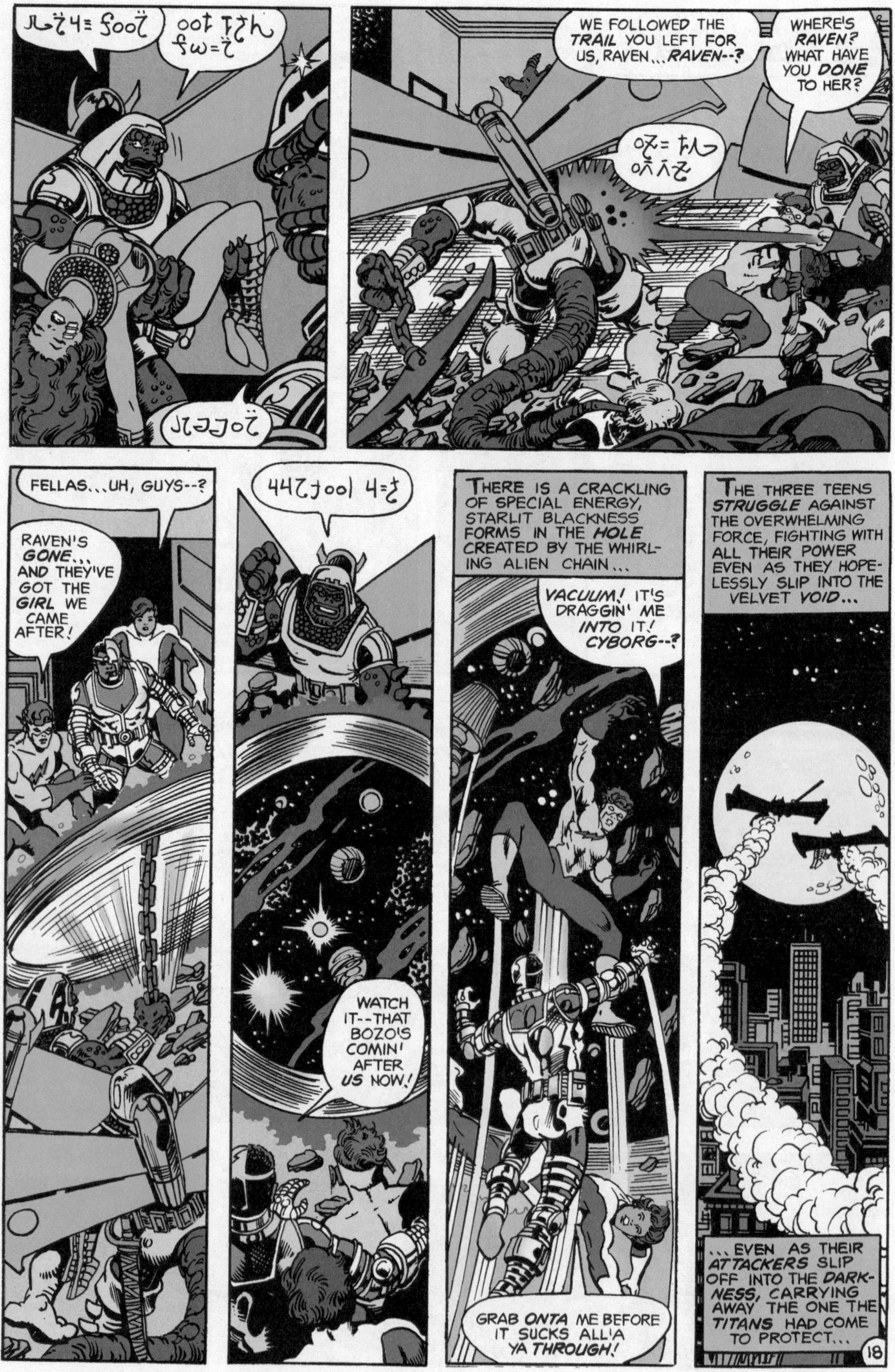
WE FOLLOWED THE TRAIL YOU LEFT FOR US, RAVEN... RAVEN--?
WHERE'S RAVEN? WHAT HAVE YOU DONE TO HER?
FELLAS...UH, GUYS--?
RAVEN'S GONE... AND THEY'VE GOT THE GIRL WE CAME AFTER!
WATCH IT--THAT BOZO'S COMIN' AFTER US NOW!
THERE IS A CRACKLING OF SPECIAL ENERGY, STARLIT BLACKNESS FORMS IN THE HOLE CREATED BY THE WHIRL-ING ALIEN CHAIN...
VACUUM! IT'S DRAGGIN' ME INTO IT! CYBORG--?
GRAB ONTA ME BEFORE IT SUCKS ALL'A YA THROUGH!
THE THREE TEENS STRUGGLE AGAINST THE OVERWHELMING FORCE, FIGHTING WITH ALL THEIR POWER EVEN AS THEY HOPE-LESSLY SLIP INTO THE VELVET VOID...
...EVEN AS THEIR ATTACKERS SLIP OFF INTO THE DARK-NESS, CARRYING AWAY THE ONE THE TITANS HAD COME TO PROTECT...
18

IT'S SOME KINDA MOTHER-LOVIN' SPACE WARP--

--AN' NOT EVEN DRAGGIN' MY BLASTED *ARM* OUTTA ITS SOCKET IS DOIN' A *BEAN'S* WORTH'A GOOD!

WE GOTTA DO *SOMETHING!*

BRIGHT BOY, GREENIE-- NOW COME UP WITH *WHAT!*

WONDER GIRL--?

ALREADY *AHEAD* OF YOU, ROB.

PRAY THIS *DOOR FRAME* DOESN'T GIVE WAY--

--BEFORE I DRAG BACK OUR FLOATING THREE-SOME!

WONDER GIRL *STRAINS* AGAINST THE TERRIBLE VOID, HER ARMS RAW WITH *PAIN*, HER TEETH SORE AS THEY GRIND AGAINST ONE ANOTHER...

HER FINGERS BEG TO LET GO, BUT...

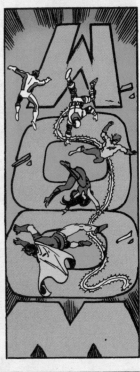

FOR LONG MOMENTS THEY LIE UPON THE FLOOR, REGAINING LOST STRENGTH, THEN...

IT IS NOT YET *DONE*, MY FRIENDS. OUR ENEMIES HAVE REGAINED THEIR *PRISONER.*

SHE MUST BE *SAVED!*

HEY! YOU CREEPS *BUSTED UP* THIS PLACE. WHAT ARE YOU GONNA *DO* ABOUT IT?

YOU'LL BE *COMPENSATED*, FRIEND. NOW, KINDLY TAKE YOUR HAND *OFF ME.*

YOU'RE THE ONE WHO *BROUGHT* THAT GIRL HERE, GRANT. IT'S NOT *THEIR* FAULT. IT'S *YOURS!*

GRANT WILSON FEELS HIS *RAGE* BUILD, A RAGE THAT WILL NOT QUICKLY *ABATE...*

19

THE CAPTAIN OF THE *CHRGA* **BELCHES** AS HIS SHIP ARCS SPACEWARD TOWARD THE ORBITING Q'ST'R...

HE WIPES HIS LIPS, THEN PLUGS IN THE *CORRESPONDER*...

⟨COMMANDER TROGAAR, WE HAVE RETAKEN *PRINCESS KORIAND'R.*⟩

⟨SHE IS HELPLESS IN THE *ENERGY-DAMPENER*...⟩

⟨DON'T FISH FOR *COMPLIMENTS*, WEEZAK.⟩

⟨YOUR *PREVIOUS* CAPTAIN IS THE ONE WHO *LOST* US KORIAND'R...⟩

⟨THAT MISTAKE WILL COST US MANY *CREDITS*, WEEZAK.⟩

⟨WE WILL *MISS* THE FIRST SESSIONS WHERE WE COULD HAVE *SOLD* THE PRINCESS FOR A PLANET'S RANSOM!⟩

⟨DO YOU REALIZE WHAT THAT LOSS WILL *COST* US, WEEZAK?⟩

⟨PERHAPS IT SHOULD COME OUT OF *YOUR* SALARY, WEEZAK?⟩

⟨YOU WON'T COMPLAIN, *WILL* YOU, WEEZAK?⟩

⟨AFTER ALL, YOU COULD INSTEAD SHARE THE *FATE* OF YOUR FORMER *CAPTAIN*, ISN'T THAT *CORRECT*, WEEZAK? *ISN'T IT?*⟩

WEEZAK'S ONLY *ANSWER* IS ANOTHER, STARTLED *BELCH*... ⑳

OUTSIDE THE MAIN BRIDGE, THE GUARD-DRONES SUDDENLY *SHIVER* AS THE CUSTOMARY HIGH TEMPERATURE SUDDENLY *DROPS*...

THE GIRL IS *HERE*-- BEHIND THAT *DOOR.*

MEBBE THE DOOR'S *SHUT,* WITCH-LADY, BUT WE CAN STILL *BLAST* OUR WAY *THROUGH!*

SKREEAKKK

HOW MANY *HAND* ATTACHMENTS DO YOU *HAVE,* CYBORG?

ENOUGH! MY FATHER KEEPS *BUILDIN'* THEM-- TRYIN' TO *MAKE UP* FOR WHAT HE *DID* TO ME...

GOOD *THING,* TOO-- THAT'S HOW WE GOT OURSELVES A *CHOPPER* SO FAST!

THOSE GUYS AT *S.T.A.R.* LABS GOT *EVERYTHIN'!*

VICTOR, I NEED YOUR KNOWLEDGE OF *COMPUTERS*...

COME WITH *ME* WHILE THE *OTHERS* LOCATE OUR FINAL *MEMBER.*

HEY, HOLD ON, RAVEN. I WANT TO--

BUT...

BLAST IT, SHE'S *GONE* AGAIN. SHE *ALWAYS* VANISHES JUST BEFORE A FIGHT.

SHE'S DOING *HER* JOB, ROBIN. WHY DON'T YOU DO *YOURS,* AND QUIT *COMPLAINING?*

I DON'T THINK *KID FLASH* LIKES YOU PUTTING RAVEN *DOWN.*

YEAH, I *NOTICED,* WONDER GIRL, I *NOTICED!*

21

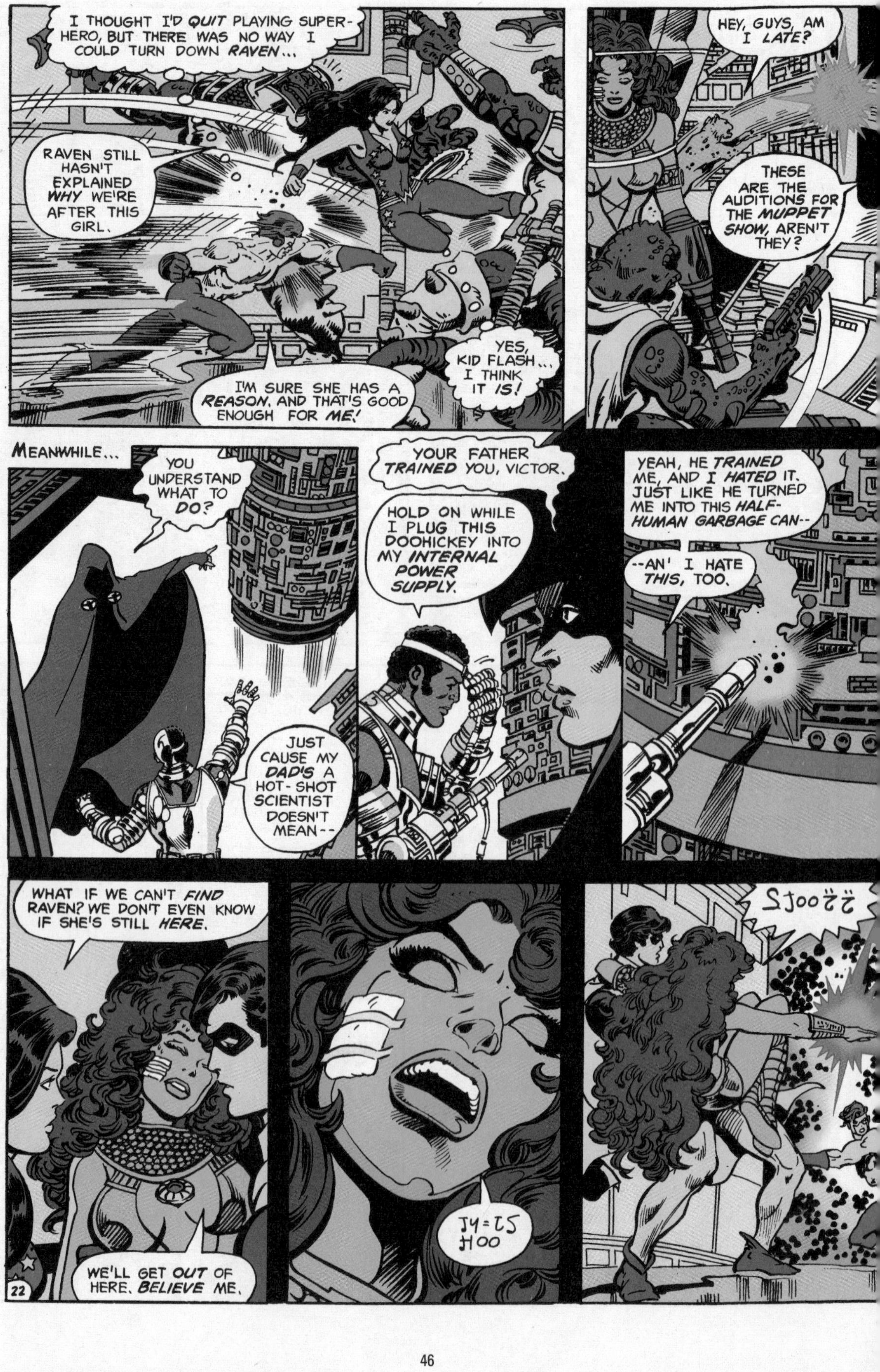
I THOUGHT I'D QUIT PLAYING SUPER-HERO, BUT THERE WAS NO WAY I COULD TURN DOWN RAVEN...
RAVEN STILL HASN'T EXPLAINED WHY WE'RE AFTER THIS GIRL.
I'M SURE SHE HAS A REASON, AND THAT'S GOOD ENOUGH FOR ME!
YES, KID FLASH... I THINK IT IS!
HEY, GUYS, AM I LATE?
THESE ARE THE AUDITIONS FOR THE MUPPET SHOW, AREN'T THEY?
MEANWHILE...
YOU UNDERSTAND WHAT TO DO?
JUST CAUSE MY DAD'S A HOT-SHOT SCIENTIST DOESN'T MEAN--
YOUR FATHER TRAINED YOU, VICTOR.
HOLD ON WHILE I PLUG THIS DOOHICKEY INTO MY INTERNAL POWER SUPPLY.
YEAH, HE TRAINED ME, AND I HATED IT. JUST LIKE HE TURNED ME INTO THIS HALF-HUMAN GARBAGE CAN--
--AN' I HATE THIS, TOO.
WHAT IF WE CAN'T FIND RAVEN? WE DON'T EVEN KNOW IF SHE'S STILL HERE.
WE'LL GET OUT OF HERE. BELIEVE ME.
22

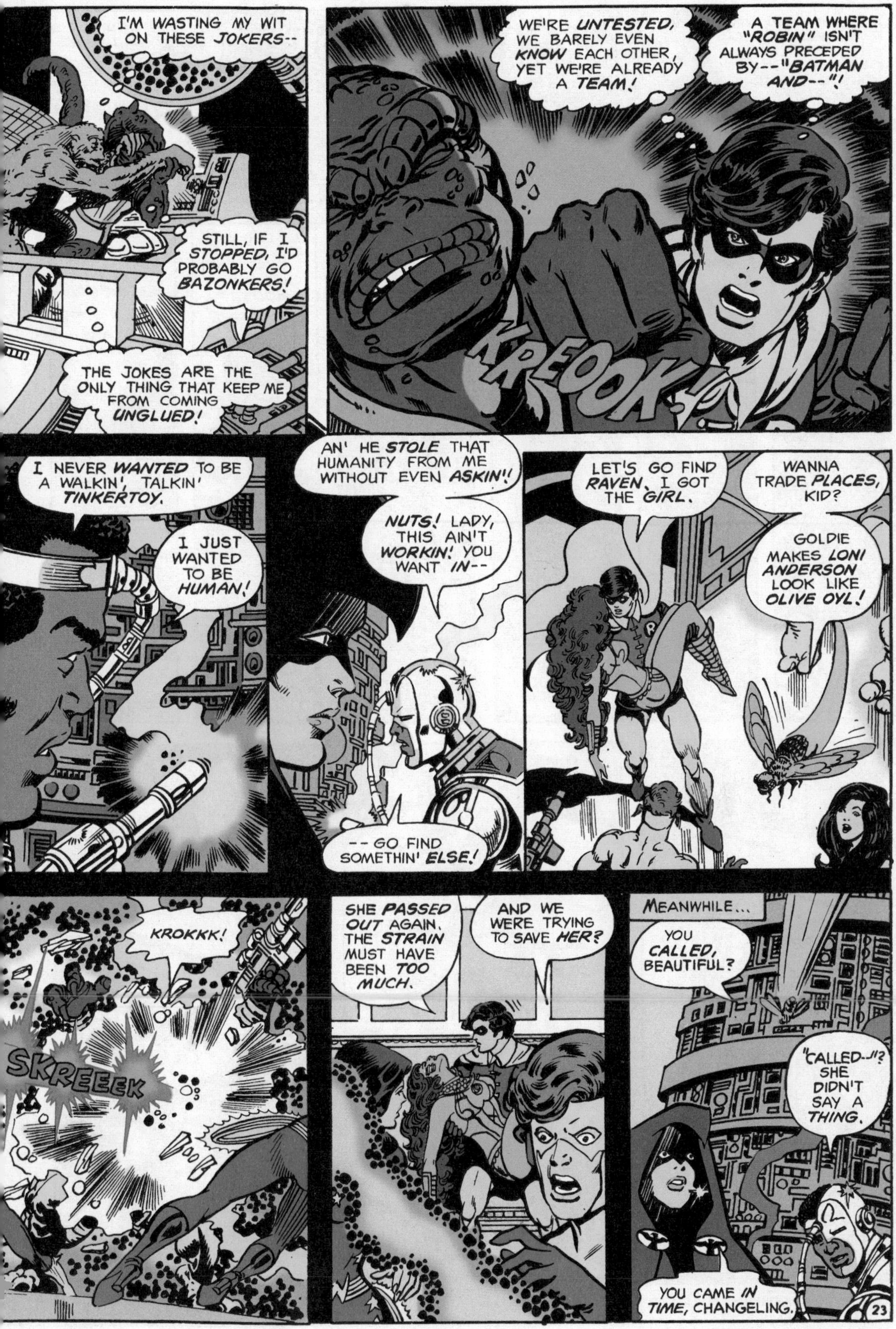

I'M WASTING MY WIT ON THESE JOKERS--
STILL, IF I STOPPED, I'D PROBABLY GO BAZONKERS!
THE JOKES ARE THE ONLY THING THAT KEEP ME FROM COMING UNGLUED!
WE'RE UNTESTED, WE BARELY EVEN KNOW EACH OTHER, YET WE'RE ALREADY A TEAM!
A TEAM WHERE "ROBIN" ISN'T ALWAYS PRECEDED BY--"BATMAN AND--"!
KREOOK!
I NEVER WANTED TO BE A WALKIN', TALKIN' TINKERTOY.
I JUST WANTED TO BE HUMAN!
AN' HE STOLE THAT HUMANITY FROM ME WITHOUT EVEN ASKIN'!
NUTS! LADY, THIS AIN'T WORKIN'! YOU WANT IN--
--GO FIND SOMETHIN' ELSE!
LET'S GO FIND RAVEN. I GOT THE GIRL.
WANNA TRADE PLACES, KID?
GOLDIE MAKES LONI ANDERSON LOOK LIKE OLIVE OYL!
KROKKK!
SKREEEK
SHE PASSED OUT AGAIN. THE STRAIN MUST HAVE BEEN TOO MUCH.
AND WE WERE TRYING TO SAVE HER?
MEANWHILE...
YOU CALLED, BEAUTIFUL?
"CALLED--"? SHE DIDN'T SAY A THING.
YOU CAME IN TIME, CHANGELING.
23

LISSEN, MAKE SURE *THIS* WIRE CONNECTS WITH THE *BLUE* ONE INSIDE, THINK YOU CAN DO IT, SHORTY?

IS THE POPE *POLISH*?

IF I DON'T *COME BACK*, GIVE MY REGARDS TO *PLUTO* AND *GOOFY*!

♪♪ HEEEERE I COME TO SAVE THE DAAYYYYY! ♪

OKAY, I'M *HERE!* NOW WHAT?

HMMM, 'BORGY SAID TO CONNECT THIS TO THE *BLUE TERMINAL!*

SO DIS *MUST* BE DE *PLACE!*

HOPE I DIDN'T *SCREW UP*, OR *TERMINAL* WILL TAKE ON AN ALTOGETHER *DIFFERENT MEANIN'!*

DID IT, 'BORGY. NOW WHEN DO I GET TO DATE *MINNIE MOUSE?*

ALL YER GONNA *GET*, SHORTY--IS THE *CLEAR OUT SIGNAL!*

TITANS-- *LET'S MOVE IT!*

THEY *DESCEND* ALMOST AS ONE...

...USING THEIR *POWERS* TO LOWER THEM TO SAFETY...

WHAT THE HECK IS THAT *WIRE* I RIGGED UP SUPPOSED TO *DO?*

KEEP YER *TRAP* SHUT, SHORTY, AN YOU'LL *FIND OUT!*

FIVE... FOUR... THREE... TWO...

24

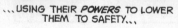

KREE-BLAMMO

⟨COMMANDER TROGAAR, THE CHRGA HAS...⟩

⟨I CAN SEE FOR *MYSELF*, DOLT.⟩

⟨OH, WELL, PERHAPS IT IS FOR THE *BEST*. I HAD DECIDED TO *SLAY* WEEZAK AT ANY RATE.⟩

⟨REPORT THIS TO THE *TRIBUNAL*. THEY WILL WANT TO SEND A *WARFLEET* TO OBLITERATE THIS INTERFERING WORLD.⟩

⟨MEANWHILE, WE STILL HAVE TO REACH KORDO-4. THERE ARE STILL *OTHER* SLAVES TO BE SOLD.⟩

IMPRESSED, SHORTY?

NAH. I'VE SEEN *BETTER*.

HEY! STOP IT! I WAS ONLY *JOKING*!

AS THE Q'ST'R STREAKS SPACEWARD...

I SEE OUR FINAL MEMBER IS *WELL*, GOOD, SHE WILL BE *NEEDED*.

NEEDED FOR *WHAT*?

YOU WERE NOT ASSEMBLED SIMPLY FOR *THIS* MISSION, MY FRIENDS.

INDEED, EVEN NOW THE MENACE IS GROWING... ONE WHICH ONLY *YOUR POWERS* CAN HOPE TO *OVERCOME*!

RAVEN'S VOICE LOWERS, FOR THAT MENACE IS STILL *MONTHS* AWAY... MONTHS WHICH WILL BE USED IN CREATING THE *GREATEST FIGHTING TEAM ALIVE*...

THERE THEY *ARE*-- THE ONES I *TOLD* YOU ABOUT.

YOU WANT THEM *DESTROYED*, GRANT? VERY WELL, THE *H.I.V.E.* SHALL SEE THAT YOUR WISHES BECOME *REALITY*!

NEXT: > TODAY--THE TERMINATOR! BE HERE!

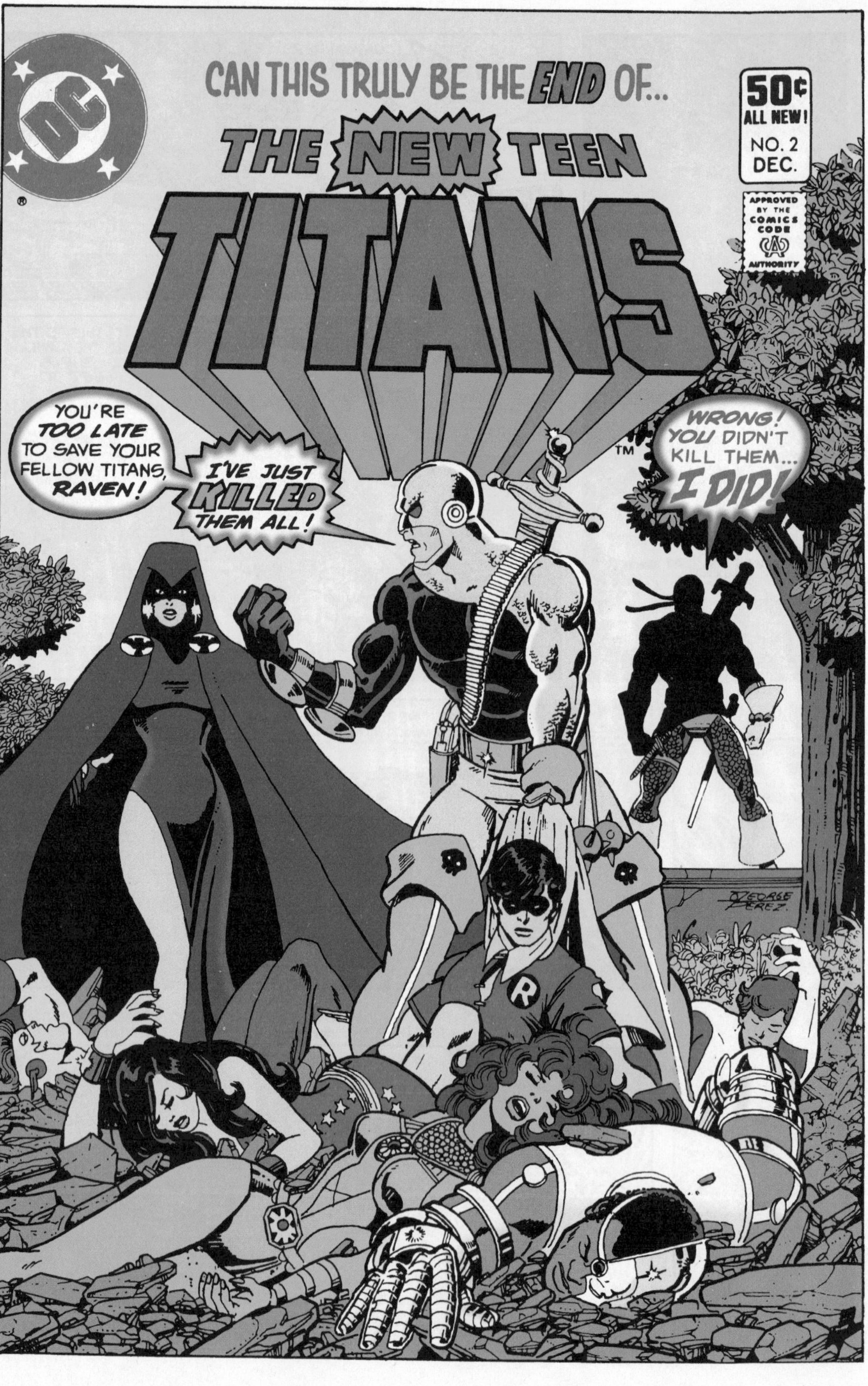
CAN THIS TRULY BE THE END OF...
THE NEW TEEN TITANS
50¢ ALL NEW!
NO. 2 DEC.
APPROVED BY THE COMICS CODE AUTHORITY
YOU'RE TOO LATE TO SAVE YOUR FELLOW TITANS, RAVEN!
I'VE JUST KILLED THEM ALL!
WRONG! YOU DIDN'T KILL THEM... I DID!
GEORGE PEREZ

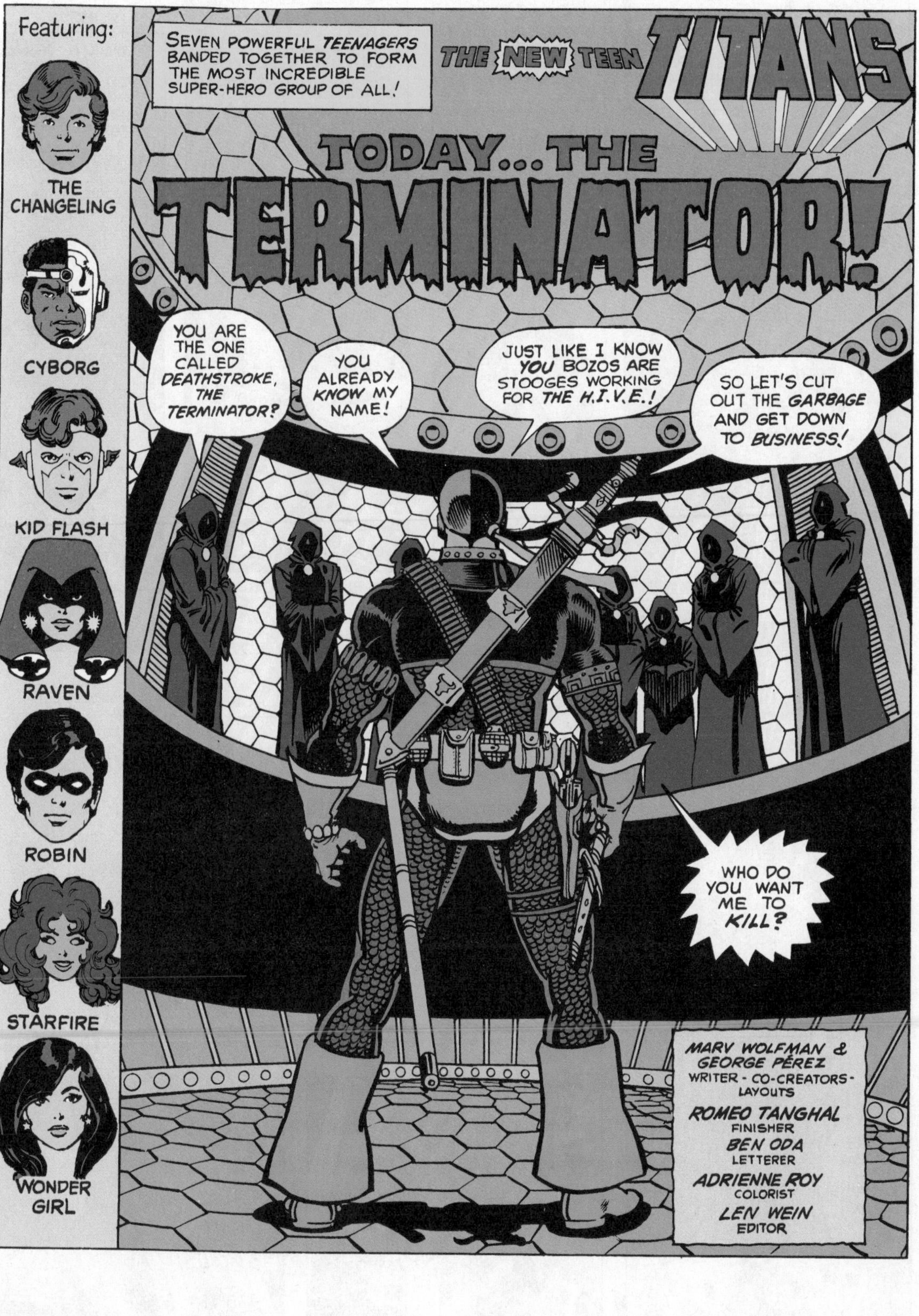
Featuring:
THE CHANGELING
CYBORG
KID FLASH
RAVEN
ROBIN
STARFIRE
WONDER GIRL
SEVEN POWERFUL TEENAGERS BANDED TOGETHER TO FORM THE MOST INCREDIBLE SUPER-HERO GROUP OF ALL!
THE NEW TEEN TITANS
TODAY... THE TERMINATOR!
YOU ARE THE ONE CALLED DEATHSTROKE, THE TERMINATOR?
YOU ALREADY KNOW MY NAME!
JUST LIKE I KNOW YOU BOZOS ARE STOOGES WORKING FOR THE H.I.V.E.!
SO LET'S CUT OUT THE GARBAGE AND GET DOWN TO BUSINESS!
WHO DO YOU WANT ME TO KILL?
MARV WOLFMAN & GEORGE PÉREZ WRITER - CO-CREATORS - LAYOUTS
ROMEO TANGHAL FINISHER
BEN ODA LETTERER
ADRIENNE ROY COLORIST
LEN WEIN EDITOR

WE WISH YOU TO DESTROY THE NEW TITANS!

YOU KNOW MY TERMS. I ANSWER TO NO ONE...

I KNOCK 'EM OFF MY WAY... AND I GET PAID IN ADVANCE!

WE WILL NOT PAY UNTIL THE JOB IS COMPLETED!

THEN YOU CAN JUST TAKE YOUR CONTRACT AND STUFF IT! I'M THE BEST IN THE BUSINESS AND YOU KNOW IT!

I'LL SEE YOU JERKS WHEN YOU WISE UP!

TERMINATOR! WE WILL NOT ACCEPT YOUR REFUSAL!

YOU WILL NOT BE ALLOWED TO LEAVE THE H.I.V.E. ALIVE!

BAM BAM BAM BAM BAM BAMB

SUDDENLY, A SECTION OF THE WALL SLIDES OPEN AND MACHINE GUNS SNAP INTO PLACE FROM THEIR CONCEALED NICHES...

BUT THE TERMINATOR IS ALREADY ON THE MOVE...

SOMEHOW I FIGURED YOU TURKEYS WERE CREEPS!

BAM BLAM

BUT THAT'S OKAY-- I'VE BEEN HANDLING CREEPS ALL MY LIFE!

NONE OF 'EM EVER STOPPED ME IN THE PAST--

BAM BLAM!

--AND FRANKLY, NO ONE'S LIKELY TO DO IT NOW!

SKA BLAMM!

THE TERMINATOR'S HAND FLASHES TO HIS SWORD, BUT...

HEY! THEY'RE FADING OUT... LIKE THEY WERE NEVER EVEN HERE...

WHAT IN BLAZES IS GOING ON?

2

NO ANSWER... THEN THESE *H.I.V.E.* CREEPS WERE JUST *ILLUSIONS,* PROBABLY *HOLOGRAMS!*

BUT *WHY?* WERE THEY TRYING TO *KILL* ME?

...OR *TEST* ME?

BAH! WHO REALLY *CARES? WHATEVER* THEY WERE UP TO--

--THEY *FAILED!*

I'M STILL *ALIVE...* STILL *LOOSE...* AND STILL *MY OWN MAN!*

KRAKK!

HE IS MORE POWERFUL THAN WE *THOUGHT!*

DID YOU SEE? HE ACTUALLY *DODGED* THAT HAIL OF *BULLETS!*

HIS REFLEXES ARE *PHENOMENAL!*

DID WE GET IT ALL ON OUR *BI-SECTORS?*

AFFIRMATIVE! X-RAYS FROM EVERY POSSIBLE ANGLE, ION SCANS, FULL BIOLOGI-CAL RECORDINGS,

THEN WE SHOULD BE ABLE TO *DUPLICATE* HIS POWERS?

SOON WE'LL BE ABLE TO *CREATE* OUR *OWN* TERMINATOR--ONE WHO WILL BELONG, BODY AND SOUL, TO THE *H.I.V.E.!*

THE SEVEN FIGURES NOD IN *AGREEMENT--*

--WHILE WE TRAVEL A THOUSAND MILES *WEST-WARD* TO A MANHATTAN APARTMENT JUST OFF COLUMBUS AVENUE...

C'MON, CAROL, I SAID I *APOLOGIZE!*

WHY WON'T YOU MOVE BACK TO *OUR* PLACE?

YOU REALLY WANT TO *KNOW,* GRANT? FRANKLY, IT'S BECAUSE YOU *FRIGHTEN* ME!

YOU HANG AROUND WITH THOSE...THOSE *THUGS.* AND I DON'T LIKE WHAT THEY'VE *DONE* TO YOU!

YOU FELL IN WITH THEM TOO *EASILY*

ARE WE BACK ON *THAT,* CAROL? I'M SORRY I EVER *TOLD* YOU ABOUT MY FATHER AND BROTHER...

AND YOU'RE GOING TO END UP JUST *LIKE* THEM!

GRANT, DO YOURSELF A FAVOR AND GO... *PLEASE?*

53

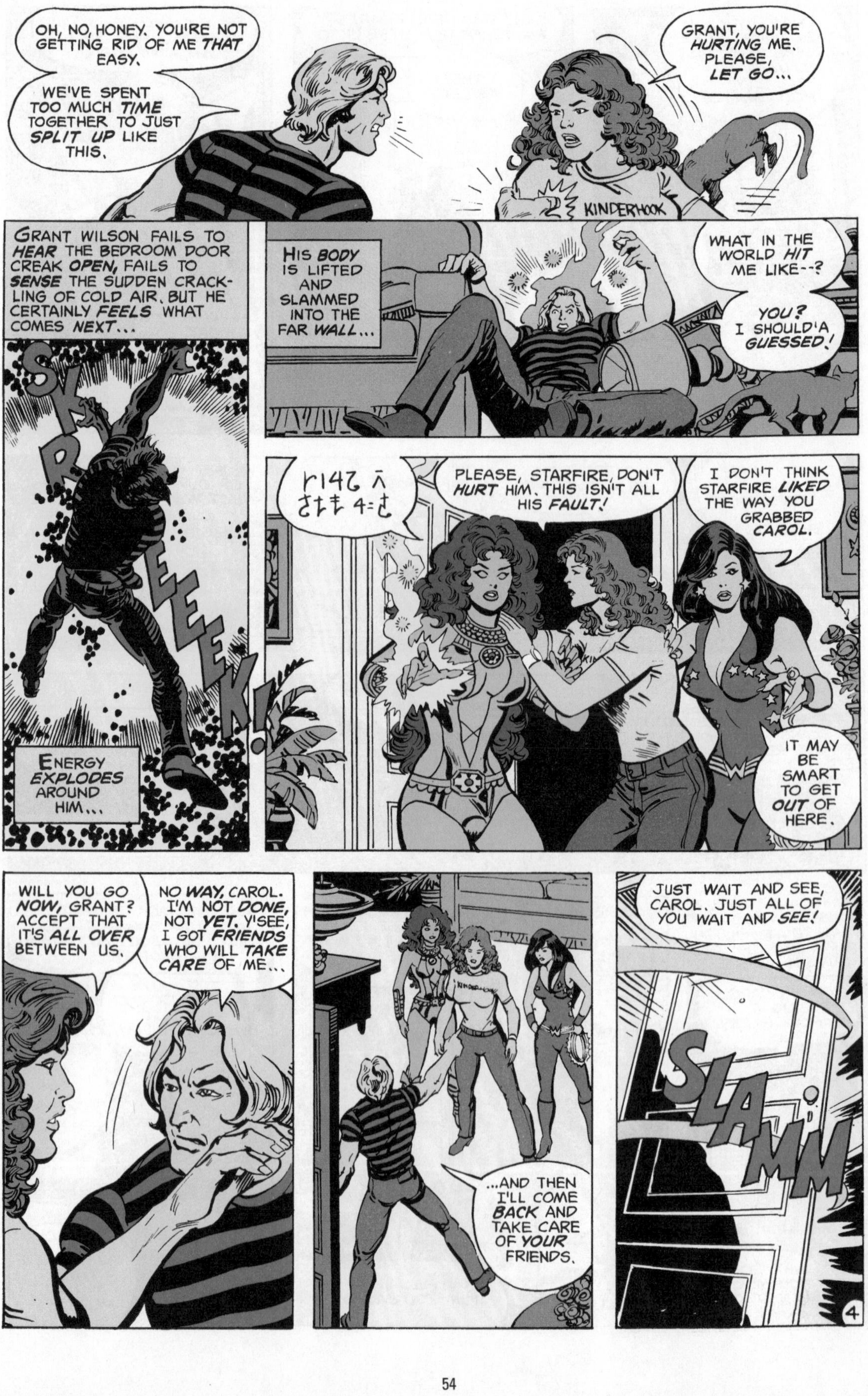

OH, NO, HONEY. YOU'RE NOT GETTING RID OF ME THAT EASY.
WE'VE SPENT TOO MUCH TIME TOGETHER TO JUST SPLIT UP LIKE THIS.
GRANT, YOU'RE HURTING ME. PLEASE, LET GO...
KINDERHOOK
GRANT WILSON FAILS TO HEAR THE BEDROOM DOOR CREAK OPEN, FAILS TO SENSE THE SUDDEN CRACKLING OF COLD AIR. BUT HE CERTAINLY FEELS WHAT COMES NEXT...
SKREEEEEK!
ENERGY EXPLODES AROUND HIM...
HIS BODY IS LIFTED AND SLAMMED INTO THE FAR WALL...
WHAT IN THE WORLD HIT ME LIKE--?
YOU? I SHOULD'A GUESSED!
PLEASE, STARFIRE, DON'T HURT HIM. THIS ISN'T ALL HIS FAULT!
I DON'T THINK STARFIRE LIKED THE WAY YOU GRABBED CAROL.
IT MAY BE SMART TO GET OUT OF HERE.
WILL YOU GO NOW, GRANT? ACCEPT THAT IT'S ALL OVER BETWEEN US.
NO WAY, CAROL. I'M NOT DONE, NOT YET. Y'SEE, I GOT FRIENDS WHO WILL TAKE CARE OF ME...
...AND THEN I'LL COME BACK AND TAKE CARE OF YOUR FRIENDS.
JUST WAIT AND SEE, CAROL. JUST ALL OF YOU WAIT AND SEE!
SLAMM
4

GOD, I KNEW THIS WAS COMING, BUT I DIDN'T THINK IT WOULD BE THIS BAD.

I'M SORRY WE GOT IN THE WAY HERE, CAROL...

...BUT AFTER VIRTUALLY DESTROYING YOUR LAST APARTMENT...*

...WE FELT OBLIGED TO SET YOU UP IN ANOTHER!

HI THERE, CAROL. WONDER GIRL, STARFIRE-- C'MON! WE'VE GOT OURSELVES A REAL EMERGENCY!

LET'S GET MOVING!

*LAST ISSUE. --LEN.

THE ALIEN STARFIRE ROCKETS AFTER THE SPEEDING KID FLASH AS WONDER GIRL SOARS UPON THE AIR CURRENTS CRISS-CROSSING MANHATTAN...

WISH I KNEW WHAT YOU WERE SAYING, STARFIRE...

"BUT SOMETHING TELLS ME YOU'RE ASKING THE SAME QUESTIONS I AM... AND THEY'LL BE ANSWERED WHEN WE GET TO WHEREVER WE'RE GOING!"

THEY'RE STILL LOADING THOSE CRATES... BUT WHAT'S KEEPING THE OTHERS?

WE GOT HERE FAST AS WE COULD. YOU THINK WE STOPPED TO POWDER OUR NOSES?

HEY, BAT-BOY ...DOWN THERE. SOMETHING'S GOIN' ON.

I SEE IT, CYBORG!

AL'RIGHT, TITANS-- LET'S GET 'EM!!

5

THE TITANS ARE A *NEW TEAM*, FORMED LESS THAN A *WEEK AGO*, BUT THEY ALREADY MOVE AS ONE...

BOOF!

SPAK!

KROK

KID FLASH RACES AT SUPER-SPEED TO CLEAR A PATH INTO THE PHARMACEUTICAL WARE-HOUSE...

...AS ROBIN'S *ACROBATIC SWINGING* DOWNS TWO MORE COSTUMED FELONS.

BTANG!

MEANWHILE, *THE CHANGELING* ROARS INTO ACTION AS ONLY A *SHAPE-SHIFTER* CAN...

YOU GUYS SEE DOROTHY OR THE TIN MAN?

THIS IS "OZ"? ISN'T IT?

FLYING HIGH, *PRINCESS KORIAND'R* UNLEASHES A DEADLY *STARFIRE BOLT* UPON ONE EIGHTEEN-WHEEL GETAWAY TRUCK...

KRAK!

...WHILE THE SCIENTIFICALLY-CONSTRUCTED *CYBORG* USES HIS *SOLAR-POWERED*, MOLYBDENUM-STEEL-REINFORCED *MUSCLES* TO WREAK *HAVOC* UPON A *SECOND* ESCAPING VAN.

YOU JERKS'VE HAD *FREE REIN* IN NEW YORK LONG ENOUGH... BUT THAT'S GONNA *STOP*--AS OF *NOW!*

'CAUSE, MISTER -- *THE NEW TITANS ARE IN TOWN!*

SPLOOSH!

6

56

UH OH, THEY'RE TRYIN' TO *HIGHTAIL* IT *OUTTA* HERE!

AN' SPEAKING OF TAILS, THOSE JERKS ALMOST RAN OVER *MINE*!

IT'S GETTING SO EVEN A *MONKEY* ISN'T SAFE IN THIS TOWN!

THEN MAYBE YOU OUGHT TO HIDE OUT IN THE *ZOO*, GAR!

THE ONLY THING YOU'D HAVE TO WORRY ABOUT *THERE* ARE KIDS WITH HOT-WIRED *RUBBER BANDS*!

HER NAME IS *WONDER GIRL*, AND IT IS WITH ASTONISHING *EASE* THAT THE AGILE YOUNG AMAZON SOMERSAULTS DOWN BEFORE THE FINAL TRUCK...

BETTER PUT ON THE *BRAKES*, MISTER. I'M NOT LETTING YOU *PASS*!

THE DRIVER SEEMS TO *SNICKER* AT THE LOVELY TEENAGER AS HIS FOOT PRESSES HARDER ON THE *GAS PEDAL*...

AND, FOR A MOMENT, THE TRUCK LURCHES *FORWARD*...

... ONLY TO FIND ITSELF ABRUPTLY *HALTED* IN ITS PATH.

KRAKKK!

NOW DON'T SAY I DIDN'T *WARN* YOU!

VOTE COSMO FOR MAYOR

... AS DOES ITS AIRBORNE *DRIVER* A MOMENT LATER...

BRKK!

CRIPES-- GEARS AND THINGIES AND ALL SORTS OF *JUNK*!

GUYS, THOSE THIEVES ARE *ROBOTS*!

BUT... 𝚺ʃ𝚥ā=𝚷

SKREEEK

SKREEEK

NO-- STOP IT.!!

WITHOUT THINKING, SHE'S USING THOSE STARFIRE *BOLTS* WE NAMED HER AFTER ON THE *OTHERS*!

SHE'LL *DESTROY* OUR ONLY *CLUES*!

BUT EVEN AS ROBIN LUNGES TOWARD HER, THE ALLURING ALIEN *FOCUSES* HER TERRIBLE POWER, AND THE ADVANCING AUTOM-ATONS ARE IN-STANTLY REDUCED TO *ASH*...

SKREEEEK!

7

IT'S *NO GOOD!*... SHE'S ALREADY *DEMOLISHED* THEM!

BLAST! WITH HER *POWER* SHE'S TOO *DANGEROUS* TO BE LEFT *FREE!*

WHAT DO YOU *MEAN?*

HAVEN'T YOU *NOTICED,* FLASHER? STARFIRE SEEMS TO *RELISH* VIOLENCE!

$\zeta \zeta \cdot \tilde{\epsilon} \times$ $\tilde{\epsilon} 4 \ddot{\epsilon}$ $=45 \downarrow$ JS↓

IF ONLY SHE COULD SPEAK OUR *LANGUAGE* ...IF ONLY WE COULD *TALK* TO HER...

QUIZZICALLY, THE YOUNG ALIEN *STARES* AT ROBIN, SENSING THE *TONE* IF NOT THE EXACT *MEANING* OF THE TEEN WONDER'S WORDS...

THEN...

HEY? HEY?!? CUT IT OU-- MMMMMMMM!!!

THE TEEN WONDER'S *PROTEST* ENDS QUICKLY...

WHILE...

ROBIN--? *ROBIN?!?*

BUZZ OFF, FLASHER...LET ROBBIE HAVE HIS *FUN!*

THOUGH WHY *HE* DESERVES IT AND NOT *ME,* I'LL *NEVER* KNOW!

GOLDIE CAN SMOTHER *ME* LIKE THAT ANYTIME!

OH, KNOCK IT *OFF,* GAR, ALL YOU THINK ABOUT IS-- *OOOHHH!*

MY BACK! I THINK I *SPRAINED* IT STOPPING THAT *TRUCK!*

8

HI, ROBIN. YOU KNOW, YOU'RE REALLY *CUTE*?

HUH? SHE *TALKS*? BUT-- *HOW*--?

PHYSICAL CONTACT, KID FLASH. I SIMPLY *ABSORBED* YOUR LANGUAGE!

Y-YOU HAD TO *KISS* ME TO DO THAT?

NOT *REALLY*. BUT IT WAS CERTAINLY MORE *ENJOYABLE* THIS WAY.

HEY, *LOOKEE HERE*, GOLDEN GIRL DIDN'T SMASH 'EM *ALL*!

GOOD *GOING*, CYBORG. NOW WE HAVE SOMETHING TO *TRACE*!

BACK STILL *HURTS*, KID?

IN PLACES I DIDN'T EVEN KNOW I *HAD*.

JUST RELAX, I C'N *FIX* IT.

HMMMMMM! YOU'RE INTO *MEDICINE*, CYBORG?

NAH! I WAS AN *ATHLETE*... I KNOW *THROWN-OUT* JOINTS WHEN I SEE 'EM!

LISTEN, *I* KNOW FRENCH. HOW ABOUT GERMAN? *CHINESE*?

NO. *ENGLISH* WILL DO FOR *NOW*. MAYBE SOME *OTHER* TIME.

BABE, I THINK THIS IS THE BEGINNING OF A BEAUTIFUL *FRIENDSHIP*!

CYBORG, DO YOU THINK YOUR *FATHER* COULD HELP US WITH--

NO WAY, *BATBOY*! I ONLY *SPEAK* TO THAT DUDE WHEN I *GOTTA*!

BUT WE *NEED* HIM. HE'S GOT ACCESS TO *S.T.A.R.*'S AUTO LAB.

*SCIENTIFIC AND TECHNOLOGICAL ADVANCED RESEARCH. --LEN.

IT'S THE ONLY WAY WE CAN *TEST* THESE ROBOTS.

LISSEN, KID, EVER SINCE HE TURNED ME INTO THIS *FREAK*, HE AND I ARE ON THE *OUTS*!

PLEASE... WE NEED *HELP* NOW.

CAN'T YOU *BURY* WHATEVER PROBLEMS YOU TWO HAVE?

NOT A *CHANCE*!

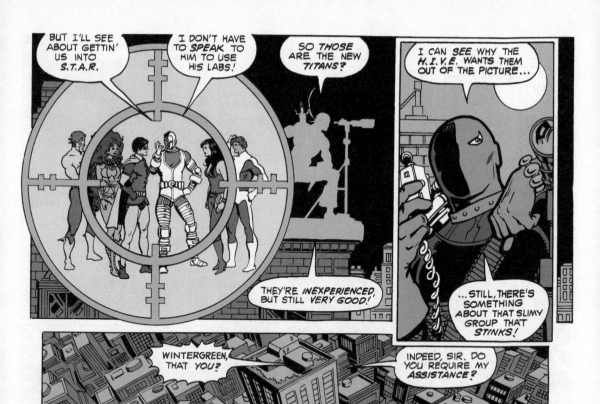

BUT I'LL SEE ABOUT GETTIN' US INTO S.T.A.R.

I DON'T HAVE TO *SPEAK* TO HIM TO USE HIS LABS!

SO *THOSE* ARE THE NEW *TITANS?*

THEY'RE *INEXPERIENCED,* BUT STILL *VERY GOOD!*

I CAN *SEE* WHY THE *H.I.V.E.* WANTS THEM OUT OF THE PICTURE...

...STILL, THERE'S SOMETHING ABOUT THAT SLIMY GROUP THAT *STINKS!*

WINTERGREEN, THAT *YOU?*

INDEED, SIR. DO YOU REQUIRE MY *ASSISTANCE?*

YEAH! I WANT YOU TO RUN A COMPUTER CROSSCHECK ON THE *H.I.V.E...*

...THAT'S AS IN THE *HIERARCHY OF INTERNATIONAL VENGEANCE AND ELIMINATIONS!*

WILL *DO,* SIR. OH, SIR, WILL YOU BE HOME FOR *DINNER* TONIGHT?

DON'T *KNOW* YET, WINTERGREEN. OH YES, I WANT SOMETHING *ELSE* CHECKED OUT...

AND WHILE THE MYSTE-RIOUS *TERMINATOR* CONTINUES HIS COMMUNI-CATION TO HIS EAST SIDE *PENTHOUSE,* WE'D BEST TAKE A LOOK AT AN *ISLAND* SOMEWHERE IN THE MID-ATLANTIC...

I'M *READY.*

YOU UNDERSTAND THE *RISKS?*

YEAH! WE'VE ONLY GONE *OVER* IT A *MILLION TIMES!*

THEN WE SHALL DO SO *ONCE AGAIN!* HUMAN BEINGS ONLY USE 1/10 OF THEIR BRAIN POWER CAPACITY. WE HAVE LEARNED THAT THE TERMINATOR *INCREASED* HIS CAPACITY TO 90%!

WE ARE GOING TO INCREASE *YOUR* CAPACITY TO *100%*

JUST IMAGINE THE *POWER* AT YOUR DISPOSAL WHEN YOU ARE FINALLY READY TO *DESTROY THE NEW TITANS!*

10

ELSEWHERE...

PLEASE, *LISTEN* TO ME. YOU MUST HEAR ME OUT. AT LEAST THIS *ONCE...*

ATOP A WINDSWEPT CRAGGY PEAK IN A PLACE WHERE NO MAN EVER TREAD, A DARKLY-DRESSED *FEMALE* RAISES HER SLENDER ARMS TOWARD THE STORM-TOSSED SKIES...

HER NAME IS *RAVEN!* ONE WEEK AGO SHE BROUGHT TOGETHER THE NEW TITANS FOR A REASON SHE HAS YET TO DIVULGE...

SPEAK!

I'VE RISKED MY *LIFE* COMING HERE WHERE NO HUMAN CAN LONG *SURVIVE!*

I'VE COME TO BEG YOUR *FORGIVENESS...*

THE FATES HAVE *SEPARATED* US TOO LONG ALREADY.

BUT NOW THERE IS A *CHANCE.* IF ONLY --

NO!

I DO NOT FORGIVE!

RAVEN IS HURLED BACKWARD...

UNNGHH!

SKROOK!

...PLUMMETING LIKE A WOUNDED BIRD...

SHE TUMBLES HELPLESSLY...

...UNTIL SUDDENLY, SHE IS *GONE!*

11

BLUE VALLEY COULD BE ANY SMALL TOWN NESTLED IN THE VAST MID-AMERICAN HEARTLAND...

PROVIDED, OF COURSE, THAT *ANY* TOWN COULD BE THE *HOME TOWN* OF A CERTAIN GOLD-AND-SCARLET-CLAD *SUPER-SPEEDSTER*...

DESPITE MY PROMISE TO HANG UP MY *RUNNING SHOES,* I'VE BECOME *KID FLASH* AGAIN!

BUT *WHY?* ALL I WANTED WAS TO BE *WALLY WEST,* ORDINARY COLLEGE STUDENT--!

SO WHAT COMPELLED ME TO *REJOIN* THE TITANS AFTER FIRST TURNING THEM--*EH*--?

YOU?!?

RAVEN! WHAT'S *WRONG?* WHAT *HAPPENED* TO YOU?

I AM SORRY TO HAVE *INTRUDED,* WALLACE... I SHOULD NOT HAVE *COME* HERE...

BUT I NEEDED A *SANCTUARY,* IF ONLY FOR--

NO! I ALREADY HAVE SAID *TOO MUCH.*

RAVEN, PLEASE DON'T *DISAPPEAR* ON ME... I HAVE TO ASK YOU--

SH-SHE'S *GONE*... LIKE SOME KIND OF *GHOST!*

BUT I HAVE TO KNOW--IS *SHE* THE REASON I CHANGED MY MIND?

DID SHE *DO* SOMETHING TO MAKE ME BECOME A *TITAN?*

12

EAST HAMPTON, THE NEXT DAY: IF YOUR INCOME IS LESS THAN *SEVEN FIGURES* IN THIS MILLIONAIRE'S PLAYGROUND, YOU CAN'T AFFORD TO BUY *DRINKING WATER*--

--LET ALONE LIVE IN THE ACCUSTOMED STYLE OF ONE *GARFIELD LOGAN*, ALSO KNOWN AS-- *THE CHANGELING*...

WHO *KNOWS?* I CAN'T *COUNT* PAST A *HUNDRED!*

...PLACE IS *INCREDIBLE*, GAR. HOW MANY *ROOMS* DO YOU HAVE?

BRUCE IS *RICH*, AND WAYNE MANOR WAS SOMETHING, BUT *THIS*... THIS IS...

IT'S NOT *TOO* BAD ...THOUGH I DID ALMOST *STARVE* TO DEATH ONCE, GOING FROM MY BEDROOM TO THE *KITCHEN*.

THE THIRD DAY OUT WAS THE *WORST!*

FACE IT, DICK, MY *STEP-DAD'S* THE KIND'A GUY WHO THINKS *HOWARD HUGHES* LIVED ON *FOOD STAMPS!*

A SMALL *COUNTRY*. YEAH, I *KNOW*. BUT EVERYONE'S GOTTA HANG HIS POUCH *SOMEWHERE!*

DICK GRAYSON AND GAR LOGAN MAKE THEIR WAY TO THE OLYMPIC-SIZE *SWIMMING POOL*, WHILE IN THE NEARBY *POOL LOCKERS*...

WONDER GIRL, I STILL DON'T QUITE *UNDERSTAND* ...WHY AM I SUPPOSED TO WEAR...

...*THIS!?!* IT CERTAINLY CAN'T BE FOR *PROTECTION*. DOES IT POSSESS ANY *SPECIAL PROPERTIES?*

YEP. IT'LL KEEP THE GUYS FROM GOING *INSANE* WHEN THEY SEE YOU. *TRUST ME,* STARFIRE.

PLEASE, CALL ME *KORIAND'R*. THAT IS MY *REAL* NAME.

ONLY IF YOU CALL ME *DONNA*. ANYWAY, ON THIS PLANET, YOU'VE *GOT* TO WEAR *CLOTHING*.

I DON'T UNDERSTAND *WHY*, BUT IF YOU *SAY* SO, I WILL *DO* IT.

HEY, THERE ARE THE GIRLS -- *WOW!*

BETTER BELIEVE IT... *AWWOOOO!*

KNOCK OFF THE *WOLF CALLS*, GAR...

WHEN YOU SAID YOU HAD *SWIM SUITS* FOR US HERE, I DIDN'T EXPECT THESE -- *THINGS!*

THESE AREN'T *BATHING SUITS*, THEY'RE *STRINGS* WITH *GLAND CONDITIONS!*

DICK! I'M SO PLEASED YOU CAME.

YOU LOOK *LOVELY*, KORIAND'R.

SO DO *YOU*, I THINK I WILL *LIKE* IT HERE ON EARTH.

SAY, CAN ALL YOUR PEOPLE CHANGE SHAPE LIKE GAR?

NO, GAR'S ONE-OF-A-KIND... I'M HAPPY TO SAY.

SUDDENLY...

SORRY I WAS *LATE*, GUYS...

BUT I HAD SOME *HOMEWORK* TO DO...

...BEFORE I COULD TAKE A *BREAK.*

HMMM. WATER LOOKS *GOOD*...

IT'S BEEN A *WHILE* SINCE I HAD A RELAXING *SWIM.*

HEY, WHAT'S *KEEPING* YOU? C'MON *IN!*

I KNOW, *ANOTHER* ONE-OF-A-KIND, RIGHT?

NOT *QUITE*, BUT DON'T WORRY, YOU'LL *LEARN!*

14

I'M TRULY SORRY I CAN'T *HELP* YOU, VICTOR--

--BUT THIS AUTOMATON IS *DAMAGED* BEYOND ANY HOPE OF *REPAIR.*

YEAH, I BET YOU'RE REALLY *CHOKED* UP, DAD.

C'MON, *LEVEL!* YOU DON'T GIVE A *HOOT* ABOUT NOTHING BUT *YOURSELF!* YOU NEVER *DID.*

IF YOU CARED, *MOM* WOULD STILL BE ALIVE, AND I WOULDN'T HAVE BECOME THIS ...*MONSTER!*

VICTOR, THAT WAS AN *ACCIDENT*...

ACCIDENT, MY *BEHIND!* YOU AND YOUR CRAZY SCIENCE FREAKS *GET OFF* ON PLAYING *GOD* WITH US LITTLE PEOPLE.

YOU NEVER THOUGHT OF ME AS YOUR *SON* --JUST AS SOME KIND OF PERSONAL *PHYSICS EXPERIMENT!*

VICTOR! WAIT...PLEASE DON'T GO! *WAIT!*

IT'S NO USE, HE'LL *NEVER* LISTEN TO THE *TRUTH!*

HE'LL NEVER BELIEVE THE ACCIDENT THAT FORCED ME TO *REBUILD* HIM--

"--IS ALSO COST-ING ME MY LIFE!"

MAN, HE'S ALWAYS FULL OF *EXCUSES!*

BUT I *KNOW* MOM WOULD STILL *BE* HERE IF IT WEREN'T FOR HIM--

--AND I WOULDN'T BE THIS BLASTED *STEEL-PINOCCHIO!*

SUDDENLY...

KRA KOOM

CYBORG FALLS *STUNNED* TO THE GROUND AS BLURRED *IMAGES* QUIVER BEFORE HIS EYES. FOR A MOMENT, ALL SEEMS VAGUE AND CLOUDY-- THEN, IN AN *INSTANT*, IT ALL SHARPENS INTO A NIGHT- MARE OF CRYSTAL CLARITY...

GET UP, CREEP... GET *UP*--

--SO I CAN *KNOCK YOU DOWN* AGAIN!!

YOU TITANS ARE REAL *BIG* WHEN IT COMES TO PUSHIN' AROUND *KIDS*--

--BUT YOU AIN'T *NOTHIN'* WHEN YOU'RE UP AGAINST-- *THE RAVAGER!*

POOM

YOU GOT A *SCREW LOOSE*, KID?

--LET ME *FIX* IT FOR YOU!

CAUSE IF YOU *DO*--

BOILING *STEAM* GUSHES FROM THE SHATTERED PIPELINE WITH ENOUGH *FORCE* TO MELT A DIAMOND...

BUT...

FDOOSH!

GOTTA DO BETTER THAN *THAT*, ROBOT!

MY *REFLEXES* HAVE BEEN SCIENTIFICALLY *INCREASED!*

I HAD *MORE* THAN ENOUGH TIME TO *DODGE* YOUR BLASTS--

--AN' STILL GET THROUGH YOUR *DEFENSES* TO PERSONALLY WRING YOUR *FAT TIN NECK!*

YOU BLASTED TITANS HAVE PUSHED *GRANT WILSON* 'ROUND LONG ENOUGH!

YOU DESTROYED MY *APARTMENT!* MADE ME LOSE MY *GIRL!*

AN' NOW THAT I GOT THE *POWER*, I'M GONNA MAKE YOU *PAY!*

GONNA MAKE YOU PAY -- *IN SPADES!*

16

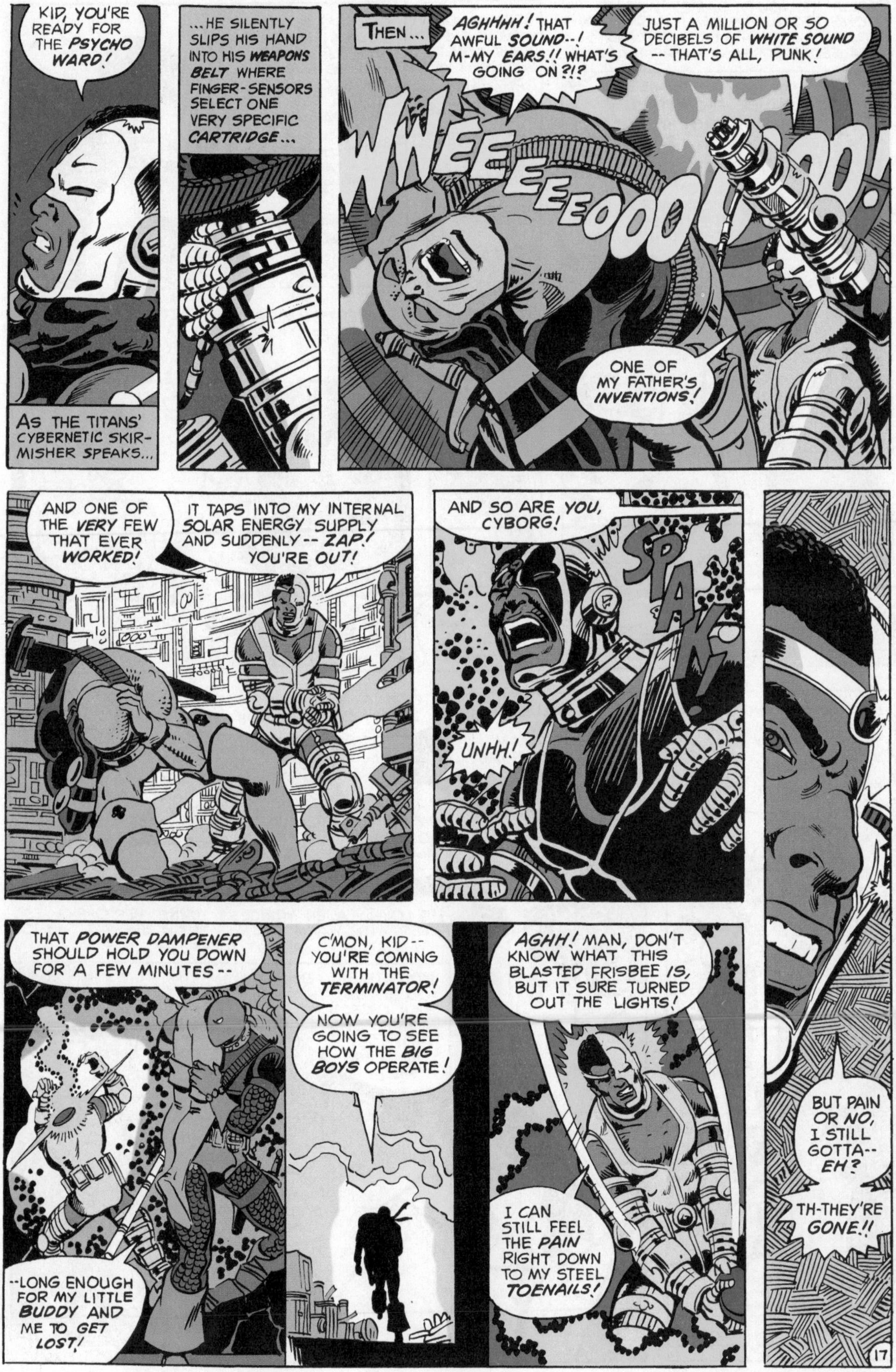
KID, YOU'RE READY FOR THE *PSYCHO WARD!*
AS THE TITANS' CYBERNETIC SKIR-MISHER SPEAKS...
...HE SILENTLY SLIPS HIS HAND INTO HIS *WEAPONS BELT* WHERE FINGER-SENSORS SELECT ONE VERY SPECIFIC *CARTRIDGE*...
THEN...
AGHHHH! THAT AWFUL *SOUND*--! M-MY *EARS!!* WHAT'S GOING ON?!?
JUST A MILLION OR SO DECIBELS OF *WHITE SOUND* -- THAT'S ALL, PUNK!
WWEEEEEOOOO
ONE OF MY FATHER'S *INVENTIONS!*
AND ONE OF THE *VERY* FEW THAT EVER *WORKED!*
IT TAPS INTO MY INTERNAL SOLAR ENERGY SUPPLY AND SUDDENLY -- *ZAP!* YOU'RE *OUT!*
AND SO ARE *YOU,* CYBORG!
SPAK!
UNHH!
THAT *POWER DAMPENER* SHOULD HOLD YOU DOWN FOR A FEW MINUTES --
--LONG ENOUGH FOR MY LITTLE *BUDDY* AND ME TO *GET LOST!*
C'MON, KID -- YOU'RE COMING WITH THE *TERMINATOR!*
NOW YOU'RE GOING TO SEE HOW THE *BIG BOYS* OPERATE!
AGHH! MAN, DON'T KNOW WHAT THIS BLASTED FRISBEE *IS,* BUT IT SURE TURNED OUT THE LIGHTS!
I CAN STILL FEEL THE *PAIN* RIGHT DOWN TO MY STEEL *TOENAILS!*
BUT PAIN OR *NO,* I STILL GOTTA-- *EH?*
TH-THEY'RE *GONE!!*
17

DAZED, THE YOUTH NAMED *VICTOR STONE* BEGINS HIS EASTWARD TREK FROM MANHATTAN'S *CROWDED* MIDTOWN TO A SECLUDED EAST HAMPTON *ESTATE...*

MMMMM! MY PLANET IS FURTHER FROM ITS *SUN* THAN YOURS. THIS *HEAT* IS QUITE... *DELICIOUS!*

...FRANKLY, WALLY, I DON'T SEE ANY *REASON* FOR SECRET IDENTITIES. I THINK THEY'D BE A *PAIN.*

I SEE WHERE HAVING *GREEN* SKIN COULD MAKE IT A *PROBLEM,* GAR...

BUT I *NEED* A SECRET IDENTITY... I GUESS TO KEEP MY PARENTS *SAFE...*

BESIDES, I COULD ALWAYS USE THE *PRIVACY!*

GUESS I'VE BEEN *LUCKY...* I DON'T WEAR A *MASK,* BUT SO FAR NO ONE'S CONNECTED *DONNA TROY* WITH WONDER GIRL.

PARENTS... MINE DON'T *NEED* PROTECTING... NOT IN THE WAY A *SECRET IDENTITY* WOULD HELP.

YOU HAVE *PARENTS?* I SHOULDN'T BE *SURPRISED,* BUT I NEVER THOUGHT...

YOU MEAN THERE ARE *OTHERS* OUT THERE LIKE *YOU?*

MY BROTHER AND SISTER ...MY PARENTS... SO *FAR AWAY.*

I DON'T SUPPOSE I'LL EVER *SEE* THEM AGAIN!

MAYBE YOU *CAN.* WE CAN SIMPLY GET *SUPERMAN* OR *GREEN LANTERN* TO TAKE YOU HOME!

DON'T GIVE UP *HOPE,* KORIAND'R.

DONNA, YOU DO NOT *UNDERSTAND.* I CANNOT *GO HOME...*

I CAN *NEVER* GO HOME *AGAIN.*

WHAT DO YOU *MEAN?*

THE LOVELY ALIEN PRINCESS TURNS, HER OPEN EYES FILLED WITH WARM *TEARS.* BUT THEN, AS SHE IS ABOUT TO *SPEAK...*

'BOUT TIME I FOUND YOU BOZOS! TRY ASKIN' *DIRECTIONS* IN THIS TOWN WHEN YOU LOOK LIKE *ME!*

VICTOR? IS SOMETHING *WRONG?*

BATBOY, YOU JUST SAID A *MOUTHFUL!* LISSEN...

18

IS HE THE *ONE*, SIR?

YEAH. THOSE *H.I.V.E.* CREEPS KNOW WHAT THEY'RE *DOING.*

HE LOOKS *FRIGHTFUL*, SIR. I SHOULD *CALL* THE HOSPITAL.

DON'T *BOTHER.* THE *H.I.V.E.* ALTERED HIS METABOLIC RATE. HE'LL *RECOVER.*

UNNHHH...WH-WHERE AM I?

TAKE IT *EASY*, KID... YOU TOOK A BAD *SPILL!*

YOU? YOU'RE *DEATHSTROKE*... THE *TERMINATOR.* MY FATHER *TOLD* ME ABOUT YOU...

...AND *THE H.I.V.E.* GAVE ME *POWERS* LIKE YOURS... MAYBE EVEN *BETTER.*

NOT *QUITE*, KID. YOUR BRAIN CAPACITY'S BEEN *INCREASED*, BUT YOU'RE FEEDING OFF YOUR BODY'S OWN *ENERGY.*

YOU KEEP *USING* YOUR POWERS -- AND YOU'LL *KILL YOURSELF!*

THE *H.I.V.E.* SAID IF YOU EVER *SAW* ME, YOU'D BE *JEALOUS.*

MY DAD USED TA SAY YOU WERE THE *BEST HIT MAN* IN THE COUNTRY.

HE SAID ONCE YOU *TOOK* AN ASSIGNMENT, YOU NEVER *FAILED.*

WELL, *I* TOOK AN ASSIGNMENT TOO -- TO DESTROY THE *TEEN TITANS!*

AN', MISTER, I'M NOT GONNA *FAIL*. NOT *NOW* ... NOT *EVER!*

THE TERMINATOR..? SHEESH... I USED TA *WORSHIP* HIM... WANTED TO BE JUST *LIKE* HIM...

WELL, NOW I'M *MORE* THAN JUST LIKE HIM. I'M *BETTER!* AN' I'M GONNA *PROVE* IT!

HE IS *DETERMINED*, SIR.

AND *FOOLISH.*

AH, WELL. PREPARE MY *WEAPONS* FOR ME, WILL YOU, WINTERGREEN?

19

...YOUTHS HE DID NOT EVEN *KNOW* SLIGHTLY MORE THAN A WEEK BEFORE...

THE REASONS ARE NO LONGER *IMPORTANT* NOW. INDEED, THEY NEVER *WERE*...

FOR THE TITANS WERE MERELY A *CATALYST* WHICH IGNITED A FLAME THAT WAS ALREADY BURNING BRIGHT...

WILSON, WE WERE *WONDERING* HOW LONG YOU'D TAKE TO GET HERE.

THE NAME'S NOW *THE RAVAGER!* DON'T *FORGET* IT!

CUT THE *KID STUFF*, GRANT. GO *HOME* BEFORE YOU GET *HURT!*

YOU'RE *OUTNUMBERED* ... SEVEN TO ONE!

SEVEN TO *TWO*...AND IN MY BOOK THAT MAKES IT *EVEN* ODDS!

YOU? YOU *FOLLOWED* ME?

COULDN'T LET YOU TACKLE THIS ONE *ALONE.* C'MON, KID--LET'S SHOW 'EM WHO'S THE *BOSS!*

THE TERMINATOR *INTERVENED* AS WE EXPECTED.

THEN THE CHOICE OF GRANT WILSON WAS A *GOOD* ONE.

FOR THE COST OF ONE MINOR *OPERATION*, WE RECEIVED THE TERMINATOR'S SERVICES -- *FREE OF CHARGE!*

TWO AGAINST THE *TITANS*. WHO DO YOU THINK WILL BE *VICTORIOUS?*

NUMBER FIVE, YOU ALREADY *KNOW*-- THE TERMINATOR HAS NEVER *FAILED.*

20

I DON'T *NEED* YOU, TERMINATOR! I DON'T NEED *ANYONE!*

WANG!

I CAN *DESTROY* THESE *CREEPS* MYSELF!

NO WAY, KID... YOU'RE *GOOD,* BUT YOU'RE *RECKLESS!*

SKREEE

DON'T JUST *ATTACK--* *THINK!*

DONNA, HE *SIDESTEPPED* MY *STARBOLT!* NO ONE HAS EVER DONE *THAT* BEFORE!

CALL ME *WONDER GIRL*...WE'RE IN *PUBLIC!*

AND DON'T WORRY, I *GOT* HIM.

LADY, WE'RE *BOTH* HOLDING THIS *GOLDEN ROPE* OF YOURS!

SO DON'T BE SO *SURE* JUST *WHO'S* GOT *WHOM!*

STARFIRE-- *WATCH OUT!*

BLAST...LOST MY *FOOTING...* GETTING TOO *CONFIDENT* ABOUT MY *AMAZON* POWERS!

NUTS! THAT *JERK'S* GOT *ROBIN* AND I DON'T EVEN KNOW IF "TONY THE TIGER" HERE CAN *STOP* HIM!

WELL, NO ONE EVER SAID I WAS *BRIGHT*... SO HERE GOES *NOTHING!*

YOO HOO, HANDSOME, *FORGET* SOMEONE?

WHOK!

I FORGET *NOTHING,* SHAPE-CHANGER! AND I DON'T NEED MY *INCREASED* STRENGTH TO TAKE CARE OF *FOOLS* LIKE *YOU!*

GAS?!?

AND *BLASTERS?* C'MON, PUNK! THEY CAN'T *STOP* ME!

21

UNGHH!

SPAK!

AND *THAT* WAY I GET *TWO* OF YOU CREEPS AT *ONCE!*

HUH? I *HAD* 'IM... BUT HE JUST *DUCKED* LIKE I WAS STANDING STILL!

SKRAK!

MAYBE *NOT,* BUT THEY'LL SURE *SLOW YOU DOWN!*

YOU'RE PICKING IT UP, KID... OUR *REFLEXES* LET US MOVE FASTER THAN *ANY* OF THEM!

ONCE YOU KNOW WHAT YOU'RE *DOING,* NOT EVEN *KID FLASH* CAN STOP YOU!

SNIK!

BUT, SUDDENLY...

SKREEEEEE!!

BLA

MMO!

DIDN'T FEEL THAT *COMING!* MAN, IF THAT HAD *CONNECTED--!*

STARFIRE? *DON'T!* YOU'LL *KILL* THEM!

IT'S ALL RIGHT, ROBIN-- I *KNOW* WHAT I'M *DOING!*

MY STARBOLTS HAVE *MORE* THAN ENOUGH POWER TO BLAST AWAY *BOTH* OF THOSE KILLERS!

STOP HER! THOSE BLASTS ARE *EVERYWHERE...* CAN'T GET AWAY!

SKREEEEEEE!

EVERYTHING'S MOVING TOO *QUICKLY...* FEEL SO *DIZZY...*

STARFIRE ISN'T *LISTENING* TO ROBIN!

SHE'S STILL FIRING THOSE *STARBOLTS!*

GOD, NO-- THE *KID!*

THE *FOOL!* I *WARNED* HIM USING HIS POWERS WOULD TAKE ITS *TOLL!*

BUT I *DIDN'T* THINK IT WOULD HAPPEN SO *QUICKLY!*

22

HOLD IT, HE'S *FALLING*-- AND I DON'T THINK THIS IS A *TRICK!*

HE LOOKS *SICK...* *DEATHLY* SICK!

TERMINATOR ...ARE YOU *THERE...?*

BUT STARFIRE NEVER *HIT* HIM!

YEAH, *HERE* I AM, KID.

LISTEN, EVERYTHING WILL BE ALL RIGHT. JUST REST.

AS THE TERMINATOR STEPS FORWARD, THE AIR SUDDENLY CRACKLES WITH ELECTRICITY...

THEN...

THE BOY IS *DYING...* LET THAT END THE *FIGHTING!*

TAKE HIM, TERMINATOR-- AND GO IN *PEACE!*

RAVEN? WHERE'VE YOU *BEEN?*

IN A PLACE BEYOND IMAGINING... LEARNING THAT THE REASON FOR THE TITAN'S *RE-CREATION* HAS FINALLY COME TO *BIRTH!*

SOON WE WILL BE NEEDED *ELSEWHERE.* I CANNOT HAVE YOU FIGHT SOME MEANING- LESS BATTLE *NOW!*

BUT *YOU*-- HOW COULD YOU LET THE BOY *DIE* LIKE THIS?

I *WARNED* HIM. I TOLD HIM WHAT USING HIS POWER WOULD DO!

BUT HE DIDN'T *BELIEVE* ME.

LOOK AT HIM ...HE'S *BURNED HIMSELF UP* FROM INSIDE...

BLAST HIM AND BLAST THE *H.I.V.E.!*

T...TERMINATOR... D-DID WE *DO* IT...?

D-DID WE KILL THE *TITANS?*

KID, UH... WE--

YOU QUESTION THE FATE OF YOUR *FOES?* LOOK *THERE*, CHILD.

SEE FOR YOURSELF THE *RESULTS* OF YOUR *HANDIWORK!*

23

HIS EYES ARE NARROW *SLITS*, BUT HE CAN STILL *SEE* THE ONES HE CAME TO HATE LYING DEFEATED AND DEAD UPON THE COLD EARTH...

THEN, AND ONLY *THEN*, HIS EYES *CLOSE* FOR THE FINAL TIME.

HIS NAME WAS *GRANT WILSON*, AGE NINETEEN, AND IN THOSE ALL-TOO-FEW YEARS HE HAD LEARNED ONLY ONE *LESSON:*

GRANT WILSON HAD LEARNED TO *HATE.*

AND IN THE END, IT WAS HATE WHICH *CONSUMED* HIM. HATE AND NOTHING *MORE*...

HATE WHICH DID NOT DIE *WITH* HIM BUT IS *PASSED ON* LIKE SOME DEMON RUNNER'S *TORCH!*

YOU DID THIS TO HIM, YOU TITANS *KILLED* HIM!

NO. *WE* DID NOTHING. THE ONES WHO GAVE HIM HIS POWERS ARE HIS *TRUE* KILLERS.

THAT'S NOT THE WAY IT *WORKS* IN MY RACKET, SISTER. THE KID TOOK A *CONTRACT!*

AND HE *DIED...* BECAUSE OF *YOU.*

POOR STUPID KID. HE NEVER REALLY HAD A *CHANCE.*

YOU'RE LETTING THEM *GO?* BUT THEY *ATTACKED* US -- THEY TRIED TO *KILL* US.

IF THERE IS A *DIFFERENCE* BETWEEN HIS KIND AND OURS, IT MUST BE IN OUR *COMPASSION* FOR AN ENEMY.

COMPASSION? I DON'T UNDERSTAND!

AND THAT MIGHT BE ENOUGH TO END THE NEW TITANS BEFORE WE'VE EVEN *BEGUN!*

24

EPILOGUE:

It *RAINS* the next day, a dark, sooty kind of New York rain that turns the world *GRAY*. But, to *ONE* young woman, the elements mean *NOTHING*.

She has come to pay her *FINAL RESPECTS* to a man she once had loved and cared for.

That's Grant's old *GIRL FRIEND*, isn't it? What's her *NAME* again, Wintergreen?

Carol... Carol Sladky, I believe, sir. I contacted the *H.I.V.E.* concerning young Grant's *CONTRACT*...

All those *STORIES* he heard about the *TERMINATOR*... no wonder he wanted to be *LIKE* me.

A *SHAME* you never really got to *KNOW* him, sir.

Yeah, and they were *DELIGHTED* that I'm gonna *FINISH* his job for him, right? Figure I *OWE* it to him.

I think I knew 'im pretty well, Wintergreen. After all, what is it they *SAY?*

"LIKE FATHER, LIKE SON!"

GRANT WILSON 1961-1980

The child died as *EXPECTED*. And now we have the *FATHER* as we anticipated!

He will not be *LOYAL*.

It does not *MATTER*. He will do his *JOB*. We gave him a reason to *HATE* the new Titans...

...and that hate will be *ENOUGH*.

"LIKE FATHER, LIKE SON" he said. So true ...so *TRUE*...

NEXT ISSUE: The origin of Starfire! More of Raven's secret! And, the creation of the most villainous super group of all! **"The FEARSOME FIVE!"** Join us, we promise to make it worth your while.

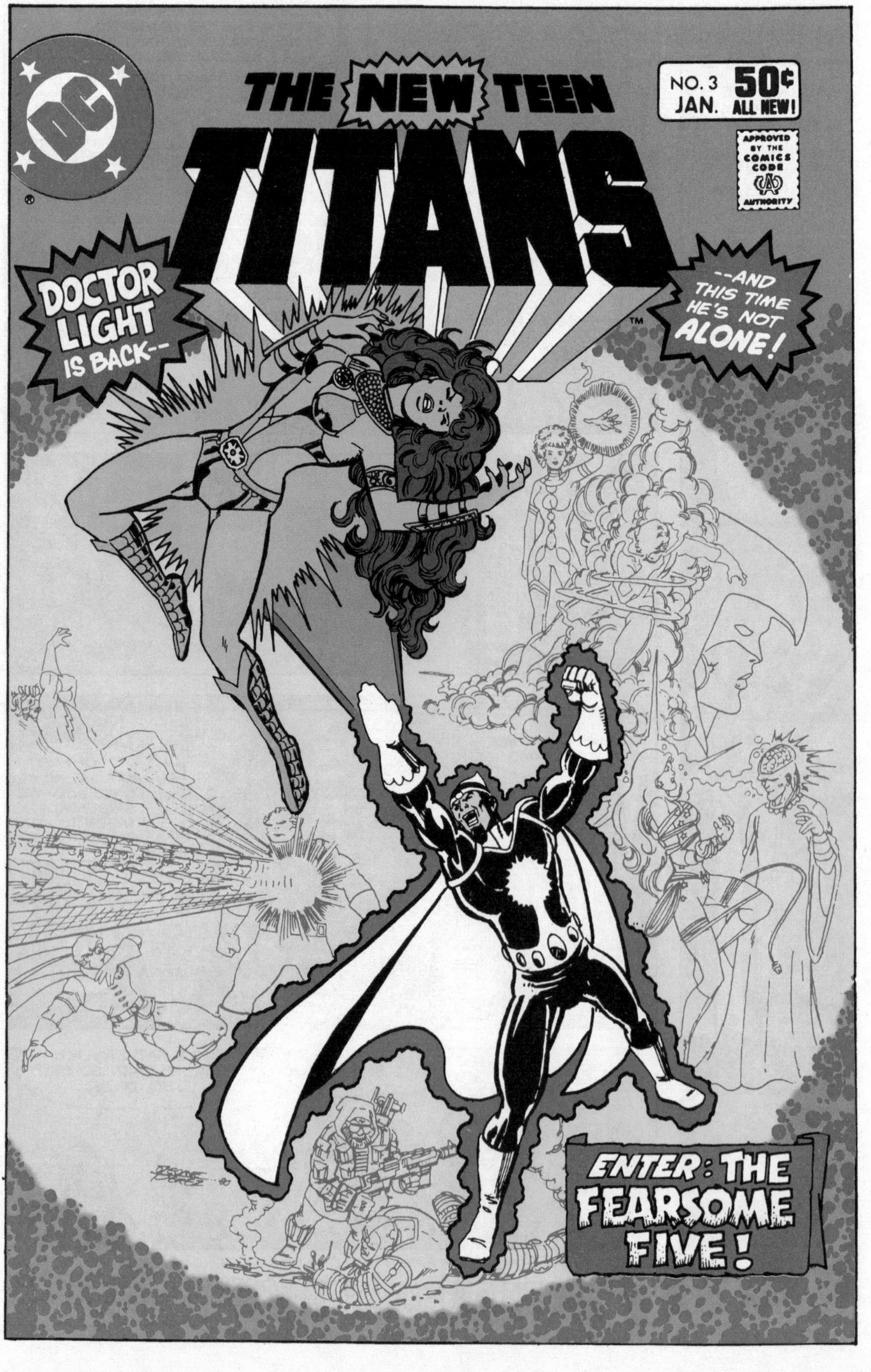
THE NEW TEEN TITANS
NO. 3 JAN.
50¢ ALL NEW!
APPROVED BY THE COMICS CODE AUTHORITY
DOCTOR LIGHT IS BACK--
--AND THIS TIME HE'S NOT ALONE!
ENTER: THE FEARSOME FIVE!

THEY ARE THE *BEST* THERE IS: *THE CHANGELING*, SHAPE-SHIFTER SUPREME; *CYBORG*, HALF MAN / HALF ROBOT; *KID FLASH*, SUPER-SPEEDSTER; *RAVEN*, MISTRESS OF MAGIC; *ROBIN*, THE TEEN WONDER; *STARFIRE*, ALIEN POWERHOUSE; AND *WONDER GIRL*, THE AMAZING AMAZON! TOGETHER THEY ARE...

THE NEW TEEN TITANS

MARV WOLFMAN & GEORGE PÉREZ / FRANK CHIARAMONTE / BEN ODA / ADRIENNE ROY / LEN WEIN
WRITER — CREATORS — LAYOUTS / FINISHES / LETTERER / COLORIST / EDITOR

THE FEARSOME FIVE!

NEW YORK CITY: SOMEWHERE IN THE EAST EIGHTIES...

THERE, YOU SEE *VEGA?* THAT IS THE STAR OF MY BIRTH!

AND *TAMARAN*, ITS *EIGHTH* PLANET, IS MY *HOME!*

IT'S BEEN SO VERY *LONG* SINCE I LAST SOARED THROUGH ITS LUSH, GREEN *VALLEYS...*

I WONDER IF IT'S *CHANGED* ANY SINCE THEN?

UP AND *AT 'EM,* GUYS. FREE COKES AND SEVEN-UPS!

BEAUTIFUL, YOUR PAD IS FAAAANTASTIC!!

BUT IT'S GOTTA SET YOU BACK A BUNDLE!

I WORK, CHANGELING. BESIDES, MY MOTHER SENDS ME A STIPEND!

STIPEND, MY TAIL! SHE'S GOTTA BE SENDING YOU THE WHOLE BANK OF ENGLAND!

SO YOU'RE ROOMING WITH KORIAND'R?

YEAH, THIS PLACE IS TOO LARGE FOR JUST ME. 'SIDES, I THINK IT'LL BE FUN.

AGAIN I THANK YOU, DONNA TROY.

I STILL FEEL LIKE A STRANGER TO YOUR PLANET, BUT YOU'VE OPENED YOUR HOME TO ME.

IT HAS BEEN SO VERY LONG SINCE I HAD A REAL HOME.

SO VERY LONG...

AS THE OTHERS TURN QUESTIONINGLY TOWARD THE GIRL KNOWN AS STARFIRE, WE TRAVEL SOUTH AND WEST TO...

YUH SURE THIS IS IS THE MEETIN' PLACE, SELINDA? IT SURE DON'T LOOK LIKE NOTHIN'!

BARAN, YOU MUST TRUST YOUR SISTER NOT TO MAKE MISTAKES.

BUT, IF THEY WUZ WAITIN' FER US, WHY'S THE DOOR LOCKED?

MEBBE I SHOULD SMASH IT DOWN, HUH?

WHY WASTE THE ENERGY, BROTHER? WHEN, WITH A SIMPLE PASS OF MY HAND--

-- I CAN TRANSMUTE THE VERY FABRIC OF THIS WOODEN DOOR INTO EASILY PASSABLE WATER VAPOR!

COME, BARAN! WE MUSTN'T KEEP THE OTHERS WAITING!

2

I DUNNO, SELINDA, THIS WHOLE SETUP *STINKS.* I DON'T *LIKE* IT NONE.

I *AGREE,* KEEP UP YOUR *GUARD.*

THIS *COULD* BE A TRAP SET UP BY THE *H.I.V.E.*

THEY STILL HAVEN'T *FORGIVEN* US SINCE WE -- *BARAN!?!*

WEAPONS-- SLIDING OUT FROM THE WALLS!

I SEE 'EM, GET *BEHIND* ME!

SWAMM!

SPLAMM!

BRAMM!

THEY GOT REAL SOUPED-UP *GUNS* --

-- BUT THEY STILL DIDN'T DENT *MY* HIDE!

NOTHIN'-- BUT *NOTHIN'* --CAN STOP *MAMMOTH!*

NOT ANY PIPSQUEAK *TOY* GUNS...

NOT ANY STUPID *BLASTERS*...

NOTHIN'!

YOU HEAR ME--? *NOTHIN'!!!*

KRANG!

WOTTA WE DO *NOW,* SELINDA? THEY TRIED TA *KILL* US.

NO, BARAN ... I THINK THEY WERE MERELY *TESTING* US!

WE *STAY.* THIS IS DEFINITELY THE RIGHT *PLACE!*

3

STAY? BUT I DON'T *LIKE* THIS, SELINDA. LET'S *GO*, HUH?

NONSENSE, YOU TWO. YOU HAVE *PASSED* THE TEST. C'MON *IN*.

ARE *YOU* THE ONE WHO PLACED THAT AD IN THE *"UNDERWORLD STAR,"* LOOKING TO RECRUIT A *SUPER-MOB?*

WHO *ELSE?* AND I BELIEVE IN *YOU*, WE'VE *FOUND* OUR FINAL TWO *MEMBERS.*

SIS, I *SEEN* THAT CREEP *SOMEWHERE* BEFORE!

OF COURSE YOU HAVE, MY BIG FRIEND. I'M *DOCTOR LIGHT,* MASTER OF ILLUMINATION!

AND TO MY *LEFT*...

I AM CALLED *PSIMON!* I AM PLEASED TO *MEET* YOU.

CAN'T STOP AN' *LOOK UP* NOW. I ALMOST GOT THIS BLASTED *NEUTRON SWEEPER* WORKIN'!

OH, BY THE WAY, MY HANDLE'S *GIZMO!*

MY NAME IS SELINDA, BUT YOU MAY REFER TO ME AS -- *SHIMMER!*

I AM A *MATTER TRANSMUTER!*

AND MY BROTHER HERE IS CALLED *MAMMOTH,* FOR RATHER OBVIOUS REASONS.

SHIMMER AND MAMMOTH, SIMPLY *PERFECT!*

WELL, MY FRIENDS, WE'VE COMPLETED THE CASTING FOR *THE FEARSOME FIVE!*

AND, FOR OUR FIRST ACT TOGETHER, WE WILL *DESTROY THE NEW TEEN TITANS!*

NOW, SHALL WE GET DOWN TO *BUSINESS?*

4

QUESTIONS? DON'T WORRY, THEY'LL BE ANSWERED SOON ENOUGH. BUT *FIRST*...

WHEN WE FIRST *FOUND* YOU, KORIAND'R, YOU WERE AN *ESCAPED SLAVE*...

BUT I WAS BORN INTO THE HOUSE OF TYKAYL, PRINCESS OF *TAMARAN*...

...AND, AS ELDEST CHILD, I WOULD HAVE BEEN OUR PEOPLE'S *QUEEN*.

BUT, I SUPPOSE RULING *PARADISE* WAS NOT MY *DESTINY*.

FOR TAMARAN WAS AS *CLOSE* TO PARADISE AS ANY WORLD I'VE SEEN SINCE *FORSAKING* ITS TROPICAL SHORES.

AND EVEN NOW, SO MANY YEARS *LATER*, WHEN I SLEEP I *DREAM* OF ITS MAGNIFICENCE AND BEAUTY. I TRULY *MISS* IT.

MY PEOPLE HAD TAMED A TROPICAL *WONDERLAND* AND WE LIVED IN HARMONY *SIDE BY SIDE* WITH OUR WILDLIFE.

OUR PEOPLE WERE NOT INDOCTRINATED INTO *SCIENCE* ...SO WE WERE RULED BY OUR *EMOTIONS*.

WE *LOVED* OUR FRIENDS WITH AN *UNRESTRAINED HEART*...

...AND *HATED* OUR CELESTIAL *ENEMIES* WITH *EQUAL FERVOR!*

5

ROBIN, YOU HAVE SAID MY BLOODLUST *STARTLED* YOU. YET, THAT IS OUR *WAY*. FROM WHAT I'VE SEEN, YOU EARTHLINGS ARE *SUSPICIOUS* OF YOUR *FRIENDS* AND SHOW *COMPASSION* FOR THOSE WHO *HATE* YOU.

"BUT, IF YOU FIND *MY* BATTLE LUST TOO GREAT, YOU SHOULD KNOW OF *THE CITADEL!*

"A MORE *BLOOD-HUNGRY* RACE HAS NEVER BEEN *KNOWN*, FOR THEY *NEVER* SHOW COMPASSION AND HAVE NEVER KNOWN *LOVE*.

"THEY *ATTACKED* TAMARAN, WOULD HAVE *DESTROYED* ALL MY PEOPLE, BUT MY FATHER, *KING MYAND'R*, NEGOTIATED A SOLEMN *PEACE*.

"THE CITADEL OVER-LORDS DISPATCHED THE *GORDANIANS*-- THEIR *WARRIOR-SOLDIERS* AND SLAVERS--

"--ON A MISSION WHICH WOULD CRUSH THE *SPIRIT* OF TAMARAN EVEN AS IT SAVED ITS *PEOPLE* FROM *ANNIHILATION!*"

THIS IS THE *CASTLE*.

MYAND'R. WE HAVE *COME*.

SO *SOON*? I HAD HOPED IT WOULD BE *LONGER*.

FATHER, PLEASE DON'T LET THEM TAKE *KORIAND'R*.

SH-SHE'S SO *YOUNG* ...SO *INNOCENT*.

I AM *SORRY*, BUT YOUR WAY SEEMS SO *WRONG* TO ME.

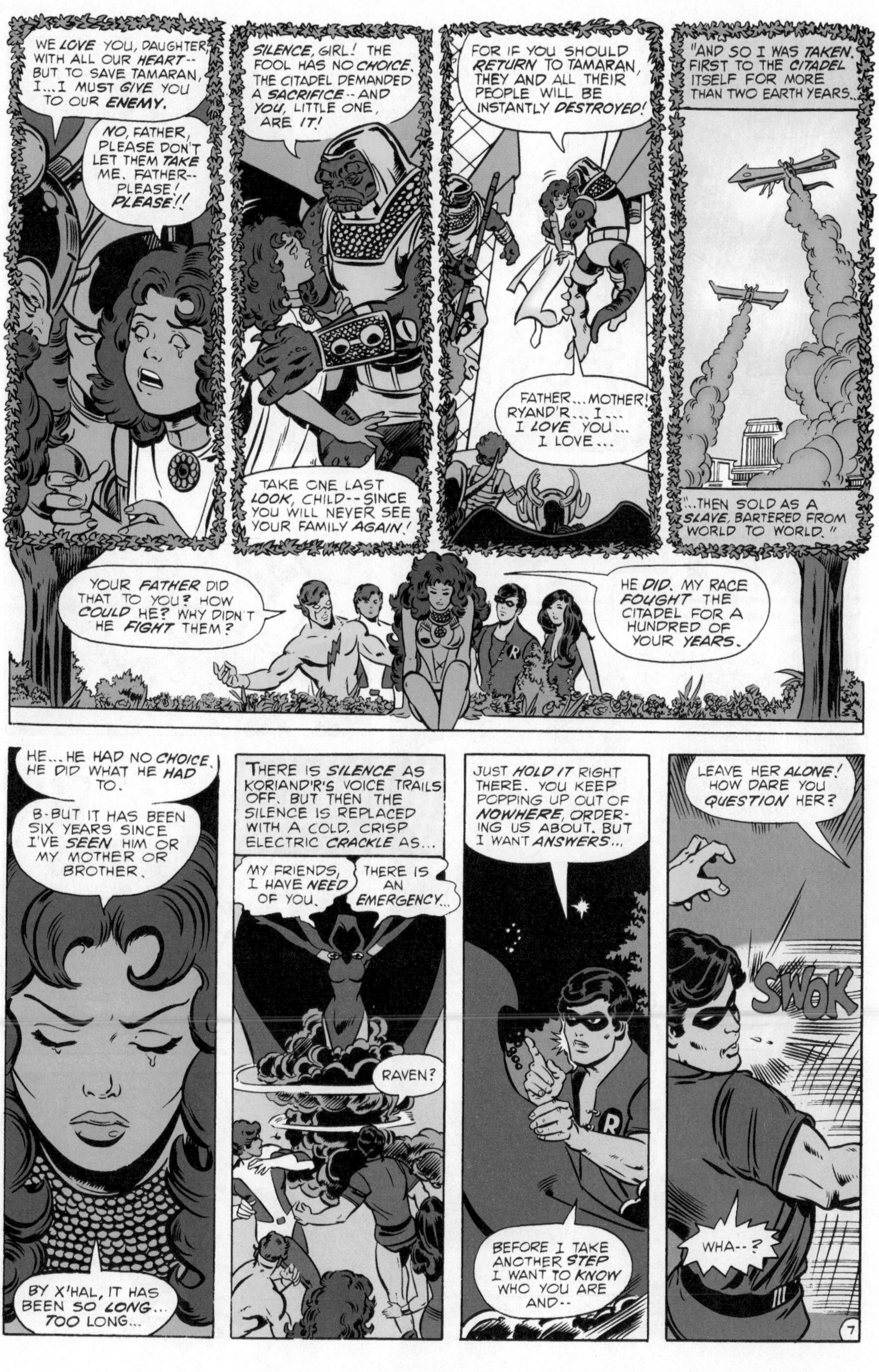

WE LOVE YOU, DAUGHTER, WITH ALL OUR HEART-- BUT TO SAVE TAMARAN, I...I MUST GIVE YOU TO OUR ENEMY.
NO, FATHER, PLEASE DON'T LET THEM TAKE ME. FATHER-- PLEASE! PLEASE!!
SILENCE, GIRL! THE FOOL HAS NO CHOICE. THE CITADEL DEMANDED A SACRIFICE-- AND YOU, LITTLE ONE, ARE IT!
TAKE ONE LAST LOOK, CHILD-- SINCE YOU WILL NEVER SEE YOUR FAMILY AGAIN!
FOR IF YOU SHOULD RETURN TO TAMARAN, THEY AND ALL THEIR PEOPLE WILL BE INSTANTLY DESTROYED!
FATHER... MOTHER! RYAND'R... I... I LOVE YOU... I LOVE...
"AND SO I WAS TAKEN. FIRST TO THE CITADEL ITSELF FOR MORE THAN TWO EARTH YEARS...
"...THEN SOLD AS A SLAVE, BARTERED FROM WORLD TO WORLD."
YOUR FATHER DID THAT TO YOU? HOW COULD HE? WHY DIDN'T HE FIGHT THEM?
HE DID. MY RACE FOUGHT THE CITADEL FOR A HUNDRED OF YOUR YEARS.
HE... HE HAD NO CHOICE. HE DID WHAT HE HAD TO.
B-BUT IT HAS BEEN SIX YEARS SINCE I'VE SEEN HIM OR MY MOTHER OR BROTHER.
BY X'HAL, IT HAS BEEN SO LONG... TOO LONG...
THERE IS SILENCE AS KORIAND'R'S VOICE TRAILS OFF. BUT THEN THE SILENCE IS REPLACED WITH A COLD, CRISP ELECTRIC CRACKLE AS...
MY FRIENDS, I HAVE NEED OF YOU.
THERE IS AN EMERGENCY...
RAVEN?
JUST HOLD IT RIGHT THERE. YOU KEEP POPPING UP OUT OF NOWHERE, ORDERING US ABOUT. BUT I WANT ANSWERS...
BEFORE I TAKE ANOTHER STEP I WANT TO KNOW WHO YOU ARE AND--
LEAVE HER ALONE! HOW DARE YOU QUESTION HER?
SWOK
WHA--?
7

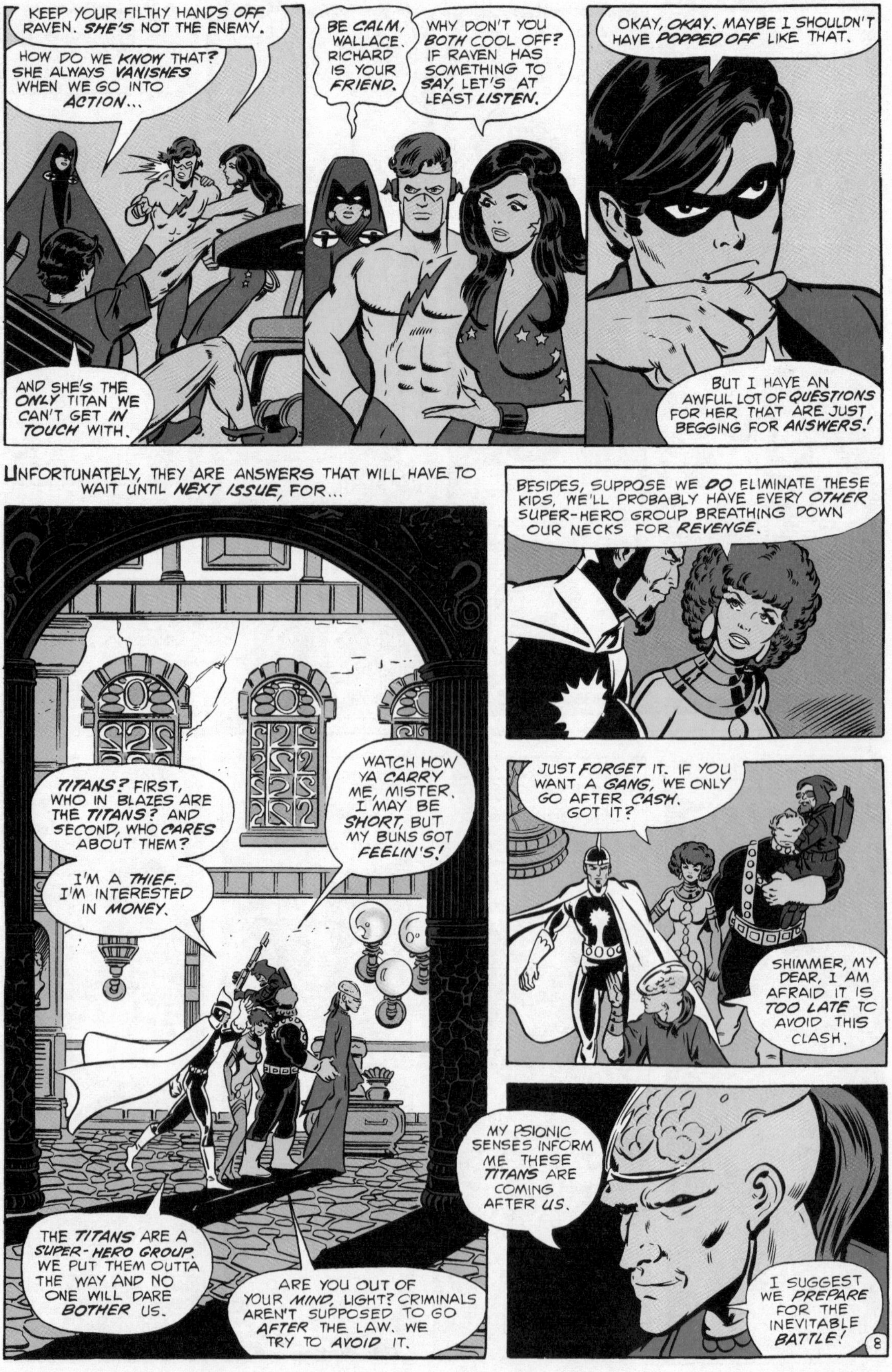

KEEP YOUR FILTHY HANDS OFF RAVEN. SHE'S NOT THE ENEMY.
HOW DO WE KNOW THAT? SHE ALWAYS VANISHES WHEN WE GO INTO ACTION...
AND SHE'S THE ONLY TITAN WE CAN'T GET IN TOUCH WITH.
BE CALM, WALLACE. RICHARD IS YOUR FRIEND.
WHY DON'T YOU BOTH COOL OFF? IF RAVEN HAS SOMETHING TO SAY, LET'S AT LEAST LISTEN.
OKAY, OKAY. MAYBE I SHOULDN'T HAVE POPPED OFF LIKE THAT.
BUT I HAVE AN AWFUL LOT OF QUESTIONS FOR HER THAT ARE JUST BEGGING FOR ANSWERS!
UNFORTUNATELY, THEY ARE ANSWERS THAT WILL HAVE TO WAIT UNTIL NEXT ISSUE, FOR...
TITANS? FIRST, WHO IN BLAZES ARE THE TITANS? AND SECOND, WHO CARES ABOUT THEM?
I'M A THIEF. I'M INTERESTED IN MONEY.
WATCH HOW YA CARRY ME, MISTER. I MAY BE SHORT, BUT MY BUNS GOT FEELIN'S!
THE TITANS ARE A SUPER-HERO GROUP. WE PUT THEM OUTTA THE WAY AND NO ONE WILL DARE BOTHER US.
ARE YOU OUT OF YOUR MIND, LIGHT? CRIMINALS AREN'T SUPPOSED TO GO AFTER THE LAW. WE TRY TO AVOID IT.
BESIDES, SUPPOSE WE DO ELIMINATE THESE KIDS, WE'LL PROBABLY HAVE EVERY OTHER SUPER-HERO GROUP BREATHING DOWN OUR NECKS FOR REVENGE.
JUST FORGET IT. IF YOU WANT A GANG, WE ONLY GO AFTER CASH. GOT IT?
SHIMMER, MY DEAR, I AM AFRAID IT IS TOO LATE TO AVOID THIS CLASH.
MY PSIONIC SENSES INFORM ME THESE TITANS ARE COMING AFTER US.
I SUGGEST WE PREPARE FOR THE INEVITABLE BATTLE!
8

AND, LESS THAN A MINUTE LATER...

OKAY, RAVEN, I APOLOGIZE. YOU WERE RIGHT. I MAY NOT KNOW *EVERYONE* HERE, BUT I SURE KNOW A CRUMB LIKE *DOCTOR LIGHT!*

APOLOGIES ARE NOT *NECESSARY.* WE'RE ALL WORKING *TOGETHER.*

I SURE *HOPE* SO.

YEAH? THEN WHAT HAPPENED TO *CYBORG?* WHERE IS *HE?*

BEING A *TITAN* ISN'T LIKE HAVING A *JOB.* WE DO THIS STUFF IN OUR *SPARE TIME!*

SURE, CYBORG'S TRYING TO RENT HIMSELF OUT FOR *STAR WARS 3*-- TO PLAY C3PO'S BROTHER--!

BESIDES WE DON'T *NEED* CYBORG TO PUT DOWN *DR. LIGHT.*

HECK, EVEN *THE ATOM* STOPPED HIM ONCE.

THAT WAS SIMPLY *LUCK,* GIRLIE, AND THAT WON'T HAPPEN *AGAIN!*

AGGHHHH!

I'VE GAINED MORE *CONTROL* OVER MY LIGHT POWERS SINCE THAT UNFORTUNATE FIASCO!

'SIDES, THIS TIME HE'S GOT *FRIENDS* BACKING HIM UP.

SMILE FOR THE *MISSILE,* KID!

HUH?

SUDDENLY...

SK RAAG!

AGGHHH!

LISSEN, SHORTY, PICKING ON ROBBIE'S A *NO-NO!*

YOU MAKE 'IM *ANGRY* AN' HE'LL SIC THE BIG, BAD *BATMAN* AFTER YA!

HITTING ME? BUT NO ONE'S EVER HIT *GIZMO* BEFORE!

SPAK!

WOTTAYAKNOW? A *FIRST!*

9

85

YOU, CREEP! WHAT'D YOU HIT MY LITTLE *FRIEND* FOR?

UH-OH.

HI THERE! *NICE* BOY! DOWN, BOY! GOT ANY THORNS YOU WANT REMOVED FROM YOUR *PAW*?

MAMMOTH WANTS TO REMOVE *YOU*!

SOMEHOW I *KNEW* YOU'D SAY THAT.

SUDDENLY, THE CHANGELING GLOWS, HIS FORM BEGINS TO SHIFT, AND...

MAMMOTH, OL' BUDDY, ANYONE EVER TELL YOU THAT YOU'VE GOT A DEFINITE *HOSTILE* STREAK?

BAM

BLAM

WHAM

BARAN! ARE YOU *HURT*?

NO, SELINDA.

INSECTS DO NOT HURT MAMMOTH!

NOTHING THAT *LIVES* CAN HURT *MAMMOTH*!

JEEZ! WHAT *IS* THAT GUY ANYWAY? A *NEANDERTHAL*?

BUT, A MOMENT LATER...

DON'T *WORRY*, RAVEN...

...I'VE GOT *THESE* TWO...

...*TRAPPED*.

ON THE *CONTRARY*, YOUNG FLASH.

WITH BUT THE *SLIGHTEST* EXPENDITURE OF MY *PSIONIC* POWERS...

...IT IS *YOU* WHO ARE SUDDENLY *TRAPPED*--

--CAUGHT IN YOUR OWN UNSTOPPABLE *WHIRLWIND*!

YAAAAAAAGGGHHHHHH

10

X'HAL'S BLOOD! HIS LIGHT SHIELD REFLECTS MY STARBOLTS!

BUT NOTHING HAS EVER DONE THAT BEFORE!

SKREEEK!

THERE'S NEVER BEEN ANYONE LIKE DR. LIGHT BEFORE.

WHEN GIZMO INTEGRATED THE CIRCUITRY OF MY LIGHTGUN INTO MY COSTUME, HE INCREASED MY ALREADY-INCREDIBLE POWERS!

NOW THERE'S ALMOST NOTHING I CANNOT DO!

BUT...

SKREEEAAKKK!

AGGGHHH! THAT GIRL'S FIRE ...IT HIT ME!

I...I'M BURNING UP!

BARAN! TRY TO MOVE ...BARAN!!

UNHHH...YEAH, WHEN THAT LIGHT HIT ME, IT HURT ME.

BUT NOTHING CAN KILL ME.

ARE YOU ALL RIGHT?

YOU HEAR ME? NOTHING CAN KILL MAMMOTH!

SKRAGG!

HERA HELP ME! HE RIPPED UP THE WHOLE FLOOR!

TRY TO MAINTAIN YOUR BALANCE!

BALANCE, SHMALANCE! I'M TAKIN' TO THE AIR!

STAND BACK, BARAN. I'VE BEEN WAITING PATIENTLY, QUIETLY, BUT NOW IT'S TIME FOR ME TO ACT!

LET'S SEE IF THEY CAN SURVIVE--

--THE ELEMENT-CHANGING POWERS OF SHIMMER!

11

BLAZES! SHE JUST WAVED HER HAND...

...THE WALLS AND FLOORS -- ROBIN, SHE'S *DONE* SOMETHING TO THEM!

CAN'T YOU SMELL IT? IT'S *ETHER!*

I-IT'S EVEN AFFECTING ME...;GASP;

;GASP; I...IT'S PUTTING US TO... SLEEP...;CHOKE;

;CHOKE;... LIMBS... SO TIRED... WANNA SLEEP... ;CHOKE;...

;GASP; ;GASP; NEED FRESH AIR... GOT TO... GET OUTTA-- *RAVEN?*

RAVEN, WHERE ARE YOU *GOING?*

;CHOKE; RAVEN!?! ;GASP; ...SH-SHE'S *DISAPPEARING* AGAINNNNN...

MEANWHILE, OUTSIDE...

HEY, WAIT FER ME.

IT TOOK A FEW SECONDS TA JURY-RIG THESE FIRE EXTINGUISHERS INTO *JETS!*

HEY, DID YOU JERKS *HEAR* ME BACK THERE? WE *HAD* THE TITANS, SO WHY DID WE *LEAVE?*

I...I DON'T *KNOW*, GIZMO. SOMETHING *FORCED* ME OUT OF THERE, BUT I DON'T KNOW *WHAT*.

PSIMON SAYS *NOTHING*, BUT A THIN, EVIL *SMILE* SNAKES ACROSS HIS PALE LIPS.

DR. LIGHT MAY HAVE *ORGANIZED* THIS FEARSOME FIVE, BUT IT WILL BE *PSIMON*, THE MIND-MASTER, WHO WILL VERY SHORTLY BE THEIR *LEADER!*

12

SOMEWHEN...

THOSE WERE THE *FIVE*, WEREN'T THEY?

WHY WON'T YOU *ANSWER* ME, TRIGON? CAN IT BE YOU *FEAR* ME?

DON'T DARE *DENY* IT, TRIGON! YOU'RE *CONTROLLING* THEM!

OR *FEAR* THE *GROUP* I'VE *ASSEMBLED* TO *FIGHT* YOU?

THE AIR SEEMS TO RIPPLE WITH *FIRE*, THEN...

WHAT *NOW*, TRIGON? ANOTHER *ATTACK*? OR IS THIS JUST TO *SCARE* ME AWAY?

WHICHEVER, I WON'T LET YOU *DO* IT, I CAN'T HELP STOP YOU DEAD --

-- THEREFORE, I'LL TAKE MY *LEAVE* BEFORE YOUR BOLT OF *DESTRUCTION* CAN *REACH* ME!

GOODBYE FOR *NOW*, TRIGON, BUT WE WILL MEET *AGAIN*, AND *SOON*--

--ON THE FIELD OF *BATTLE*!

THE MYSTERIOUS GIRL NAMED RAVEN *VANISHES* IN A CLOUD OF EBON SMOKE, BUT TRIGON BARELY *NOTICES*. TO ONE OF HIS POWER, SHE IS *NOTHING*...

STILL, HE MUST *WONDER*: WHY COULDN'T HE STRIKE *FASTER*? WHY COULDN'T HE *SLAY* HER BEFORE SHE *FLED*?

THE QUESTIONS AND THEIR FRIGHTENING IMPLICATIONS *GNAW* AT HIM.

13

NEW YORK CITY, 44TH STREET AND ELEVENTH AVENUE...

IF TAMARAN WAS *PARADISE*, THEN THIS DARK, SEAMY SIDE STREET IS MOST DEFINITELY *HELL*...

OR MEBBE YOU WERE TOO *THICK* TO UNDERSTAND WHAT I *MEANT* WHEN I SAID I NEVER WANTED TO *SEE* YOU AGAIN.

PLEASE, VICTOR, I'VE BEGGED YOU TO *FORGIVE* ME. I NEVER MEANT TO *HURT* YOU. I ONLY WANTED TO *HELP*.

YEAH, LIKE YOU HELPED *MOM* INTO THE *GRAVE*, AND ME INTO THIS BLASTED *ROBOT SUIT* I GOTTA WEAR JUST TO STAY ALIVE.

WHY WON'T YOU *LISTEN* TO ME, *VICTOR*?

I *HAD* TO KNOW WHERE YOU LIVED... FOR YOUR OWN *GOOD*.

LISTEN, POP, WITH THE TITANS, I'M STARTING TO *FORGET* THE PAST, ALMOST STARTING TO BE *HAPPY* AGAIN.

SO YOU HAD THOSE GOONS OVER AT *S.T.A.R.* SEARCH ME OUT. THAT *STINKS*, POP, WITH A CAPITAL "*S*".

I MOVED OUTTA OUR HOME TO GET *AWAY* FROM YOU, TO BE BY *MYSELF*.

SO DO ME A *FAVOR* AND GET OUT OF HERE BEFORE YOU *SPOIL* IT ALL.

BUT YOU'VE GOT TO *KNOW*, VICTOR ... YOU'VE GOT TO KNOW I'M *DYING*.

AND BEFORE I'M *DEAD*, I'VE GOT TO CONVINCE YOU OF THE *TRUTH*.

MAN, EVERY TIME I SEE HIM, IT TAKES *DAYS* TO GET *HAPPY* AGAIN.

WHY DOESN'T HE JUST... EH? THAT *LETTER*.

CYBORG: YOU ARE CORDIA[LLY INVI]TED TO THE [GRAND] OPENING OF [THE] TITANS' TOWER. [PLEASE] BE THERE TOMO[RROW] AT NOON. LOCAT[ION] AND MAP ENCLOS[ED].

DIDN'T SEE *THIS* BEFORE. MAYBE THE POSTMAN GAVE IT TO MY *DAD*.

HUH?!?

14

24 HOURS LATER, ON A SMALL ISLAND OFF MANHATTAN IN THE EAST RIVER...

CHUKCHUKCHUKCHUKCHUKCHUKCHUK

WELL, DON'T IT MAKE MY BROWN EYES BLUE!

SONUVAGUN! *TITANS' TOWER,* JUST LIKE THE LETTER SAID.

ONLY QUESTION IS, WHO *BUILT* IT?

WELL, DON'T LOOK A *GIFT MANSION* IN THE *DOOR,* I ALWAYS SAY.

ANYONE GIVES ME AN ALL-EXPENSE-PAID PALACE, I *TAKE* IT...

...UNLESS WHOEVER GAVE IT TO ME IS PREPARING A *TRAP.*

NOW, WHY DID I HAVE TO GO AND *SPOIL* EVERY-THING BY THINKING THE WORST?

JEEZ! GUESS I'M JUST TOO *USED* TO THINKING THAT WAY, CONSIDERING VIRTUALLY NOTHING *GOOD* HAS EVER HAPPENED TO ME IN THE *PAST.*

MY REAL PARENTS *KILLED,* AND NO SOONER DO I GET *ADOPTED* THAN MY *FOSTER MOTHER* GETS HERSELF KILLED AS WELL!

AND I HAVEN'T EVEN *SEEN* MY STEP-DAD IN OVER A *YEAR*... HE'S STILL OUT THERE SEARCH-ING FOR THE *KILLERS!*

KERMIT THE FROG IS *RIGHT*--IT'S NOT *EASY* BEING GREEN!

AND IF I DIDN'T KEEP TELLING *JOKES* ALL THE TIME, I THINK MY HEAD WOULD BLOW UP FROM *DEPRESSION.*

TROUBLE IS, THE JOKES ARE STARTING TO GET *STALE,* AND THE... *EH?*

I *HEAR* SOMETHING... COMING THIS WAY. UH-OH, THE DOOR'S *OPENING...*

YOU?!? YOU!?!?

15

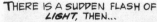
THERE IS A SUDDEN FLASH OF *LIGHT*, THEN...

YOU BOZOS SCARED ME OUTTA TEN YEARS' *GROWTH!*

SHEESH! YOU EVER HEAR OF GIVING A GUY A LITTLE *WARNING?*

JEEZ! NOW THE JERK'S PLAYIN' *BUGS BUNNY!*

I'D PROBABLY GET *SUED* DOING *CRUSADER RABBIT.* YOU GUYS GOT THE LETTER, *TOO?*

YEAH, AND WHAT'S *BOTHERING* ME IS--WE DON'T KNOW WHO *BUILT* THIS OR *WHY!*

NOBODY GIVES AWAY A *HEADQUARTERS* LIKE THIS UNLESS THERE ARE *ROPES* ATTACHED. CYBORG?

YEAH, YEAH, LEADER-MAN. YOU WANT ME TO TAP INTO THE *COMPUTER*, RIGHT?

A SAP DOING A *TAP*. I LOVE IT!

YOU'RE LIVING *DANGEROUSLY*, GREENIE.

I CHECKED OUT THE WHOLE *PLACE*. EVEN THE *DUST* IS CLEAN.

SOMEHOW I'M STILL NOT *CONVINCED.*

YOU AND ME *BOTH*, DONNA. SOMETHING HERE STINKS LIKE THREE-DAY-OLD *HAMBURGER!*

SUDDENLY...

THIS PLACE IS OF NO *IMPORTANCE*. WE HAVE A MISSION *ELSEWHERE.*

EVEN NOW OUR FOES PREPARE TO *STRIKE.*

FORGET IT, RAVEN.

WE'RE NOT GOING *ANYWHERE* UNTIL WE GET SOME *ANSWERS!*

I WARNED YOU *BEFORE*, ROBIN, HANDS OFF--

HOLD, *WALLACE...*

RICHARD IS *CORRECT*. I HAVE GIVEN YOU LITTLE REASON TO *TRUST* ME.

HERE THEN IS THE *TRUTH*, SO YOU WILL KNOW WHY THIS WORLD IS NOW *IMPERILED!*

16

KNOW FIRST WHERE I WAS TRAINED, FOR THE *TEMPLE AZARATH* PREPARED ME IN ALL THE MYSTIC ARTS!

IT WAS *THERE*, DEEP IN THE DEEPEST OF ALL *TRANCES*, THAT I SAW THE DEADLY VISAGE OF *TRIGON THE TERRIBLE!*

HE WHO HAD TORN AN ENTIRE *UNIVERSE* ASUNDER!

"THEN THAT IMAGE BEGAN TO *CHANGE*. I SAW GREAT *HEROES* HERE ON EARTH UNLEASH THE MIGHTIEST OF TRIGON'S *DEMONS*. AFTER A MILLENNIUM OF IMPRISONMENT, *GORONN* WAS *FREE* ONCE MORE!

"AND IN HIS FRIGHTFUL WAKE DID THOSE HEROES FALL *DEAD* ON THE FIELD OF BATTLE!

"THE VISIONS WERE DARK AND TERRIBLE, FOR I SAW OUR MOTHER WORLD CAUGHT IN TRIGON'S EVIL GRIP...

"...CAUGHT AND *CRUSHED* LIKE SOME OVERRIPE MELON, FOR TRIGON'S POWER IS *IMMEASURABLE* AND TERRIBLE BEYOND ANY HUMAN *COMPREHENSION!*

⑰

93

TRIGON'S IMAGE *FADED* AND WAS REPLACED WITH THOSE OF THE *FEARSOME FIVE.* SOMEHOW THEY APPEARED TO ME AS A *WARNING...*

...THOUGH NEVER BEFORE HAD I POSSESSED SUCH POWERS OF *PRECOGNITION.*

YOU'RE SAYING THERE'S A *LINK* BETWEEN THOSE FIVE AND SOME OTHER-DIMENSIONAL *DEMON?*

INFORMATION HAS HAS BEEN GIVEN TO ME, RICHARD. THOSE FIVE *WANT* US TO *FIGHT* THE HEROES I SAW IN MY VISION.

MAN, THAT'S LIKE SENDING *GNATS* AGAINST THE *SEVENTH FLEET!*

YOU ARE *WRONG,* VICTOR. SOMEHOW I SENSE IT IS IN *OUR* INTEREST, AND THE INTEREST OF THIS *WORLD,* TO DO AS THOSE VILLAINS *WISH.*

US TAKE ON THE *WHOLE BLAMED JUSTICE LEAGUE OF AMERICA?*

'SIDES, WE'RE ON THE *SAME SIDE!*

WE MUST NOT ONLY *BATTLE* THE JUSTICE LEAGUE, BUT WE MUST *DEFEAT* THEM AS WELL!

THE NEW JERSEY PALISADES OVERLOOKING UPTOWN MANHATTAN...

...YOU WANT THE JUSTICE LEAGUE DEFEATED BECAUSE THEY'LL SOMEHOW CAUSE YOUR *DEATH?*

IT SOUNDS *INSANE,* LIGHT.

NEVERTHELESS, IT IS *TRUE.* AND SINCE I HAVE REPEATEDLY *LOST* ALL MY BATTLES WITH THE LEAGUE--

--THIS TIME I SHALL SEND *OTHERS* TO DO MY FIGHTING *FOR* ME.

SOUNDS KINDA *ROUNDABOUT* TO ME, LIGHT. WHAT MADE YOU THINK OF THESE *TITAN* CREEPS ANYWAY?

I, UHHH... I DON'T *KNOW,* BUT...

YOU DO NOT *KNOW,* LIGHT, BECAUSE THE TITANS FIT INTO *MY* PLAN AND NOT *YOURS!*

18

PSIMON, ARE YOU CRAZ-- ARRRRGHHH!

SILENCE, YOU DIMWITTED BUFFOON!

ALL THAT HAS TRANSPIRED HERE HAS BEEN *MY* DOING!

I HAVE EVEN PLANTED OUR CURRENT *LOCATION* INTO THE THOUGHTS OF THE TITAN KNOWN AS *RAVEN!*

SELINDA, YOU WANT FOR ME TO *SMASH* HIM?

NO, BARAN, LET'S HEAR HIM OUT.

A WISE *DECISION,* SHIMMER.

"KNOW THEN *THAT* ONCE I WAS MERELY SIMON JONES, PHYSICIST... OBSESSED WITH PIERCING THE BARRIERS BETWEEN DIMENSIONS.

"THEN, YESTERDAY, I *SUCCEEDED...*

"...AND THE RESULTS--

"...WERE BEYOND MORTAL UNDERSTANDING!"

RISE! YOU ARE NOW IN THE POWER OF *TRIGON THE TERRIBLE!*

TITANS! HEED THE WRATHFUL WORD OF *PSIMON!*

WE AWAIT YOU ON THE FIELD OF *BATTLE!* COME AND LEARN WHO YOUR *SUPERIORS* TRULY *ARE!*

I HAD BEEN CHANGED INTO A *LIVING PSIONIC!* ALL MY MIND COULD *CONCEIVE,* I COULD *CREATE!*

BUT TRIGON HAD A *MISSION* PLANNED FOR ME, ONE THAT REQUIRED ASSISTANCE .... *YOUR* ASSISTANCE.

HOLY *CRIPES!* IT'S *WINDOW-HEAD* AGAIN!

ALL RIGHT, TITANS, THIS IS *IT!*

WHEN I SAW *LIGHT'S* REQUEST FOR *PARTNERS,* I KNEW I COULD USE THAT GROUP FOR *MY* PURPOSES. AND *NOW*--

STAND ASIDE AS I *SUMMON* OUR *ENEMIES* TO US FOR A SECOND AND *FINAL* TIME.'

19

YOU'RE *WAITIN'* FOR US, CRUMB? OKAY, MISTER, WE'RE *COMIN'*--

--BUT WE'RE GONNA MAKE YA WISH YOU WERE NEVER *BORN!*

NO, CYBORG... PLEASE DO NOT *GO.* THERE ARE *ALTERNATIVES!*

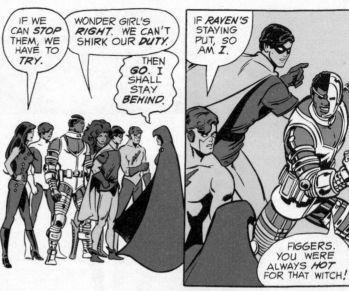

IF WE CAN *STOP* THEM, WE HAVE TO *TRY.*

WONDER GIRL'S *RIGHT.* WE CAN'T SHIRK OUR *DUTY.*

THEN *GO.* I SHALL STAY *BEHIND.*

IF *RAVEN'S* STAYING PUT, SO AM *I.*

FIGGERS. YOU WERE ALWAYS *HOT* FOR THAT WITCH!

C'MON, WE'VE GOT A *JOB* TO DO!

THIS BATTLE IS *USELESS.* OUR TIME SHOULD BE SPENT IN CONVINCING THE *JUSTICE LEAGUE.*

CAN'T *WE* DO THAT?

WE'RE GONNA *SHOW* THOSE JOKERS WHAT THE NEW TITANS ARE *MADE OF!*

I DO NOT *KNOW,* WALLACE. AND PERHAPS *THAT* IS WHY I SUFFER SUCH *SORROW!*

RAVEN SAID THEY'D BE *WAITING* FOR US ON THAT *SHIP!*

I SEE *MAMMOTH.* THE OTHERS MUST BE *WITH* HIM.

YOU'RE KIDDING. YOU CAN SEE THAT *FAR?*

CAN'T *EVERYONE?*

PSIMON WAS *RIGHT.* THOSE CREEPS ARE *COMIN'!*

WELL, *LET 'EM* COME!

MAMMOTH AIN'T AFRAID OF *NO ONE!*

AN' *NO ONE* CAN STOP *MAMMOTH!*

UGLY, WE'LL JUST HAVE TO *SEE* ABOUT THAT, WON'T WE?

SHUMP!

SKUNCH!

20

LOOK AT THEM, STARFIRE, THEY'RE *BAITING* US.

MAYBE RAVEN WAS *RIGHT* -- MAYBE WE *SHOULDN'T* FIGHT THEM.

BUT WHAT *ELSE* CAN WE DO?

YOU CAN *SURRENDER*, GIRL.

BAH! TALKIN'S A WASTE OF TIME, *CREAM* 'EM!

YOU ARE ALWAYS *IMPATIENT*, GIZMO. BUT PERHAPS THIS TIME YOU ARE *RIGHT!*

OH, *NO!* I LET GO OF *ROBIN!*

A MINOR LIGHT BLAST SHOULD PROVE *DEADLY* ENOUGH!

IN AN INSTANT, THE TEEN WONDER *DROPS*...

... AND VANISHES DEEP BENEATH THE BRACKISH WATERS OF THE HUDSON RIVER...

ONE DOWN, TWO MORE HELPLESS.

I'M ALMOST DISAPPOINTED AT THE *EASE* OF YOUR *DEFEAT!*

BAWHAMM

CRIPES! THE DECK'S BLOWIN' UP, LIGHT!

DON'T PLAN ON STRUTTIN' YOUR STUFF JUST YET, JERK!

WH-WHAT'S GOING ON?

WE GOT *COMPANY*, LIGHT.

AN' IF I KNOW MY *MACHINES*, HE COMES EQUIPPED WITH A *SONIC AMPLIFIER!*

BELIEVE IT, SHORTY. I GOT ENOUGH *POWER* HERE TO GIVE YOU *EARACHES* FOR THE REST OF THE *CENTURY*.

21

ONLY IF YOU GET THE CHANCE TO *USE* IT, PUNK!

SPLANG

AN' GIZMO AIN'T GONNA *LET YA!*

HUH? WHAT IN THE WOR--

SKREEAMMM

ARRGHHH!! MY ARM!!

HMMM. THAT TOTALIZER STILL AIN'T *WORKIN'* RIGHT. IT SHOULD'A BLOWN HIM UP *COMPLETELY!*

WONDER GIRL, CYBORG IS *INJURED!* HELP HIM WHILE *I* STOP DR. LIGHT!

SKREEEE

NOT WHEN I HAVE POWER OVER *ALL* LIGHT! EVEN *STAR* LIGHT!

DON'T *SWEAT* IT, DOC. I GOT A *GIZMO* HERE TO TAKE CARE OF THIS *STAR-BROAD!*

MY *HANDS!* WHAT ARE YOU DOING?

OH, JUST SETTIN' UP A *GRAVITY TOW!*

IT USES YOUR OWN *STAR POWER* TO PULL YOU STRAIGHT INTO THE *CENTER OF THE EARTH!*

SKREEEEEE

I-- I CAN'T STOP...

STARFIRE? *STARFIRE?!* GREAT HERA, I CAN'T *SEE* HER!!

WHERE *IS* SHE?

PROBABLY IN *HELL* BY NOW, FOOL. JUST WHERE *YOU'RE* GOING!

A WAVE OF MY HAND TRANSMUTES ENOUGH OF THIS STEEL TO *GAS*--

THE SMOKE-STACK... *FALLING!*

22

UNNHH! ARMS ...STRAINING... I FEEL EVERY *TENDON* PULLING...

I'M *STRONG* ...BUT *THIS* IS JUST *TOO HEAVY!*

...CAN'T *SUPPORT* IT ANY...

WHAT? SOMETHING'S *PULLING* AT ME... CAN'T MOVE A *MUSCLE*...

PSIMON? I SHOULD HAVE *KNOWN.*

BUT YOU *DIDN'T*. AND THAT IS WHY I AM YOUR *SUPERIOR*.

BALONEY! AND WRAPPING THIS *LAMP WIRE* AROUND ME ISN'T PROVING YOUR CASE.

I CAN *SNAP* THIS WIRE LIKE -- *HUNH?* STILL CAN'T *MOVE*...

AND THE WIRE'S *CONSTRICTING* ...GROWING *TIGHTER*...

YES, MY DEAR. YOU SEE, MY *PSIONIC* POWERS PERMIT ME TO DO ALMOST *ANYTHING*...

...INCLUDING PUTTING YOU INTO A *DEEP SLEEP* WITH BUT A TOUCH OF MY HAND.

SLEEP *WELL*, MY DEAR, FOR WHEN YOU *AWAKEN*--

--YOUR VERY *SOUL* WILL BELONG TO *PSIMON!*

MEANWHILE... MAN, EVERY BONE IN MY BODY IS CRYING FOR *HELP*. ALMOST BLACKED OUT FROM THE *IMPACT* OF THAT FALL...

BUT FORTUNATELY I *HELD ON*...AND FORTUNATELY I CAN GET BACK TO DRY LAND BEFORE ANYONE SEES...

UH OH!

23

LESS THAN TWO MILES AWAY, THE WIND MOANS AS IF IN AGONY AS IT TEARS ACROSS THE HIGH ROOF OF *TITANS' TOWER*...

I DON'T *UNDERSTAND*, RAVEN -- WHY DO THE OTHERS KEEP COMING DOWN ON YOU? ESPECIALLY *ROBIN*.

HE TREATS YOU LIKE YOU WERE A *LEPER!*

HE NEEDS *FACTS* TO WORK WITH, NOT *FAITH*, AND I HAVE GIVEN PRECIOUS LITTLE OF *EITHER!*

PERHAPS *NOW*, AS TRIGON MAKES HIS FINAL MOVE, IT IS TIME TO REVEAL THE *WHOLE* TRUTH AND--

NO!!

ALL ARE *UNCONSCIOUS* SAVE STARFIRE AND THE CHANGELING.

"WALLACE, OUR FRIENDS NEED HELP!"

GOTTA HELP... EVEN IF I DON'T PARTICULARLY *LIKE* 'EM.

JUST ONE THING WORRIES ME, THOUGH--

WHAT DID RAVEN MEAN BY "THE *WHOLE* TRUTH"?

FINALLY SHATTERED THOSE *SHACKLES*, BUT-- X'HAL'S BLOOD! MY STARBOLTS ARE *USELESS* AGAINST THE MASSIVE ONE! BUT WHY? *WHY?*

HOOWWWWW!!

BRA

IT'S WORSE THAN I *THOUGHT* ...SEEING ROBIN AND CYBORG *DEFEATED*.

NOW I'VE REALLY GOT TO *STOP* HIM SOME --

FOOLS! MAMMOTH'S BODY IS SO *DENSE* NOTHING CAN HURT IT. *NOTHING!*

WE'LL, DON'T BREAK YOUR ARM PATTING YOURSELF ON THE BACK!

KRA MM

WHAT? *ANOTHER* TITAN? I THOUGHT THEY WERE ALL *SMASHED!*

SURPRISE!

AND NOW FOR MY *NEXT* NUMBER I...I... UNHHH...

YAAWWNNNN...

24

...SLEEPY...UNHNN ...GREAT... JUST...

...GREAT...

AN' I GOT *THIS* ONE, SELINDA.

X'HAL'S *BLOOD!* HIS GRIP IS SO *POWERFUL*, I CANNOT BREAK FREE!

BUT *I* CAN BREAK *YOU!*

W-MMMP

THEY'RE ALL *DOWN*, BECAUSE I *WASN'T* HERE TO *HELP* THEM EARLIER!

BUT I'M GONNA MAKE UP FOR THAT *NOW*, MISTER. YOU BETTER *BELIEVE* IT!

MAMMOTH, HE MOVES TOO *QUICKLY* FOR YOUR *SLOW* REFLEXES. LET MY *MIND* *CONTROL* YOUR ACTIONS...

DO WHAT YOU *WANT*, DOME-HEAD...

BUT, NOTHING'S *FASTER'N* KI--

THUNK!

HUH? I DIDN'T EVEN *SEE* 'IM, BUT I KNOCKED 'IM OUT *ANYWAY!*

WE GOT 'EM *ALL*, PSIMON, JUST LIKE YOU *SAID.*

WOTTA WE GONNA DO *NOW?*

PRECISELY WHAT DR. *LIGHT* HAD *PLANNED*, MY FRIEND.

HUH? YOU MEAN WE'RE *BOTH* AFTER THE *SAME* THING?

NO, LIGHT. *YOU* WISH TO DESTROY YOUR *FOES*. *I* WISH TO DESTROY A *WORLD!*

I HAVEN'T ANY *CHOICE* NOW... AND EVEN THOUGH THEY ONCE *SCORNED* ME, I MUST AGAIN VISIT THE ORBITING SATELLITE HEADQUARTERS OF THE...

JUSTICE LEAGUE of AMERICA

101

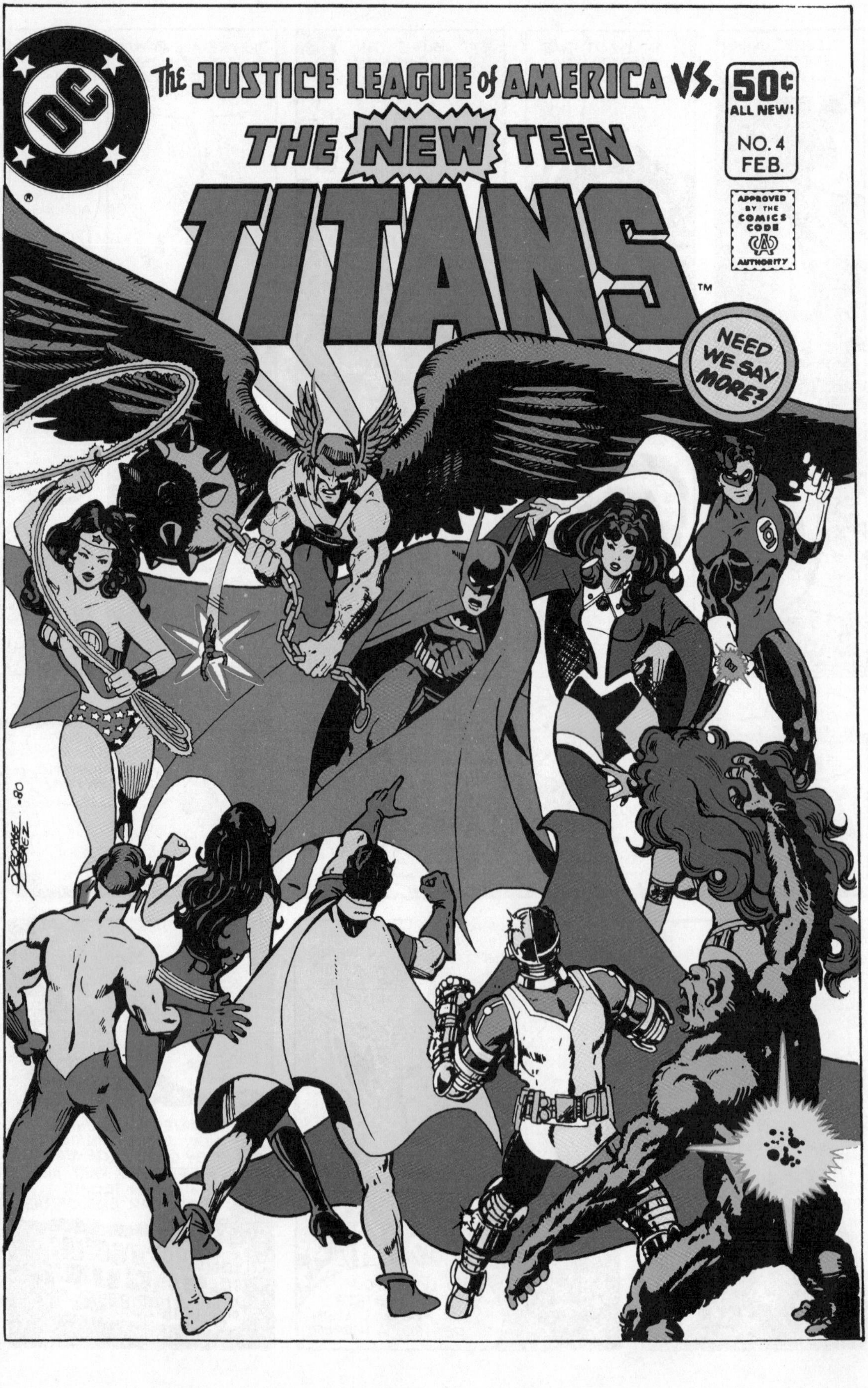
DC
The JUSTICE LEAGUE of AMERICA VS.
THE NEW TEEN
TITANS
50¢
ALL NEW!
NO. 4
FEB.
APPROVED BY THE COMICS CODE AUTHORITY
NEED WE SAY MORE?

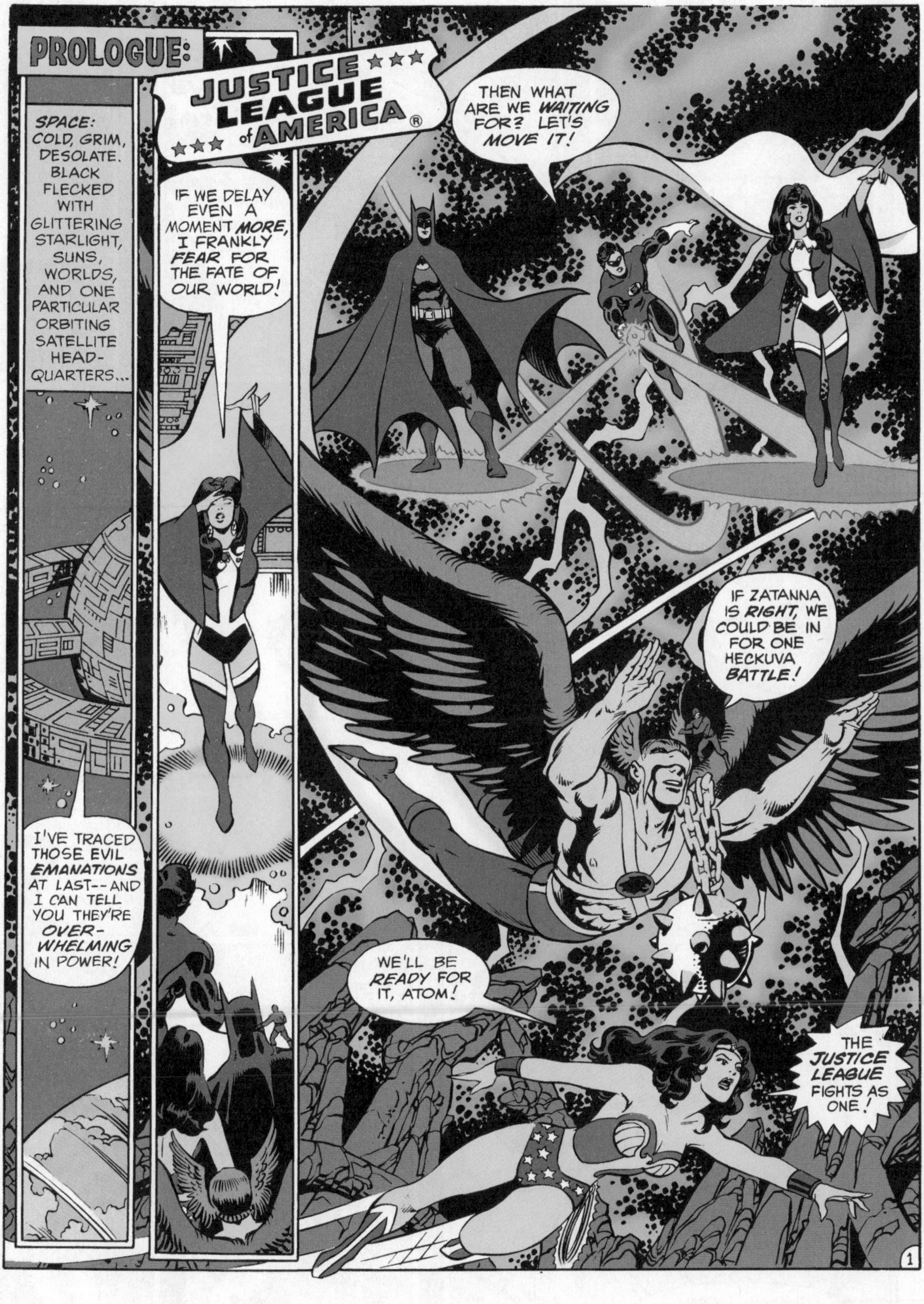
PROLOGUE:
JUSTICE LEAGUE of AMERICA®
SPACE: COLD, GRIM, DESOLATE. BLACK FLECKED WITH GLITTERING STARLIGHT, SUNS, WORLDS, AND ONE PARTICULAR ORBITING SATELLITE HEAD-QUARTERS...
IF WE DELAY EVEN A MOMENT MORE, I FRANKLY FEAR FOR THE FATE OF OUR WORLD!
THEN WHAT ARE WE WAITING FOR? LET'S MOVE IT!
I'VE TRACED THOSE EVIL EMANATIONS AT LAST--AND I CAN TELL YOU THEY'RE OVER-WHELMING IN POWER!
IF ZATANNA IS RIGHT, WE COULD BE IN FOR ONE HECKUVA BATTLE!
WE'LL BE READY FOR IT, ATOM!
THE JUSTICE LEAGUE FIGHTS AS ONE!
1

THIS IS UP *YOUR* ALLEY, ZATANNA. WHAT ARE WE *LOOKING* AT?

IT'S A *MYSTIC CEREMONY* OF SOME SORT!

A *MAGIC* GREATER THAN ANY I'VE EVER BEFORE *ENCOUNTERED,* GREEN LANTERN!

HAWKMAN! WE'VE BEEN *SPOTTED!*

M-MIND GOING *NUMB* ...CAN'T USE MY *RING...*

NO! THEIR *POWER!* I-- CAN'T *FIGHT* IT!

SUCH *POWER* ...AND THEY DON'T SHOW ANY SIGNS OF *STRAIN!*

WE'RE STILL IN *ONE PIECE,* I SEE.

I THINK I CAN CONJURE A SPELL TO--

BUT...

MY MOUTH-- CLAMPED *SHUT! CAN'T SPEAK!*

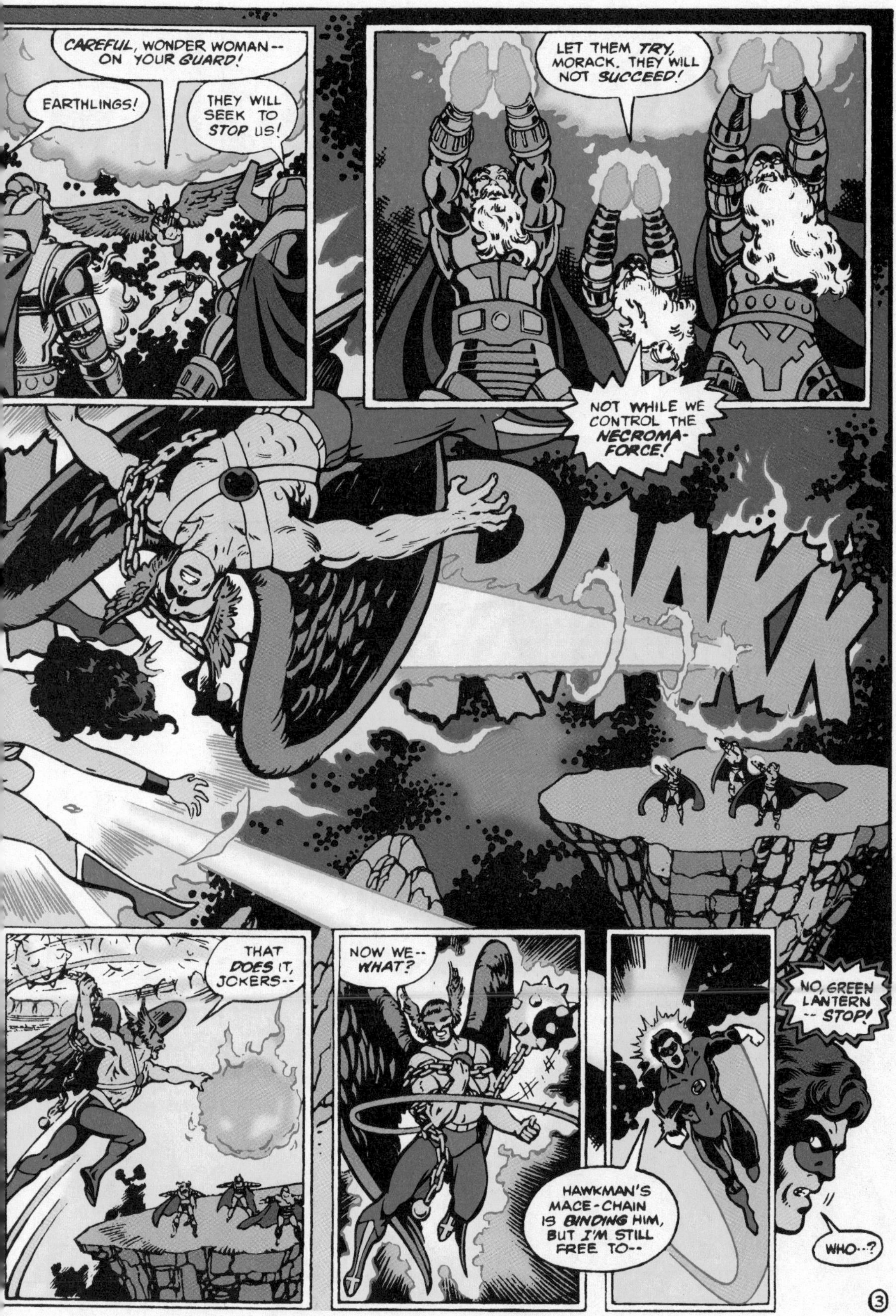
CAREFUL, WONDER WOMAN-- ON YOUR GUARD!
EARTHLINGS!
THEY WILL SEEK TO STOP US!
LET THEM TRY, MORACK. THEY WILL NOT SUCCEED!
NOT WHILE WE CONTROL THE NECROMA-FORCE!
THAT DOES IT, JOKERS--
NOW WE-- WHAT?
HAWKMAN'S MACE-CHAIN IS BINDING HIM, BUT I'M STILL FREE TO--
NO, GREEN LANTERN -- STOP!
WHO--?
3

GREEN LANTERN, PLEASE, I *BESEECH* YOU...

YOU!

LET THOSE SORCERERS DO WHAT THEY *MUST!*

YOU KNOW WE *CAN'T,* RAVEN. YOU WERE TOLD THAT *BEFORE!*

AND I CAN'T LET YOU *INTERFERE* WITH US NOW!

YOUR POWER CAGE MAY HOLD MY *MORTAL* FORM...

...BUT IT IS *USELESS* IN STOPPING MY *SOUL SELF!*

I AM *SORRY,* BUT THE SORCERERS MUST COMPLETE THEIR MISSION.

SWOK

HOW MANY TIMES DO WE HAVE TO *TELL* YOU-- HUH?!

I CAN SEE THAT THIS IS ALL *USELESS.*

TO ACHIEVE *VICTORY,* MY ANSWERS LIE *ELSEWHERE!*

HER ASTRAL IMAGE SLIPPED PAST MY *BEAM!*

THE GIRL FAILED TO *STOP* THEM!

THEN IT IS UP TO *US!*

OUR MISSION IS TOO *VITAL!* NO ONE MAY BE PERMITTED TO INTERFERE WITH US. *NO ONE!*

BPAK!

4

GO, RAVEN. TIME IS OF THE *ESSENCE!*

THEN, I WILL DELAY *NO LONGER!*

FAITH BE *WITH* YOU, MY FRIENDS!

SHE IS *GONE,* BUT TO *WHERE?* TO SOME STRANGE, FARAWAY *CITY?* TO SOME DISTANT *CONTINENT?* OR TO SOME *WORLD* THAT EXISTS NEITHER IN TIME NOR SPACE?

THERE CAN BE NO READY *ANSWER;* FOR SHE IS IN A PLACE LIKE NO OTHER...

THIS IS THE *TEMPLE AZARATH,* AND IT SPARKLES WITH A BEAUTY SEEN ONLY ONCE BEFORE...

...IN AN ANCIENT EARTHIAN *GARDEN* LOST A MILLION MILLENNIA AGO...

5

IF THERE IS ANYONE HERE WHO CAN HELP ME, IT IS *ARELLA*.

SHE HOLDS THE ULTIMATE KEY!

BUT, CAN I PERSUADE HER TO *USE* IT?

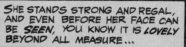

SHE STANDS STRONG AND REGAL, AND EVEN BEFORE HER FACE CAN BE *SEEN*, YOU KNOW IT IS *LOVELY* BEYOND ALL MEASURE...

IT WAS A *MISTAKE* FOR YOU TO *COME* HERE, RAVEN.

YOU *KNEW* OUR RULES WHEN YOU LEFT. TO FORSAKE AZARATH MEANS NEVER TO RETURN.

BUT I NEED YOUR *HELP*. OUR *HOME WORLD* NEEDS THE HELP ONLY *YOU* CAN GIVE.

CAN YOU TURN YOUR *BACK* ON THE WORLD OF YOUR *BIRTH*?

CAN YOU PERMIT UNTOLD MILLIONS TO BE *CRUSHED* IN THE MERCILESS GRIP OF *TRIGON THE TERRIBLE*?

CAN YOU LET YOUR OWN *DAUGHTER* DIE? CAN YOU... *MOTHER*?

ARELLA KNOWS HER *BOND*, RAVEN. MORE THAN *YOU*, IT WOULD SEEM.

THERE IS A *WILL* TO ALL. IF TRIGON *DESTROYS* THE EARTH, THAT, *TOO*, IS WILLED.

YOU'RE GIVING *EXCUSES* AS ALWAYS. YOU *RUN* INSTEAD OF *FIGHTING* FOR WHAT YOU BELIEVE.

WE BELIEVE TO *FIGHT* IS TO *DEGRADE* ONESELF.

N-NO! YOU'RE *WRONG*. YOU'RE *ALL WRONG*!

6

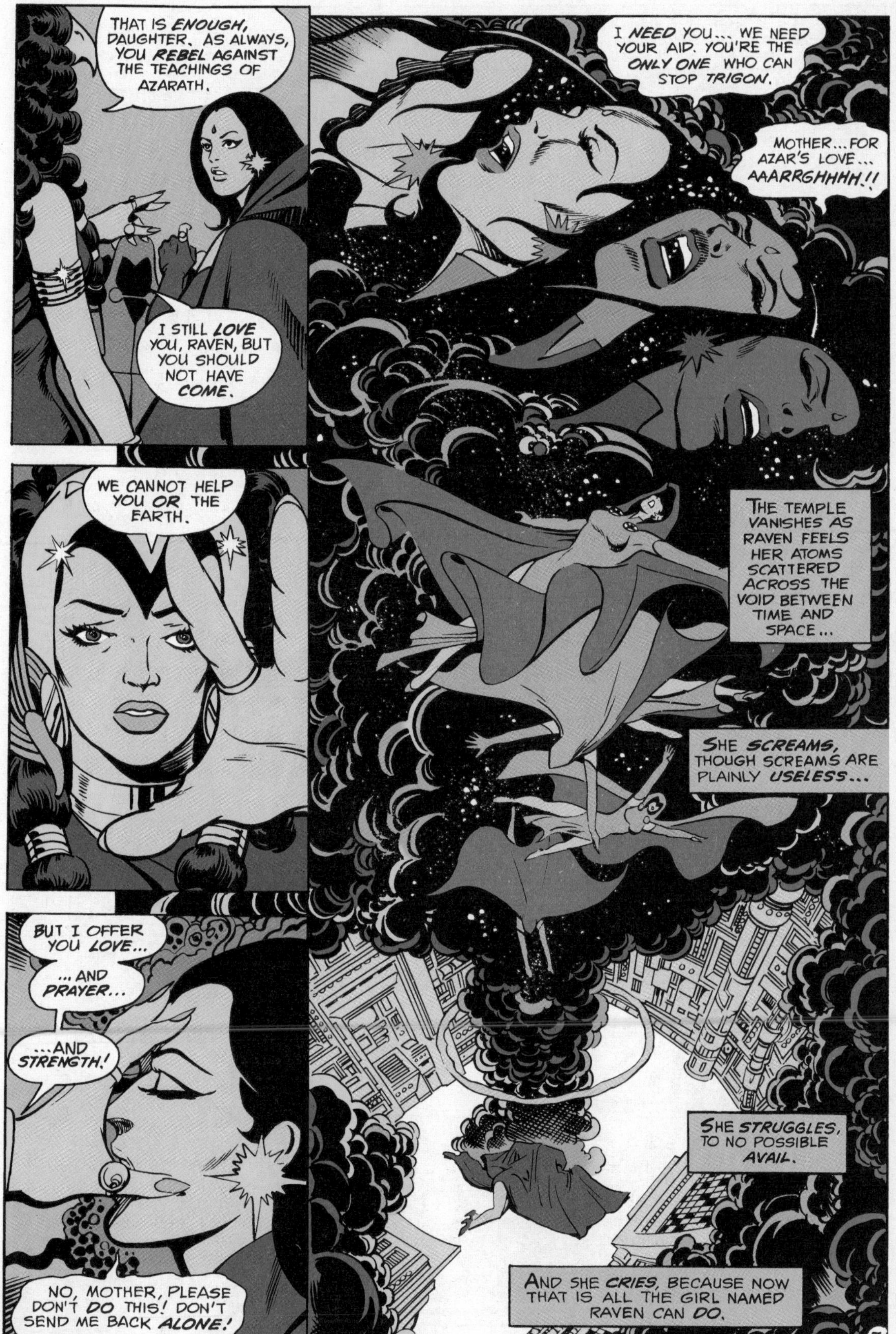
THAT IS ENOUGH, DAUGHTER. AS ALWAYS, YOU REBEL AGAINST THE TEACHINGS OF AZARATH.
I STILL LOVE YOU, RAVEN, BUT YOU SHOULD NOT HAVE COME.
WE CANNOT HELP YOU OR THE EARTH.
BUT I OFFER YOU LOVE...
...AND PRAYER...
...AND STRENGTH!
NO, MOTHER, PLEASE DON'T DO THIS! DON'T SEND ME BACK ALONE!
I NEED YOU... WE NEED YOUR AID. YOU'RE THE ONLY ONE WHO CAN STOP TRIGON.
MOTHER...FOR AZAR'S LOVE... AAARRGHHHH!!
THE TEMPLE VANISHES AS RAVEN FEELS HER ATOMS SCATTERED ACROSS THE VOID BETWEEN TIME AND SPACE...
SHE SCREAMS, THOUGH SCREAMS ARE PLAINLY USELESS...
SHE STRUGGLES, TO NO POSSIBLE AVAIL.
AND SHE CRIES, BECAUSE NOW THAT IS ALL THE GIRL NAMED RAVEN CAN DO.
7

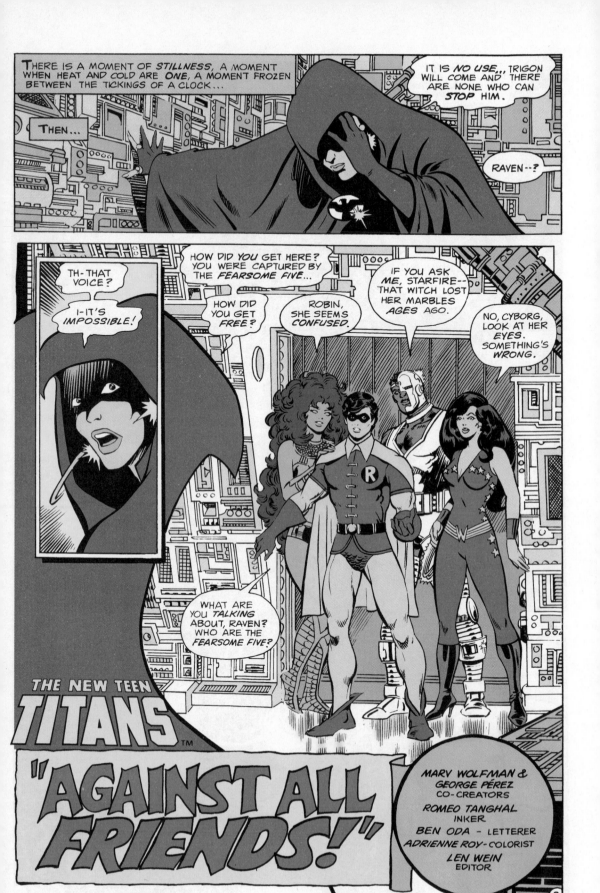

THERE IS A MOMENT OF *STILLNESS*, A MOMENT WHEN HEAT AND *COLD* ARE *ONE*, A MOMENT FROZEN BETWEEN THE *TICKINGS* OF A CLOCK...

THEN...

IT IS *NO USE*,.. TRIGON WILL COME AND THERE ARE NONE WHO CAN *STOP* HIM.

RAVEN--?

TH-THAT VOICE?

I-IT'S IMPOSSIBLE!

HOW DID *YOU* GET HERE? YOU WERE CAPTURED BY THE *FEARSOME FIVE*...

HOW DID YOU GET *FREE?*

ROBIN, SHE SEEMS *CONFUSED*.

IF YOU ASK *ME*, STARFIRE-- THAT WITCH LOST HER *MARBLES AGES* AGO.

NO, CYBORG, LOOK AT HER *EYES*. SOMETHING'S *WRONG*.

WHAT ARE YOU *TALKING* ABOUT, RAVEN? WHO ARE THE *FEARSOME FIVE?*

THE NEW TEEN TITANS ™

"AGAINST ALL FRIENDS!"

MARV WOLFMAN & *GEORGE PÉREZ* CO-CREATORS

ROMEO TANGHAL INKER

BEN ODA – LETTERER

ADRIENNE ROY – COLORIST

LEN WEIN EDITOR

8

THE FEARSOME FIVE ARE PROBABLY MARKED DOWN FROM THE FEARSOME *TEN*, WHAT ELSE?

GARFIELD! *YOU* SURVIVED AS WELL?

IF YOU MEAN *CYBORG* HASN'T *SMASHED* ME YET, YEAH!

I'VE CHECKED THE WHOLE BUILDING AND I STILL DON'T KNOW WHO *BUILT* THIS PLACE.

RAVEN? WHEN DID *YOU* GET HERE?

NONE OF YOU *REMEMBER.*

ARE YOU *ALL RIGHT,* RAVEN?

YOU LOOK LIKE YOU'VE JUST SEEN A *GHOST!*

PLEASE, MY FRIENDS, YOU MUST *BELIEVE* ME. WE BATTLED A GROUP WHO CALLED THEMSELVES THE *FEARSOME FIVE.* THEY *CAPTURED* YOU AS I *VANISHED.*

YOUR *DISAPPEARING ACT* IS SOMETHING I WANT TO *TALK* ABOUT, RAVEN.

NOT *NOW,* ROBIN. GIVE THE LADY A *BREAK!*

WAIT, I CAN *PROVE* IT. CYBORG'S *HAND* WAS CRUSHED IN -- *NO!*

WANNA *COUNT* 'EM, SISTER? FIVE FULLY-OPERATIN' HYDRAULIC FINGERS. *BATTERIES* NOT INCLUDED!

THERE CAN BE ONLY ONE *ANSWER.* FOR REASONS OF THEIR OWN, THE FEARSOME FIVE ERASED YOUR *MEMORIES*... SENT YOU BACK HERE TO *TITANS' TOWER!*

BUT, BY AZAR -- WHY? *WHY?*

C'MON *OUTSIDE,* RAVEN. YOU NEED SOME *FRESH AIR.*

THEN WE'RE *ALL* GONNA HAVE A REAL LONG *TALK!*

9

111

ELSEWHERE...

THE *OMNI-SCOPE* YOU PLACED IN CYBORG'S REPAIRED HAND WORKS *WELL*, GIZMO.

AS WELL AS MY OWN PSIONIC TAMPERING WITH THEIR *MINDS*.

AT THE PROPER MOMENT, THEY WILL INDEED *DESTROY* THE JUSTICE LEAGUE FOR US.

HOLD IT, PSIMON, I FORMED THE FEARSOME FIVE, REMEMBER?

HOW DARE *YOU* TAKE CONTROL?

HOW DARE I, DR. LIGHT?

AGHH!

MY INCREDIBLE POWER ALLOWS ME TO DARE *ANYTHING!*

WITH BUT A *THOUGHT*, I COULD *MELT* YOU WHERE YOU STAND--

--OR SEND YOU HURTLING LOST FOREVER THROUGH ENDLESS *SPACE...*

...OR EVEN *BANISH* YOU TO THE DISTANT *PAST* TO MEET A MORE *GRISLY* END...

PSIMON NOW CONTROLS THIS LITTLE GROUP, AND BE GLAD HE *DOES.*

OR ELSE YOUR PLAN TO DESTROY THE JUSTICE LEAGUE WOULD END-- AS HAVE ALL YOUR *OTHER* LUDICROUS ATTEMPTS-- IN *FOLLY!*

NOW, LEAVE ME TO *PREPARE.* THE TIME QUICKLY COMES FOR *FINAL BATTLE!*

LOUSY FILTH. I SHOULD *KILL* HIM FOR HUMILIATING ME.

MAMMOTH AND I DON'T LIKE HIM ANY MORE THAN *YOU* DO, LIGHT.

THEN YOU AND YOUR *BROTHER* WILL *JOIN* ME, SHIMMER?

YOU CAN COUNT ON *GIZMO,* TOO.

GOOD! AFTER *PSIMON* DESTROYS THE JUSTICE LEAGUE, WE SHALL DESTROY *HIM!*

THEN, WHATEVER'S *LEFT* OF THIS WORLD, WE DIVIDE-- *FOUR WAYS!*

10

MEANWHILE...

FRANKLY, GUYS, RAVEN'S AWFULLY CONVINCING!

SHE'S TELLING THE TRUTH. I'M SURE OF IT.

SO WE FOUGHT SOME CREEPS AND DON'T REMEMBER IT. SO WHAT?

IN YOUR CASE, CYBORG, MIND CONTROL COULD ONLY HELP!

KNOCK IT OFF, CHANGELING. SOMEONE'S OBVIOUSLY USING US, BUT WHY?

THE ANSWER LIES WITH TRIGON.

ONLY HE COULD MANIPULATE SUCH FORCES SO CASUALLY AND FROM SO GREAT A DISTANCE!

IT IS TIME, MY FRIENDS, FOR YOU TO KNOW OF TRIGON THE TERRIBLE-- AND TO LEARN AT LAST WHY THE TITANS HAVE BEEN FORMED!

"TRIGON'S STORY BEGAN LONG AGO, ON ANOTHER WORLD IN ANOTHER DIMENSION. THERE, THE PLANET'S LAST INHABITANTS ASSEMBLED FOR A CEREMONY OF BLASPHEMOUS INTENT!

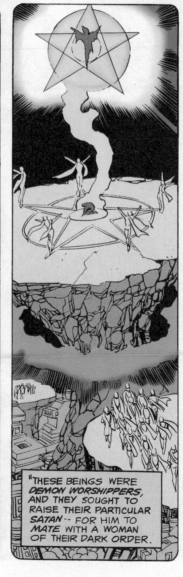

"THESE BEINGS WERE DEMON WORSHIPPERS, AND THEY SOUGHT TO RAISE THEIR PARTICULAR SATAN-- FOR HIM TO MATE WITH A WOMAN OF THEIR DARK ORDER.

"THEIR CHANTS REACHED THE NETHERWORLD, AND THEY CALLED UPON THEIR DARK DEMON TO APPEAR BEFORE THEM IN HIS SHADOW FORM."

11

"Nine months later, a child spawned of *evil* was born, and this child was *Trigon*. Instantly he *slew* all around him -- including the woman who had *birthed* him. Trigon grew more malevolent with every passing day. He *ruled* his world at the age of *one*, and he *destroyed* that world when he turned *six*.

By the time this supreme evil was *thirty*, he ruled his entire *dimension* and the million million planets contained within. He had a *universe* to play with as he saw fit. But even *this* was not enough. Trigon wanted more... *much* more."

AND THEN HE LEARNED OF *OUR* UNIVERSE!

AND NOW, BECAUSE OF THE *JUSTICE LEAGUE*, TRIGON WILL BE ABLE TO *BRIDGE* THE GULF BETWEEN DIMENSIONS...

... AND DO TO *US* WHAT HE'S DONE TO ALL THE *OTHERS*.

HOLY COW! NO *WONDER* YOU WANTED US TO STOP THEM!

BUT WE KNOW WHAT TO DO *NOW*, DON'T WE?

BELIEVE IT, BATBOY.

LET'S GO, TITANS!

WE'VE GOT TO DESTROY THE *JUSTICE LEAGUE*!

DESTROY--? *NO!* THERE IS *ANOTHER* WAY TO--

CURSE ME FOR A *FOOL!* OF COURSE, *THAT* IS WHY THE FEARSOME FIVE FREED THEM...

THEY'VE TURNED THE TITANS INTO *MIND-CONTROLLED ASSASSINS!*

AS RAVEN'S MIND RACES FOR ANSWERS, SHE *FAILS* TO HEAR THE SOUND OF METAL SWIVELLING ON METAL...

JUST AS SHE FAILS TO NOTICE A PARTIALLY-HIDDEN *CAMERA* AIMED DIRECTLY TOWARD HER...

A CAMERA WHOSE PICTURE IS BEING CAREFULLY SCRUTINIZED BY A SHADOWY FIGURE IN A SECLUDED CONTROL ROOM...

FASCINATING... THESE TITANS *ALREADY* WORK AS *ONE*.

WELL, SOON ENOUGH I'LL LEARN IF MY *PRESENTING* THEM WITH TITANS' TOWER ACCOMPLISHES *ALL* I'VE INTENDED.

QUITE SOON ENOUGH!

MEANWHILE, 22,300 MILES STRAIGHT UP IN SPACE...

WHAT ELSE COULD WE *DO*, ZATANNA?

THOSE SORCERERS WERE *GONE* WHEN WE AWOKE.

WE SHOULD BE *SEARCHING* FOR THEM.

SEARCHING? WHERE? MY *RING* CAN'T HELP. EVEN YOUR *MAGIC* FAILED YOU.

IT'S BEST TO *CONSERVE* OUR ENERGY, PLAN OUR NEXT MOVES SO WE'LL BE *READY* THIS TIME...

JUST THEN...

WE'VE GOT VISITORS COMING UP IN THE TRANSPORTER TUBE, FRIENDS.

VISITORS? *WHO--?*

13

WHO IS IT, HAWKMAN? AND WHY ARE YOU LETTING THEM USE THE TUBE?

IT'S ONLY SET TO BRING UP JUSTICE LEAGUE MEMBERS!

IT'S ALL RIGHT, I JUST RESET THE PROGRAMMING. I DON'T THINK YOU'LL MIND.

AFTER ALL, WHEN WAS THE LAST TIME THEY VISITED US?

I THOUGHT YOU DISBANDED THE TEEN TITANS.

WE DID, BUT THIS IS A NEW TITANS... WITH SOME OTHER MEMBERS.

SHALL WE SHOW THEM, ROBIN?

WE MAY AS WELL. WONDER GIRL?

GREAT HERA! KID FLASH, ROBIN, AND WONDER GIRL, TOGETHER?

IT'S GOOD TO SEE YOU AGAIN. WHAT BRINGS YOU UP HERE?

READY WHEN YOU ARE, ROB.

THEN LET'S ATTACK!

ALREADY IN ACTION, PAL. MY WIND STORM SHOULD KEEP THEM BUSY!

YOU GET TO THE TRANSPORTER.

WHAT ARE YOU COMPLAINING ABOUT? I CAN'T EVEN GRAB ANYTHING!

MERCIFUL MINERVA! CAN'T KEEP MY BALANCE--!

THEY'VE GOT TO BE IMPOSTERS!

14

BUT THEY'RE *NOT!* THE COMPUTER *CLEARED* THEM BEFORE TRANS-PORTING THEM UP!

WELL, *SOMETHING'S* SURE TURNED THEM AGAINST US!

HOLD IT! ROBIN'S TAMPERING WITH THE *TRANSPORTER* --

I'M JUST *RESETTING* THE CONTROLS, LANTERN!

IF WE'RE TO STOP THE *JUSTICE LEAGUE,* WE'LL NEED *ALL* OUR POWER!

DONNA, THIS *MADNESS* HAS GONE ON LONG ENOUGH. EXPLAIN YOUR-SELF *NOW!*

WONDER GIRL, DON'T WASTE YOUR *BREATH!*

MY *STARBOLT* WILL TAKE CARE OF HER!

SKREEEK!

THAT *DOES* IT, GOLDIE!

YOU *WANT* A FIGHT, YOU'VE *GOT* ONE!

BUT, EVEN AS GREEN LANTERN'S POWER RING FLASHES...

FORGET IT, LANTERN. I KNOW YOUR POWER RING IS USELESS AGAINST ANYTHING *YELLOW!*

AND *THAT* INCLUDES MY *CAPE!*

THE CAPE STOPS YOUR *RING,* AND A SAVATE KICK STOPS *YOU!*

ALL RIGHT, ROBIN. THAT'S QUITE *ENOUGH!*

BATMAN?!!

15

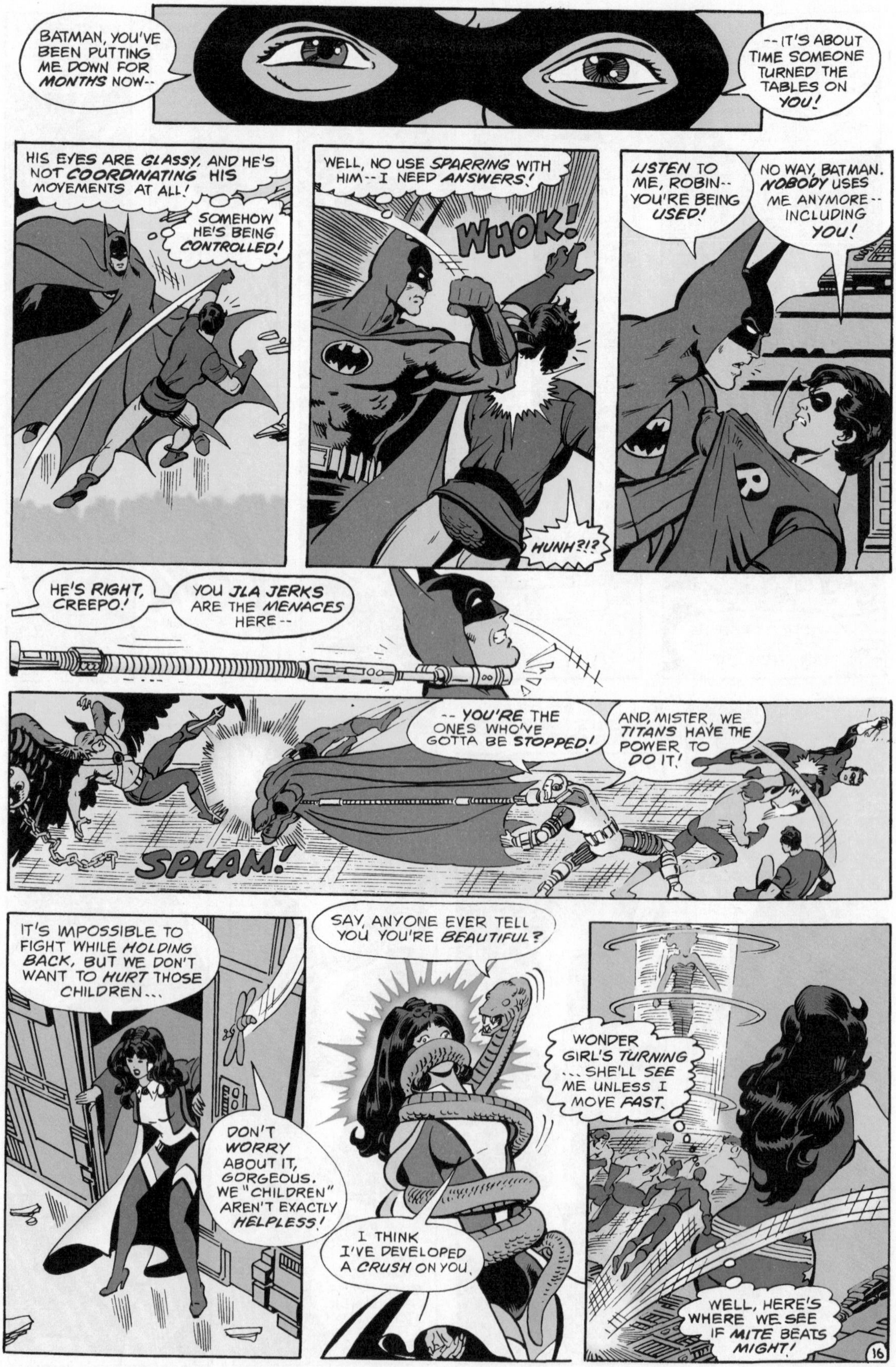
BATMAN, YOU'VE BEEN PUTTING ME DOWN FOR MONTHS NOW--
--IT'S ABOUT TIME SOMEONE TURNED THE TABLES ON YOU!
HIS EYES ARE GLASSY, AND HE'S NOT COORDINATING HIS MOVEMENTS AT ALL!
SOMEHOW HE'S BEING CONTROLLED!
WELL, NO USE SPARRING WITH HIM--I NEED ANSWERS!
WHOK!
HUNH?!?
LISTEN TO ME, ROBIN--YOU'RE BEING USED!
NO WAY, BATMAN. NOBODY USES ME ANYMORE--INCLUDING YOU!
HE'S RIGHT, CREEPO!
YOU JLA JERKS ARE THE MENACES HERE--
--YOU'RE THE ONES WHO'VE GOTTA BE STOPPED!
AND, MISTER, WE TITANS HAVE THE POWER TO DO IT!
SPLAM!
IT'S IMPOSSIBLE TO FIGHT WHILE HOLDING BACK, BUT WE DON'T WANT TO HURT THOSE CHILDREN...
DON'T WORRY ABOUT IT, GORGEOUS. WE "CHILDREN" AREN'T EXACTLY HELPLESS!
SAY, ANYONE EVER TELL YOU YOU'RE BEAUTIFUL?
I THINK I'VE DEVELOPED A CRUSH ON YOU.
WONDER GIRL'S TURNING... SHE'LL SEE ME UNLESS I MOVE FAST.
WELL, HERE'S WHERE WE SEE IF MITE BEATS MIGHT!
16

AN INSTANT IS ALL IT TAKES FOR THE ATOM TO *DECREASE* HIS SIZE AND WEIGHT...

...TO LAUNCH HIMSELF WITH UNERRING AIM TOWARD THE YOUNG AMAZON'S *EAR*...

WH-WHAT HAPPENED? EVERYTHING'S SPINNING?!?

...AND TO DIVE DEEP INTO HER *AURAL* CANAL, THE HUMAN BODY'S CENTER OF BALANCE!

THEY'RE ATTACKING US FOR NO REASON!

YOU THINK THOSE SORCERERS WE FOUGHT HAVE SOMETHING TO DO WITH THIS?

THEY MUST... THERE'S NO OTHER ANSWER-- AGHHH!

THE MAID OF MAGIC RECITES HER BACK- WARDS SPELL...

TNEPRES TREVER OT NAMUH!

AND, AS A HUMAN GARFIELD LOGAN CRUMPLES TO THE GROUND...

PLEASE, ZATANNA, YOU MUSTN'T HARM THEM.

RAVEN--?

THEY KNOW YOU MUST BE STOPPED, BUT THEY ARE BEING CONTROLLED ...FORCED TO SLAY YOU.

BUT TO STOP THEM BEFORE THEY ACCOMPLISH THAT--

-- THE JUSTICE LEAGUE MUST DIE!

17

THERE IS A MOMENT OF *SILENCE,* FOLLOWED BY A HEARTRENDING CRY OF HORROR...

AS ONE, THE MEMBERS OF THE MIGHTY JUSTICE LEAGUE BEGIN TO *AGE...*

...THEIR ONCE-POWERFUL BODIES *CRUMBLING* INTO TIME-WORN DUST...

...AND THE NAUSEATING SULPHURIC SMELL OF *DECAY.*

HUH? THEY'RE *DEAD...* BUT *HOW?*

THIS IS *HORRIBLE.* THIS IS NOT THE WAY A NOBLE ENEMY SHOULD *PERISH.*

ENEMY, MY *SNEAKERS,* THEY WERE *FRIENDS.* WHY DID--

SOMETHING TELLS ME WE'RE ABOUT TO *FIND OUT.*

WHAT DID YOU DO TO THE *LEAGUE,* RAVEN? THEY AREN'T *DEAD,* ARE THEY?

NO, THEY *LIVE.* YOU SAW AN *ILLUSION* SIMILAR TO THE ONE I LET GRANT WILSON SEE.*

TT #2.-- Len.

THEY ARE BEING HELD IN TIME STASIS.' AS FOR US--

--ALL WILL SOON BECOME *CLEAR,* MY FRIENDS-- WHEN WE REACH THE *CEREMONY.*

BLAST, THAT WITCH IS *DISAPPEARING* AGAIN.

LET 'ER. THIS TIME I JUST *DON'T...*

18

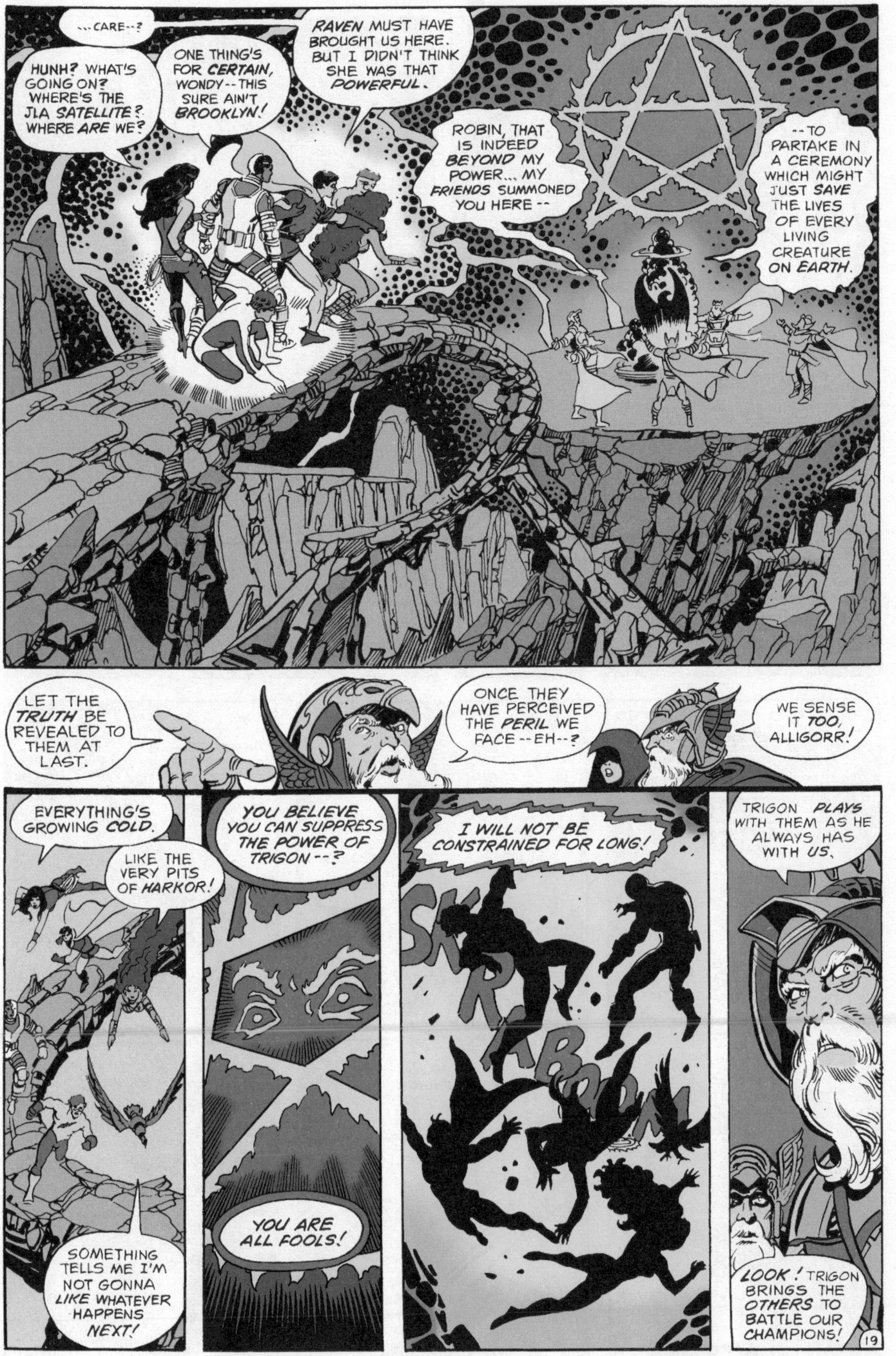
...CARE--?
HUNH? WHAT'S GOING ON? WHERE'S THE JLA SATELLITE? WHERE ARE WE?
ONE THING'S FOR CERTAIN, WONDY--THIS SURE AIN'T BROOKLYN!
RAVEN MUST HAVE BROUGHT US HERE. BUT I DIDN'T THINK SHE WAS THAT POWERFUL.
ROBIN, THAT IS INDEED BEYOND MY POWER... MY FRIENDS SUMMONED YOU HERE --
--TO PARTAKE IN A CEREMONY WHICH MIGHT JUST SAVE THE LIVES OF EVERY LIVING CREATURE ON EARTH.
LET THE TRUTH BE REVEALED TO THEM AT LAST.
ONCE THEY HAVE PERCEIVED THE PERIL WE FACE--EH--?
WE SENSE IT TOO, ALLIGORR!
EVERYTHING'S GROWING COLD.
LIKE THE VERY PITS OF HARKOR!
SOMETHING TELLS ME I'M NOT GONNA LIKE WHATEVER HAPPENS NEXT!
YOU BELIEVE YOU CAN SUPPRESS THE POWER OF TRIGON--?
YOU ARE ALL FOOLS!
I WILL NOT BE CONSTRAINED FOR LONG!
SKRABOOM
TRIGON PLAYS WITH THEM AS HE ALWAYS HAS WITH US.
LOOK! TRIGON BRINGS THE OTHERS TO BATTLE OUR CHAMPIONS!
19

YOU *FOUND* THEM, ZATANNA.

I WISH I *HAD*, HAWKMAN...BUT SOMEONE *ELSE* BROUGHT US HERE.

WELL, IT DOESN'T MATTER *WHODUNNIT*.

THERE ARE THE *TITANS*, SO LET'S GET THIS *OVER* WITH.

WAIT, GREEN LANTERN, LET *ME* TRY FIRST.

NIATNOC EHT SNATIT. OD TON TEL MEHT OG EERF!

GOOD GOING, ZATANNA, THAT'S SEVEN *DOWN*--

--AND ONLY SIX MORE TO GO!

NO, WE ARE *NOT* THE ENEMY-- YOU MUST *BELIEVE* US!

LISTEN, POPS -- ZATANNA PICKED UP MAGIC EMANATIONS WHICH WERE CREATING MASSIVE *HOLES* IN THE EARTH'S *OZONE* LAYER--

--AND THREE GUESSES WHERE THOSE EMANATIONS CAME FROM-- *HUNH?*

LANTERN, HE *REPELLED* YOUR RING BLAST!

YOU WILL NOT *LISTEN* TO US, AS YOU FAILED TO BELIEVE *RAVEN*.

WE HAVE NO *CHOICE* THEN. YOU MUST BE *DESTROYED*.

ONLY OUR *MISSION* IS IMPORTANT NOW.

WE HAVE *PRECEDED* TRIGON TO A HUNDRED DIFFERENT *PLANETS* AND A HUNDRED *TIMES* WE HAVE FAILED TO *STOP* HIM.

BUT WE MUST NOT FAIL *AGAIN*--

WE MUST NOT PERMIT HIM TO RAVAGE A BRAND- NEW *DIMENSION* AND A MILLION WORLDS *MORE!*

20

THEREFORE, LET OUR CHAMPIONS BE *FREE.*

THE JUSTICE LEAGUE MUST BE KEPT *OCCUPIED*--

--WHILE WE DEAL WITH MATTERS OF FAR *GREATER* IMPORT!

HUNH? THE SHELL'S *BROKEN!*

AND THE LEAGUE IS *WAITING* FOR US!

THEY DON'T *UNDERSTAND* ...THEY JUST WON'T *BELIEVE.*

SO THAT'S WHY THEY'VE GOTTA BE *STOPPED*--

--AND THAT'S JUST WHAT I'M GONNA *DO!*

MOVING AT SUPER-SPEED...

...NOT EVEN *WONDER WOMAN* CAN CATCH ME...

SPO-OOM

...BUT MY SONIC *BACKLASH* CAN SEND HER *REELING!*

CHANGELING, WE ONLY WANT TO *STOP* THE LEAGUERS. DON'T *HURT* HIM.

WONDY, YOU'RE A *SPOIL-SPORT.*

DON'TCHA KNOW I *LOVE* HAVING BATS FOR DINNER?

GOING SOMEWHERE, PAL?

HUH? WHERE'D *THAT* COME FROM?

SKRROK!

X'HAL'S BLOOD! I *RECOGNIZE* THAT UNIFORM -- HE'S A *THANAGARIAN.*

BACK OFF, I WOULD HATE USING MY *STARBOLTS* ON A FELLOW OUTWORLDER.

YOU'RE GOING TO *HAVE* TO, GIRL.

THE J.L.A. IS *OVERPOWERING* US, RAVEN...ISN'T THERE ANY WAY WE CAN *CONVINCE* THEM?

I HAVE *TRIED,* ROBIN, BUT TO NO-- *WHAT?* IT IS SUDDENLY ALL *TOO LATE!*

21

TRIGON IS FREE!

THOSE SORCEROUS FOOLS FAILED TO STOP ME AGAIN!

WILL THEY NEVER LEARN THAT TRIGON IS INVINCIBLE?!

SKROOM

TRIGON, PLEASE-- WHILE THERE IS STILL *TIME*--GO *ELSEWHERE!* LEAVE THIS WORLD ALONE!

THE DIMENSION YOU RULE IS *LARGE ENOUGH* FOR YOU.

NO!

TRIGON HUNGERS FOR EVEN GREATER POWER! A POWER I CAN ONLY CLAIM BY CONQUERING A NEW DIMENSION!

FROOOM

I WILL NOT FORFEIT SUCH POWER FOR ANY MAN OR BEAST!

THE PATHWAY IS NOW CLEAR INTO YOUR DIMENSION.

GORONN SHALL BE THE FIRST TO ARRIVE.

AND ONCE HE HAS TAMED YOUR PEOPLE'S FLESH--

--THEN I SHALL ARRIVE TO CLAIM THEIR *FRAGILE SOULS!*

22

THE GROUND IS COLD AND HARD, AND THOSE WHO LIE UPON IT ARE RACKED WITH TERRIBLE *PAIN*...

SLOWLY THEY FEEL THEIR CONSCIOUSNESS RETURN... AND SLOWLY THEY RISE TO THEIR FEET...

HE'S *GONE*. BUT HE WILL *RETURN*.

I-I DON'T KNOW *HOW*, BUT I COULD ACTUALLY FEEL HIS *EVIL*. *TRIGON* WAS BORN *WITHOUT* A HEART OR A SOUL. HE IS CAPABLE OF THE MOST BLASPHEMOUS *EVILS*.

ALL RIGHT, ROBIN, WHAT WAS THIS ALL *ABOUT*? YOU KIDS BETTER HAVE *EXPLANATIONS*.

FIRST OFF, WE'RE NOT *KIDS*. WE'RE THE *TITANS*-- NOT SOME JUNIOR *JUSTICE LEAGUE*.

SECOND, YOU BIG SHOTS REALLY *BLEW IT* THIS TIME. THOSE SORCERERS YOU WERE SO ANXIOUS TO GET *RID OF*...

...WELL, THEY WERE TRYING TO *STOP* SOME CREEP NAMED *TRIGON* FROM *DESTROYING* OUR WORLD.

23

AND BECAUSE OF *YOU* SELF-RIGHTEOUS SUPER-HEROES, THOSE SORCERERS WERE *THWARTED*. TRIGON IS *FREE.*

AND HOW DO *YOU* KNOW ALL THIS?

RAVEN *TOLD* US... SHE'S THE ONE WHO BROUGHT US *TOGETHER.*

HER? WEEKS AGO SHE APPEARED BEFORE THE LEAGUE, TELLING *US* THE SAME STORY.

I USED MY MAGIC TO *CHECK HER OUT,* AND I DISCOVERED AN INCREDIBLE *EVIL* WITHIN HER.

NO! THAT EVIL IS IN MY *HERITAGE,* NOT IN *ME.*

PLEASE, YOU MUST *BELIEVE* ME. TRIGON WILL DESTROY *OUR* WORLD AS HE HAS SO MANY *OTHERS.*

I NEEDED HELP AND YOU *REJECTED* ME. IS IT ANY *WONDER* I CREATED THESE NEW *TITANS* TO STAND BESIDE ME?

IT'S A GROUP BUILT ON *LIES,* RAVEN. YOU EVEN USED YOUR POWERS TO MAKE KID FLASH THINK HE *LOVED* YOU SO HE WOULD *JOIN* YOU AFTER FIRST *TURNING YOU DOWN.*

I'M *SORRY,* RAVEN, I HAD TO *TELL* WHAT I KNEW TO BE *TRUE.*

WAIT. WHAT DO YOU *MEAN* SHE USED HER POWER TO *MAKE* ME LOVE HER?

RAVEN, TELL THEM THAT'S A *LIE.*

I... I *CARE* FOR YOU, BUT YOUR POWER WAS ONE I DESPERATELY *NEEDED.*

PLEASE UNDERSTAND... PLEASE FORGIVE ME.

24.

IF YOU USED *HIM*, YOU MUST HAVE USED *ALL* OF US. HOW COULD YOU, *RAVEN?* WE *TRUSTED* YOU.

BUT TRIGON HAS TO BE *STOPPED*, AND ONLY YOU COULD--

TRIGON? WHO'S *HE*, WITCH-LADY? YOUR *EX-BOYFRIEND* FINDING OUT YOU LIED TO *HIM*, TOO?

HIS EVIL IS *REAL!*

NO, PLEASE DON'T *GO*. TRIGON *IS* COMING.

PLEASE, I NEED ALL OF YOU *BESIDE* ME.

DON'T YOU *UNDERSTAND?* OUR WORLD COULD BE *DOOMED!*

PLEASE... BELIEVE ME..., YOU MUST *BELIEVE* ME...,

THEY PART SILENTLY LIKE GRIEF-STRICKEN *MOURNERS...*

AND, IN A SENSE THAT IS EXACTLY WHAT THEY *ARE:*

FOR THE CORPSE IN QUESTION IS THE GROUP CALLED THE NEW TEEN TITANS, BORN LESS THAN A *MONTH* BEFORE, NOW *DEAD*, ALL TOO SUDDENLY AND ALL TOO TRAGICALLY...

NEXT ISSUE: **TRIGON LIVES!** THE ORIGIN OF RAVEN! AND SURPRISES GALORE!

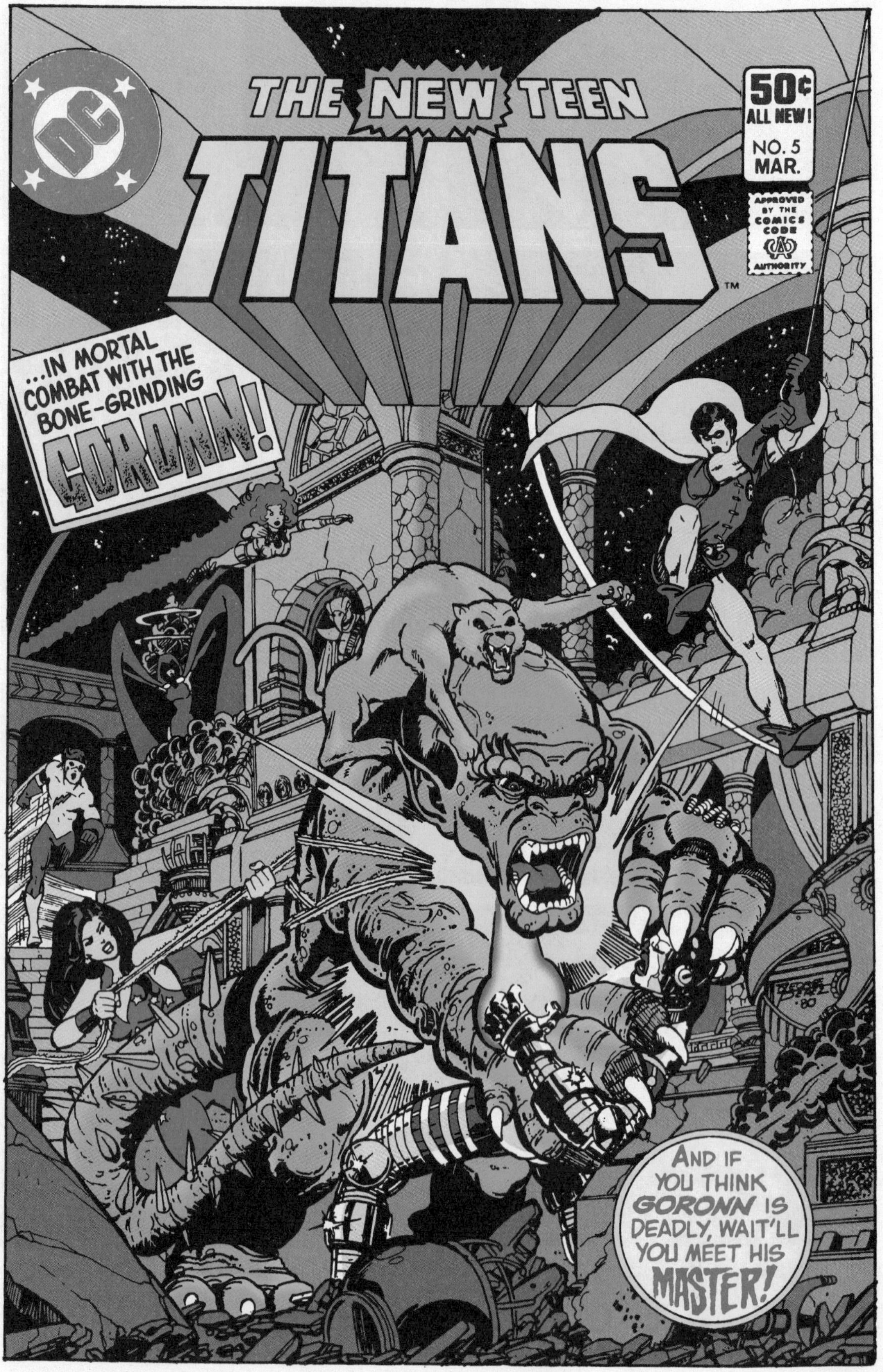
THE NEW TEEN
TITANS
50¢
ALL NEW!
NO. 5
MAR.
APPROVED BY THE COMICS CODE AUTHORITY
...IN MORTAL COMBAT WITH THE BONE-GRINDING
GORONN!
AND IF YOU THINK GORONN IS DEADLY, WAIT'LL YOU MEET HIS MASTER!

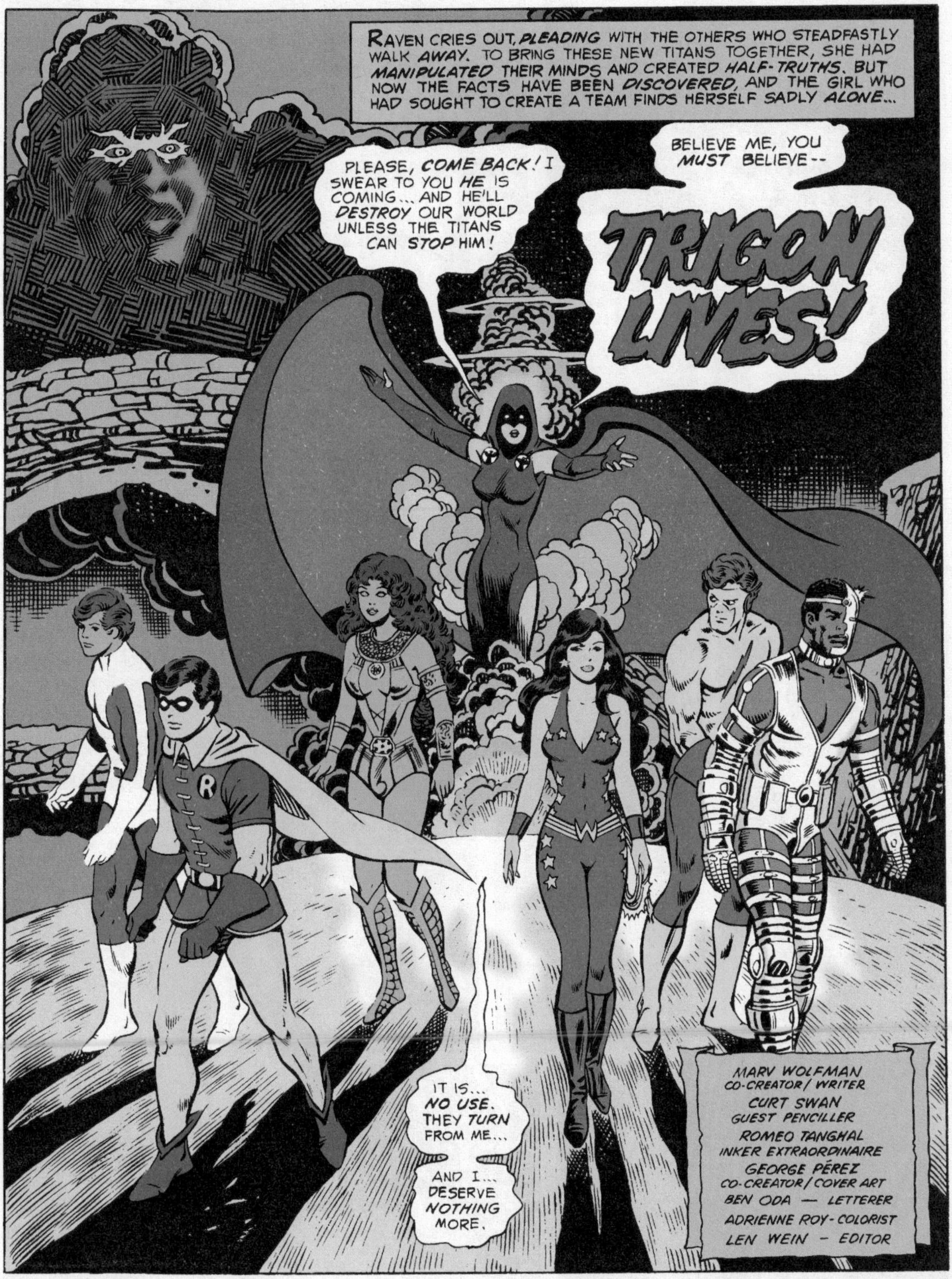
RAVEN CRIES OUT, PLEADING WITH THE OTHERS WHO STEADFASTLY WALK AWAY. TO BRING THESE NEW TITANS TOGETHER, SHE HAD MANIPULATED THEIR MINDS AND CREATED HALF-TRUTHS. BUT NOW THE FACTS HAVE BEEN DISCOVERED, AND THE GIRL WHO HAD SOUGHT TO CREATE A TEAM FINDS HERSELF SADLY ALONE...
PLEASE, COME BACK! I SWEAR TO YOU HE IS COMING... AND HE'LL DESTROY OUR WORLD UNLESS THE TITANS CAN STOP HIM!
BELIEVE ME, YOU MUST BELIEVE--
TRIGON LIVES!
IT IS... NO USE. THEY TURN FROM ME...
AND I... DESERVE NOTHING MORE.
MARV WOLFMAN CO-CREATOR/WRITER
CURT SWAN GUEST PENCILLER
ROMEO TANGHAL INKER EXTRAORDINAIRE
GEORGE PÉREZ CO-CREATOR/COVER ART
BEN ODA — LETTERER
ADRIENNE ROY - COLORIST
LEN WEIN - EDITOR

YOU LIED TO THEM!

...AND THE RAGING THUNDER ECHOES THE *PAIN* THAT GROWS IN HER EMPATHIC SOUL...

ALL MY LIFE I WAS TAUGHT THE VIRTUE OF *PEACE* AND THE FOLLY OF *BATTLE.* ALL MY LIFE I HAVE BELIEVED THAT TO *FIGHT* WAS TO CAUSE YOUR SOUL TO *WITHER* AND *DIE.*

TO *ENRICH* MY *POWER!* TO QUENCH MY *ENDLESS* THIRST FOR DESTRUCTION!

YOU KNOW YOUR *POWERS* PREVENTED ME FROM TELLING THEM THE WHOLE *TRUTH.*

BUT MY MOTHER AND THE OTHERS IN THE *TEMPLE AZARATH* ARE *WRONG!* LIFE IS TOO PRECIOUS AND TOO IMPORTANT TO LET *YOU* WASTE IT SO IGNOBLY.

I CAN NO LONGER STAND IDLY BY AND SIMPLY PERMIT THE DESTRUCTION OF UNTOLD *BILLIONS* OF LIVES.

GOD, TRIGON-- YOU HAVE AN ENTIRE *DIMENSION* TO DEVASTATE-- WHY MUST YOU DESTROY *OURS* AS WELL?

THEN, TRIGON GROWS *SILENT,* AND ONCE AGAIN RAVEN AGONIZES AS IMPOTENT *FRUSTRATION* OVERWHELMS HER. *TEARS* STREAM FROM HER *STEEL-GRAY* EYES...

AND I SWEAR I SHALL FIND A WAY TO *DEFEAT YOU--* EVEN IF *I* MUST DIE TO SEE THAT *YOU* NEVER KILL *AGAIN!*

TRIGON, *LISTEN* TO ME: NOW, AS ALWAYS, WE ARE *ENEMIES!*

THE THUNDER ROARS LIKE *MOCKING LAUGHTER,* THEN *LIGHTNING* SHATTERS THE COAL-DARK SKIES...

2

...BRINGING WITH ITS FIERY FURY A BEING OF *MONSTROUS PROPORTIONS*...

AHH, LITTLE ONE --COME AND MAKE ME A *TASTY MEAL!*

I *HUNGER*, DEAR RAVEN. I HUNGER FOR *YOU!*

HIM? HE'S BEEN SENT HERE *SOONER* THAN I EXPECTED!

THEN THE OTHERS *MUST* BE CONVINCED!

I STILL CAN'T TELL THEM THE *FULL* TRUTH... BUT THEY MUST BE MADE TO *BELIEVE!*

MY *SOUL-SELF* MUST *SUCCEED* SOMEHOW! GOD, IT *MUST SUCCEED!*

RAVEN'S ASTRAL SELF RISES FROM HER BODY LIKE SOME GREAT EBON *SHADOW*...

...CHARTING A MYSTIC PATH ACROSS HALF A CITY TO THE LOOMING TEN-STORY EDIFICE KNOWN AS *TITANS' TOWER*, WHERE...

I WAS A *FOOL* TO BELIEVE HER. A *DAMNED FOOL!*

LIGHTEN UP, WALLY. YOU COULDN'T *HELP* IT.

"LIGHTEN UP"? ARE YOU *CRAZY*, DICK?

I WAS THE ONE SHE USED HER BLASTED *POWERS* ON, REMEMBER? SHE MADE ME REJOIN THE TITANS BY MAKING ME *FALL IN LOVE WITH HER!*

GOD, I FEEL LIKE SOME SORT OF *PUPPET.*

I *HATE* KNOWING I COULD BE *USED* LIKE THAT, DICK. I *HATE* IT!

I CAN *UNDERSTAND* THAT, BUT--

DON'T GIVE ME THAT *GARBAGE*, DICK. YOU CAN'T *BEGIN* TO UNDERSTAND WHAT I FEEL LIKE.

BUT I CAN *TRY.* AND I WANT TO *HELP*...

HEY, *BATBOY* AIN'T THE *ENEMY*, KID.

REALLY? ACTUALLY, WHO *CARES?* I'M *QUITTING!*

NO *WAY*, KID. YOU'RE *STAYING PUT!*

OKAY, SO SOME *WITCH* GETS YOU ALL HOT'N BOTHERED, THEN *SPLITS*, AIN'T NO REASON TO GO *CRYIN'* IN YOUR MILK.

WATCH IT, STONE. YOU DON'T HAVE ANY *RIGHT* TO TALK TO ME LIKE THAT.

MEBBE NOT. BUT *SOMEBODY'S GOTTA* TELL YOU TO ACT YOUR *AGE* AN' NOT YOUR *SNEAKER SIZE!*

3

ACTUALLY, FRIENDS, I DON'T THINK RAVEN *WAS* LYING.

WHAT WOULD *YOU* KNOW, STARFIRE? YOU DON'T UNDERSTAND *HUMAN* EMOTIONS!

OH, WALLY, YOU'RE VERY *WRONG.* ON TAMARAN WE ARE *GUIDED* BY OUR EMOTIONS AND PASSIONS. WE LET THEM *CONTROL* US THE WAY YOU LET YOUR *INTELLECT* GUIDE YOU.

I HAVE ALWAYS SENSED *TRAGEDY* IN RAVEN... AND GREAT *SORROW.* AS IF SHE FIGHTS AGAINST HER *OWN* EMOTIONS FOR REASONS I CAN'T POSSIBLY *COMPREHEND.*

FRANKLY, GUYS, YOU SHOULD'A FIGGERED IT ALL OUT *LONG AGO.*

ISN'T IT *OBVIOUS?* RAVEN FORMED THE TITANS JUST TO *MEET ME!*

WAY I SEE IT, SHE WAS TOO *EMBARRASSED* TO ASK ME OUT FOR A *DATE,* SO SHE CAME UP WITH THIS TITANS IDEA AS A *COVER!*

CRIPES. WILL SOMEONE LOCK THAT JERK UP IN A *SAFE* OR SOMETHIN'?

CHANGELING, WILL YOU BE *SERIOUS* FOR ONCE?

I AM *SERIOUS,* ROBBY. YOU JUST HAVEN'T *SEEN* THE *EFFECT* I HAVE ON THE MORE *PULCHRITUDINOUS SEX.*

FACE IT, PAL. I COULD GIVE *WARREN BEATTY* LESSONS IN LOVING!

As WONDER GIRL RETORTS WITH A LOUD *SNORT,* THE AIR IN TITANS' TOWER GROWS COLD AND *ELECTRIC.* THEN...

FRIENDS -- YOU MUST *LISTEN* TO ME.

I HAVE SENT MY *SOUL-SELF* TO PLEAD WITH YOU. THE TIME HAS *COME...*

THIS WORLD'S BEING *INVADED.* PLEASE ... YOU'VE GOT TO *BELIEVE* ME.

GET *OUT* OF HERE, RAVEN. WE DON'T NEED ANY MORE *LIES.*

THIS IS NO *LIE,* WALLACE. THE *REASONS* I FORMED THE TITANS WERE *NEVER* A LIE.

I DON'T WANT TO *HEAR* ANY MORE. GO! DON'T YOU KNOW WHEN YOU'RE NOT *WANTED?*

BUT THERE *IS* NO PLACE TO GO. MY TRUE FORM *FIGHTS* FOR ITS LIFE WHILE I *PLEAD* WITH YOU FOR THE LIFE OF OUR *WORLD.*

RAVEN'S IN *TROUBLE?*

BATMAN WOULD PROBABLY CALL ME *CRAZY,* BUT DESPITE ALL THE *FACTS...*

...I'M GOING TO GO WITH MY *HUNCH.* I THINK RAVEN'S TELLING THE *TRUTH.*

I'M *STAYIN'* HERE.

NO ONE *OWNS* YOU, VIC. DO WHAT YOU *WANT.*

BUT I'M *GOING.*

AND I WILL *JOIN* YOU, ROBIN.

WE'RE *ALL* GOING.

YEAH. THERE'S NOTHING ON *TV* TONIGHT ANYWAY.

4

FIGGERS, KID. YOU AN' ME ARE THE ONLY ONES *SMART* ENOUGH TO STAY *BEHIND.*

DO YOU *MIND?* I'D RATHER BE *ALONE* RIGHT NOW.

SURE, KID, I KNOW HOW YOU FEEL! WE'RE THE ONLY ONES WHO *KNEW* THAT WITCH WAS PLAYIN' US FOR *FOOLS.*

SO WHAT IF SHE HAD A *REASON* TO BRING US TOGETHER? SO WHAT IF THIS *TRIGON* CREEP IS *REAL?* THAT DOESN'T *MATTER* NOW, DOES IT?

SHE *NEEDED* YOU, SO SHE MADE A *PLAY* FOR YOU, OR MEBBE YOU ONLY *THOUGHT* SHE DID, DOESN'T *MATTER.*

SHE STILL DIDN'T HAVE ANY RIGHT TO MAKE YOU THINK YOU *LOVED* HER.

SO, EVEN IF SHE IS *DYIN'* NOW -- WHO CARES, RIGHT? *WHO CARES?*

GOD, THAT'S WHAT I *HATE* ABOUT ALL THIS, STONE.

I *CARE.* I *STILL* CARE.

I CAN'T GET HER OUT OF MY *MIND.*

AND NOW... SHE SAYS SHE'S *HURT.*

'SCUSE ME, STONE. I GOTTA *GO.*

RAVEN MAY *REALLY* NEED ME.

YEAH...

WHO'S *STOPPING* YOU? JUST *YOURSELF,* THAT'S WHO!

SO *GO!* WHO'S *STOPPIN'* YA?

AS KID FLASH RACES OFF, VICTOR STONE ALLOWS HIMSELF A QUICK *SMILE.* EVER SINCE CRUEL FATE ROBBED HIM OF HIS *HUMAN BODY* AND TURNED HIM INTO THIS MAN-MACHINE CALLED *CYBORG,* HE HAS KNOWN HOW TERRIBLY SELF-CREATED PITY CAN *TORTURE* THE MIND...

AND, PERHAPS, THAT IS WHY HE HAS *STAYED BEHIND;* TO KEEP A NEWFOUND *FRIEND* FROM SINKING EVER DEEPER INTO HIS OWN SELF-MADE *HELL.*

THOUGH VICTOR STONE MAY COME ACROSS LIKE SOME STREETWISE *BRAWLER* JUST WAITING FOR A FIGHT, IN TRUTH, HE IS ANYTHING *BUT.*

YET, SADLY, THIS GENTLE SIDE OF HIM IS NOT *SEEN* BY HIS FELLOW *TITANS* WHO BELIEVE HIM TO BE CALLOUS AND CRUEL, BUT ONLY BY A MAN WHO IS HIDING DEEP IN THE *SHADOWS* OF THE NEWLY-BUILT TITANS' TOWER.

HE STARES AND WATCHES IN *SILENCE,* AND A THIN *SMILE* CROSSES HIS FLESHY FACE...

5

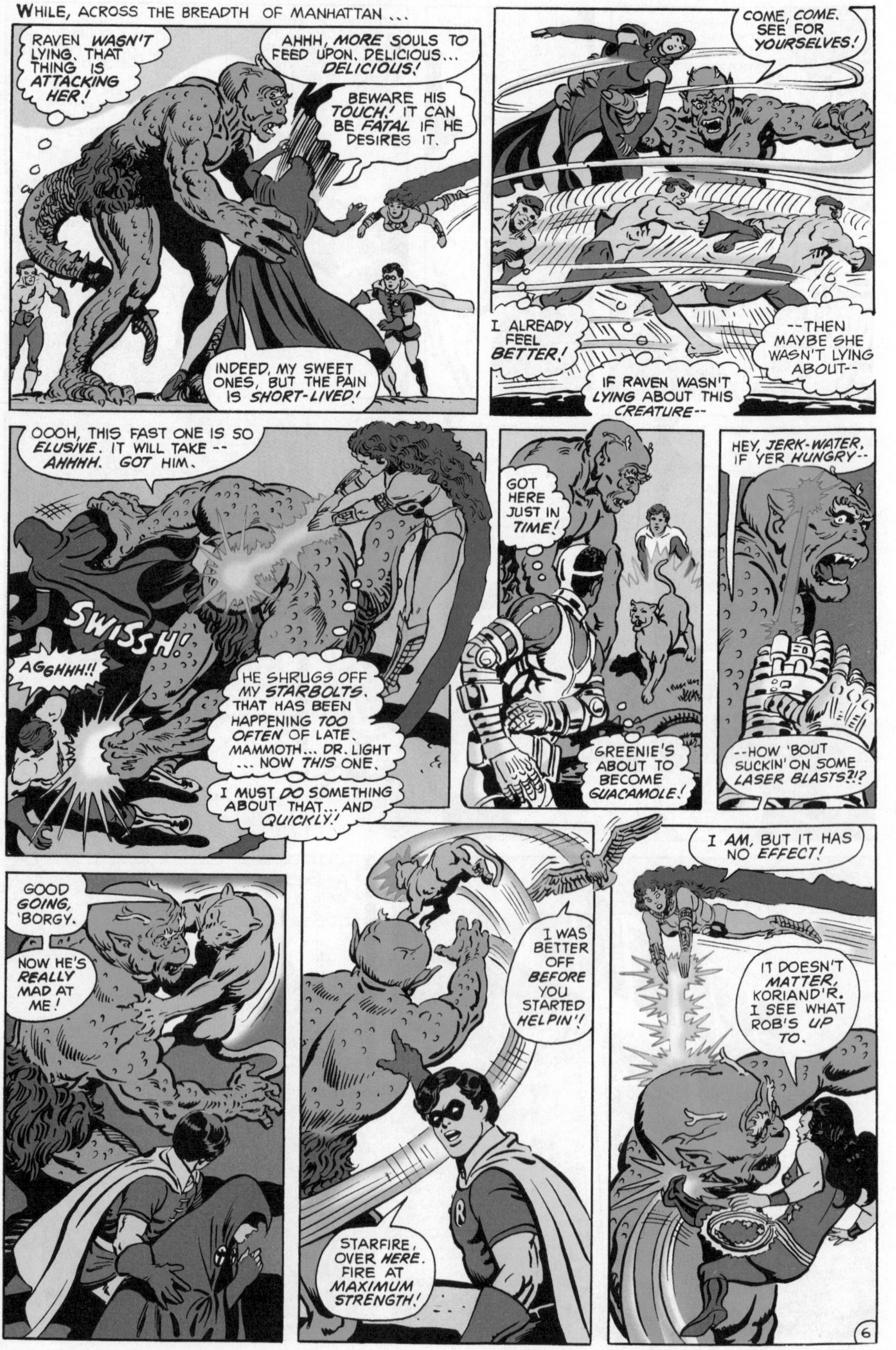
WHILE, ACROSS THE BREADTH OF MANHATTAN ...
RAVEN WASN'T LYING. THAT THING IS ATTACKING HER!
AHHH, MORE SOULS TO FEED UPON. DELICIOUS... DELICIOUS!
BEWARE HIS TOUCH! IT CAN BE FATAL IF HE DESIRES IT.
INDEED, MY SWEET ONES, BUT THE PAIN IS SHORT-LIVED!
COME, COME. SEE FOR YOURSELVES!
I ALREADY FEEL BETTER!
IF RAVEN WASN'T LYING ABOUT THIS CREATURE--
--THEN MAYBE SHE WASN'T LYING ABOUT--
OOOH, THIS FAST ONE IS SO ELUSIVE. IT WILL TAKE -- AHHHH. GOT HIM.
SWISSH!
AGGHHH!!
HE SHRUGS OFF MY STARBOLTS. THAT HAS BEEN HAPPENING TOO OFTEN OF LATE. MAMMOTH... DR. LIGHT ... NOW THIS ONE.
I MUST DO SOMETHING ABOUT THAT... AND QUICKLY!
GOT HERE JUST IN TIME!
GREENIE'S ABOUT TO BECOME GUACAMOLE!
HEY, JERK-WATER, IF YER HUNGRY--
--HOW 'BOUT SUCKIN' ON SOME LASER BLASTS?!?
GOOD GOING, 'BORGY.
NOW HE'S REALLY MAD AT ME!
I WAS BETTER OFF BEFORE YOU STARTED HELPIN'!
STARFIRE, OVER HERE. FIRE AT MAXIMUM STRENGTH!
I AM, BUT IT HAS NO EFFECT!
IT DOESN'T MATTER, KORIAND'R. I SEE WHAT ROB'S UP TO.
6

IT'S *MY* TURN NOW TO KEEP HIM OFF GUARD... TOO CONFUSED TO *ATTACK!*

GREAT HERA! I'M USING ALL MY *STRENGTH*, BUT I'M HAVING AS MUCH EFFECT AS A *FLEA* NIPPING AT AN ELEPHANT!

ROB, I NEED *HELP* HERE.

DON'T WORRY, IT'S *COMING!*

CYBORG, INTO *POSITION THREE!*

SMART MOVE, SHORT-PANTS. I'M GETTIN' YOUR *DRIFT!*

--BUT I'M ALMOST *AFRAID* OF WHAT I'D LEARN.

I WISH I *UNDERSTOOD* RAVEN. SHE *CALLED* US HERE, BUT THE FIGHTING SEEMS TO *BOTHER* HER.

AND I WANT TO *REACH OUT* TO HER--

SO I GUESS I'LL DO WHAT I ALWAYS DO *BEST*--

JUST KEEP *FIGHTING* INSTEAD OF COMING TO *GRIPS* WITH *WHO I AM!*

I ALREADY KNOW THE *ANSWER*, BUT I'VE GOT TO ASK HER *ANYWAY.*

RAVEN, WE NEED YOU *IN* THIS BATTLE. WILL YOU *JOIN US?*

I CANNOT, ROBIN, PLEASE, DON'T ASK ME.

I CAN'T BELIEVE RAVEN'S A *COWARD*, BUT WHY WON'T SHE *JOIN* US? THIS IS *HER* FIGHT.

YOU WILL *NEVER* DEFEAT HIM BY FIGHTING *SEPARATELY.* YOU MUST ACT *TOGETHER!*

THAT'S THE *PLAN*, WITCH, IF YOU SHOWED UP AT *HALF* OUR MEETIN'S, YOU'D *KNOW* THAT.

--AN' *BINGO!* I GOT AN *ELECTRIFIED LEASH* ALL READY FOR ACTION.

F'RINSTANCE, I LOCK ON A NEW *HAND-MECH* FROM MY *FIGHTIN'* BELT--

NOW, ALL OF YOU-- *ATTACK!*

WONDER GIRL, GET YOUR LASSO *AROUND* HIS NECK... CYBORG, KEEP UP YOUR *LEASH*, STARFIRE, MAINTAIN FULL *POWER*--

HEY, LEADER-MAN WHAT ABOUT *ME?*

THE REST OF YOU-- *PULL!*

GET BACK AND STAY OUT OF *TROUBLE.*

7

ARMS FEEL LIKE THEY'RE BEING WRENCHED FROM THEIR *SOCKETS*, BUT AT LEAST WE'RE FINALLY MAKING SOME *HEADWAY*.

WE GOT 'IM *DOWN*, NOW TO *KEEP* HIM THIS WAY.

WHUUMP!

Y/////KES! NOW I KNOW HOW *JACK* FELT WHEN THE *BEANSTALK* STARTED *FALLIN'!*

THE *WINNER*, AN' STILL *CHAMPEEEEEN!*

MY *MAGIC LASSO* WILL KEEP HIM *BOUND* UNTIL WE DECIDE WHAT TO *DO* WITH HIM.

OKAY, *WITCH-LADY*. HE'S *YOUR* BUNDLE. WHAT *NOW?*

YOU WERE *RIGHT*, ROBIN. BY WORKING *TOGETHER*, WE *DEFEATED* HIM. WE'RE A REAL *TEAM!*

NO-- JUST *STARTING* TO BE ONE, STARFIRE. THAT'S THE *FIRST* TIME WE DIDN'T FIGHT *SEVEN SEPARATE* BATTLES.

BUT WE STILL HAVE *PLENTY* OF *WORK* AHEAD OF US.

THEN YOU WILL HAVE TO LEARN *QUICKLY*, MY FRIENDS.

WHAT DO YOU *MEAN?* WE TOOK CARE OF *TRIGON* FOR YOU.

THIS *MONSTER* WAS *NOT* TRIGON. HE IS *GORONN*, TRIGON'S *ADVANCE WARRIOR*.

TRIGON'S POWER *DWARFS* THAT OF *THIS* ONE. WE MUST PREPARE BEFORE--

ALL YOUR *PREPARATIONS* ARE *MEANINGLESS*.

THE *TIME* HAS NOW *COME!*

TRIGON IS READY TO ENTER YOUR DIMENSION--

--AND TO *DESTROY* IT!

SKREEAKKK!

8

THE AIR GROWS THICK WITH THE STENCH OF SULPHUR AND BRIMSTONE AS BRUMOUS *CLOUDS* GATHER WITH SATANIC FURY. THERE IS A RUMBLING OF *THUNDER,* THEN...

NOW, I STAND BETWIXT OUR TWO MIGHTY UNIVERSES--

--AND I REVEL IN THE POWER THAT BELONGS ONLY TO TRIGON!

TRIGON, *GO BACK!* YOU'LL FACE *RESISTANCE* HERE UNLIKE ANY YOU'VE EVER ENCOUNTERED *BEFORE!*

RESISTANCE IS FUTILE TO ONE WHO IS THE DESTROYER OF ALL THAT EXISTS!

BUT, THIS WORLD ISN'T LIKE THE *OTHERS* YOU'VE CONQUERED. WE WON'T *CATER* TO YOUR MAD *WHIMS!*

GIRL, YOU WILL *CATER!* YOU WILL *GROVEL!* YOU WILL BEG FOR MERCY!

AND I WILL SHOW YOU *NONE!*

THERE ARE *OTHERS* WITH ME. THEY WILL *FIGHT* YOU!

THEY WILL *DIE* BEFORE THEY RAISE A FIST IN *REBELLION!*

TRIGON, YOU MUSTN'T. WITH ALL THE *POWER* AT YOUR COMMAND, FOR ONCE CAN'T YOU RISE *ABOVE* YOUR *LUSTS* AND SHOW *COMPASSION?*

9

137

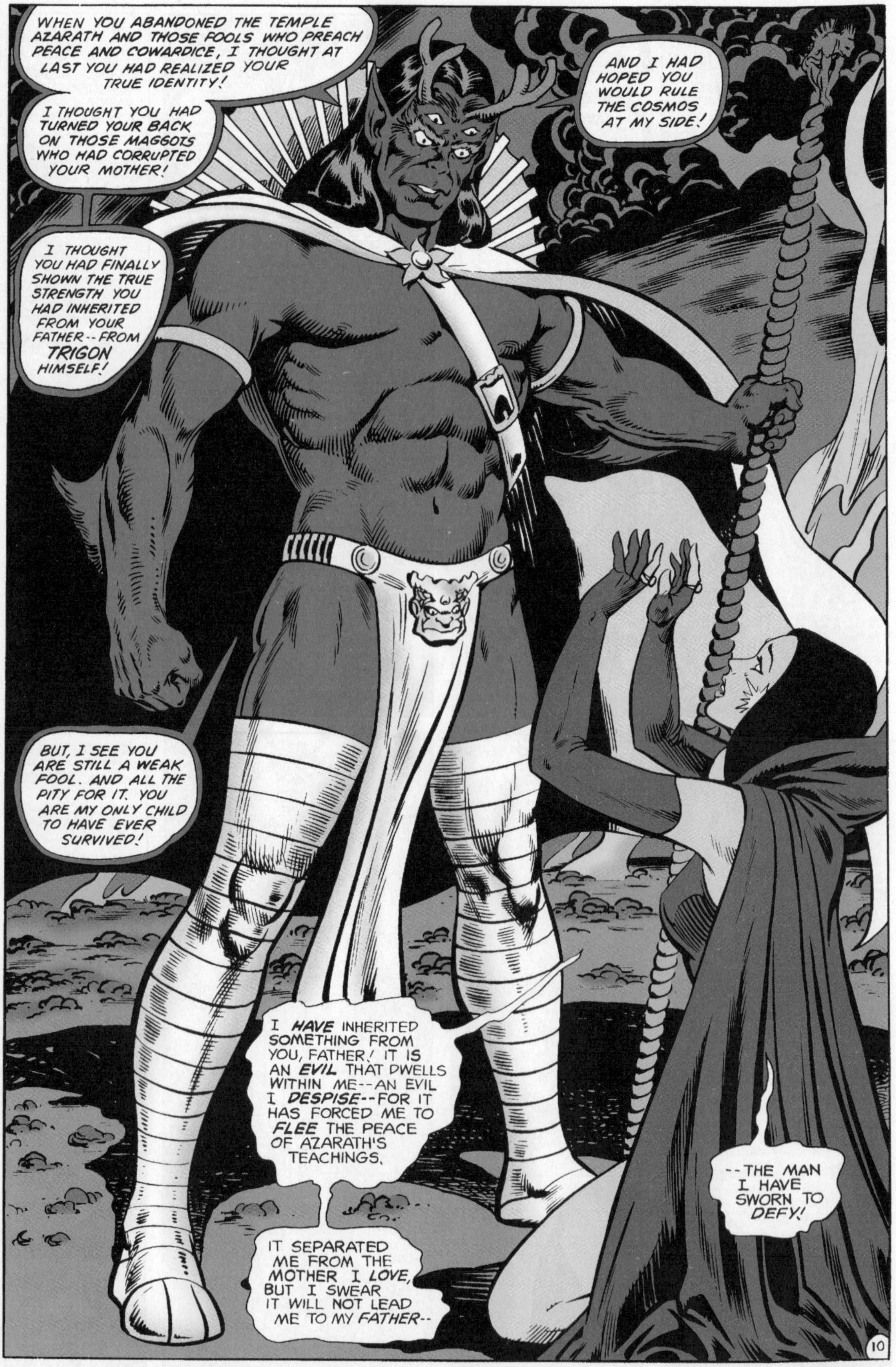
WHEN YOU ABANDONED THE TEMPLE AZARATH AND THOSE FOOLS WHO PREACH PEACE AND COWARDICE, I THOUGHT AT LAST YOU HAD REALIZED YOUR TRUE IDENTITY!
I THOUGHT YOU HAD TURNED YOUR BACK ON THOSE MAGGOTS WHO HAD CORRUPTED YOUR MOTHER!
AND I HAD HOPED YOU WOULD RULE THE COSMOS AT MY SIDE!
I THOUGHT YOU HAD FINALLY SHOWN THE TRUE STRENGTH YOU HAD INHERITED FROM YOUR FATHER--FROM TRIGON HIMSELF!
BUT, I SEE YOU ARE STILL A WEAK FOOL. AND ALL THE PITY FOR IT. YOU ARE MY ONLY CHILD TO HAVE EVER SURVIVED!
I HAVE INHERITED SOMETHING FROM YOU, FATHER! IT IS AN EVIL THAT DWELLS WITHIN ME--AN EVIL I DESPISE--FOR IT HAS FORCED ME TO FLEE THE PEACE OF AZARATH'S TEACHINGS.
IT SEPARATED ME FROM THE MOTHER I LOVE, BUT I SWEAR IT WILL NOT LEAD ME TO MY FATHER--
--THE MAN I HAVE SWORN TO DEFY!
10

SMOKE SURROUNDS RAVEN AS SHE WRAPS HER CAPE ABOUT HER, AND, WHEN IT CLEARS A MOMENT LATER, THE MYSTIC MISTRESS IS *GONE.* TRIGON *SHRUGS* HIS MASSIVE SHOULDERS AS IF *UNCONCERNED.* HE WILL DEAL WITH HIS ERRANT DAUGHTER *LATER,* BUT FIRST HE MUST STILL CONFRONT....

PSIMON! AT LAST I HAVE MY QUISLING BEFORE ME!

YOU ACTUALLY BROKE THROUGH THE DIMENSIONS? BUT -- *HOW --?*

BE SILENT AND BOW BEFORE THE MASTER YOU TRIED TO HAVE SLAIN!

PRESSURE -- FORCING ME GROUND-WARD!

I GAVE YOU YOUR POWERS TO AID ME IN BREACHING THE DIMENSIONS, TO DESTROY THE SORCERERS WHO SOUGHT TO DESTROY ME!

INSTEAD, YOU USED THOSE POWERS TO SAVE THOSE MYSTIC DOLTS! ONLY MY OWN SUPERIOR POWER LET ME PREVAIL!

I SAID *SILENCE!* I SHOULD SLAY YOU, TRAITOR, BUT DEATH WOULD BE TOO PAINLESS.

INSTEAD I SHALL MERELY DISSIPATE YOUR ATOMS THROUGH-OUT THE LIGHT STREAM --

-- WHERE YOU SHALL SUFFER BY BEING *ALIVE* FOREVER, AND *FOREVER* HELPLESS!

TRIGON, I DIDN'T KNOW -- I COULDN'T *SUSPECT* --

AND NOW, AS FOR YOU, FAILURE I CALL GORONN...

OooH, MASTER, YOU WOULDN'T HARM YOUR SWEET, LOYAL GORONN, EHHH?

I ONLY LIVE TO *SERVE* MY DEAR ONE!

YOU SNIVEL BEFORE ME, GORONN, AND I DESPISE SNIVELING WORMS!

BUT, I SHALL BE MERCIFUL, WHEREAS PSIMON SHALL SURVIVE A PAINFUL ETERNITY --

-- TO YOU I GRANT A SUDDEN PAINLESS DEATH!

NOOOO, PLEASE, MASTER, I ONLY SEEK TO SERVV-- ACHHHHH!!

GORONN'S SCREAM IS CUT SHORT, AND THEN THE ONLY SOUND TO BE HEARD IS THAT OF A MAD GOD'S LAUGHTER...

(11)

139

AND, WHILE TRIGON'S LAUGHTER BOOMS FORTH LIKE THE DISTANT THUNDER ON A SMALL *ISLAND* IN NEW YORK'S *EAST RIVER*...

WH-WHAT *HAPPENED?* HOW DID WE GET BACK *HERE?*

I WISH I *KNEW*, WALLY!

WOW! MY HEAD'S STILL *RINGING* FROM THE PAIN. EVEN MY *HAIR* HURTS.

WHATEVER TRIGON *BLASTED* US WITH, I STILL FEEL IT RIGHT DOWN TO MY *TOENAILS!*

HALF THE *BLASTED* CIRCUITS IN MY HEAD ARE SPUTTERIN' *STATIC!*

OKAY, RAVEN --*TALK* TO US! WHAT'S *GOING* ON?

IT'S STILL DIFFICULT TO EVEN *LOOK* AT HER. I WANT *US* TO TALK, BUT NOT IN FRONT OF THE *OTHERS!*

I WILL ATTEMPT TO ANSWER *ALL* YOUR QUESTIONS, WALLACE, EVEN YOUR *UNSPOKEN* ONES.

SHE *KNOWS?* DOES THAT MEAN SHE'S ALSO A *TELEPATH?*

SOMETHING TELLS ME THIS IS THE TITANS' *CRUCIAL* MOMENT. EITHER RAVEN'S GOING TO KEEP US AS A *TEAM* ...OR THE TITANS WILL BE *DISBANDED...FOREVER.*

BELIEVE ME, PLEASE, WHEN I SAY I DID NOT *LIE* TO ANY OF YOU. NOT EVEN TO *YOU*, WALLACE.

UNDERSTAND I AM AN *EMPATH*, AND THROUGH MY EMPATHIC POWERS I LEARNED OF *TRIGON'S* COMING, AND I KNEW HOW *TERRIBLE* HIS POWER COULD BE.

THEREFORE I *FORSOOK* MY HOME, THE *TEMPLE AZARATH* --AND I SOUGHT *AID* HERE IN THIS OUTSIDE WORLD.

FIRST I APPEARED BEFORE THE *JUSTICE LEAGUE OF AMERICA.* I EXPLAINED ALL I *COULD*, BUT...

I SENSE A TERRIBLE *EVIL* WITHIN HER. SHE COULD BE LEADING US INTO A *TRAP.*

12

THE EVIL THAT ZATANNA SENSED IN ME WAS THE EVIL OF TRIGON--MY FATHER--NOT MY OWN. I KNEW THEN MY HOPES DID NOT LIE WITH THE JUSTICE LEAGUE.

"I HAD TO FIND OTHERS TO JOIN ME, AND THROUGH MY EMPATHIC SENSES I LEARNED OF YOU SIX, EACH WITH THE SPECIFIC ABILITIES I NEEDED TO DEFEAT TRIGON BEFORE HE DESTROYS US."

HOLD IT, RAVEN. I'LL BUY EVERYTHING, EXCEPT--WHY ME? THE OTHERS ALL HAVE POWERS, ALL I'VE GOT IS SOME ACROBATIC SKILL!

I DID NOT NEED SEPARATE INDIVIDUALS, RICHARD. I NEEDED A TEAM. WITHIN YOU IS THE CAPACITY TO BE A LEADER, TO MAKE US WORK AS ONE.

THAT IS WHY I APPEARED BEFORE YOU FIRST. THAT IS WHY I HAD YOU SEEK OUT THE OTHERS.

WE SHOULD HAVE HAD MONTHS TO PREPARE, MONTHS TO LEARN HOW TO WORK TOGETHER--BUT TRIGON HAS ALREADY COME.

MORE THAN EVER NOW, I NEED YOU ALL BESIDE ME. AND I NEED YOU, RICHARD, TO CARRY ON AS LEADER. FOR, UNLESS WE WORK AS A TEAM, WE ARE ALREADY DOOMED!

BUT BEFORE THE TEEN WONDER CAN REPLY...

KLANG

THE ALARM!

SOMETHING MUST BE WRONG!

CHANGELING, DO A RECON--QUICKLY.

SURE, SURE, ALWAYS SEND OUT THE KID WITH THE GREEN FACE, RIGHT?

WELL, EVERYTHING SEEMS CLEAR, EXCEPT--HOLD IT!

HEY, GUYS--WHAT'S GOT FOUR EYES AND FLIES?

'CAUSE WHATEVER IT IS, IT'S COMIN' THIS WAY--AND FAST!

GAR, GET BACK HERE--PRONTO!

PRONTO? WASN'T HE THE LONE RANGER'S PARTNER?

CHANGELING!!?

SPOILSPORT!

13

141

AND, JUST MOMENTS LATER...

IT'S DEFINITELY RAVEN'S *POP*, AND HE DOESN'T LOOK LIKE HE'D BE MUCH *FUN* AT PARTIES!

SO WHAT *NOW*, *WITCH-LADY?* ARE WE *READY?* DO WE *ATTACK*, OR--?

THIS ISN'T THE *TIME* FOR OUR BATTLE. I SENSE SOMETHING *AMISS!*

WAIT! RAVEN, DON'T *DISAPPEAR* ON US!

I *MUST*, WALLACE, ONLY IN THE *TEMPLE AZARATH* CAN I HOPE TO FIND MY ANSWERS.

SHE DID IT *AGAIN!* SHE *ALWAYS* DISAPPEARS ON US!

THERE'S STILL SO MUCH WE DON'T *KNOW* ABOUT HER. SHE MUST HAVE HER *REASONS*.

YEAH, SHE PROBABLY *DOES*, BUT THIS TIME I *DON'T CARE!*

WHEN THIS MISSION'S OVER WITH, I'M *QUITTING* THE TITANS AS FAST AS I CAN!

TALK ABOUT YOUR *OPTIMISTS*. HE ACTUALLY THINKS WE'RE GONNA *SURVIVE!*

HEY, GUYS-- WAIT UP FOR *ME!*

YOU ALWAYS *CARRY* ME, KORIAND'R. I'VE GOT TO GET SOME SORT OF *VEHICLE*.

WHY? I *LOVE* HAVING YOU NEAR ME, DICK.

HMMM, EVERYONE TOOK OFF BUT 'BORGY. HE'S STILL IN FRONT OF THE TOWER.

BETTER SEE WHAT'S *GOIN'* DOWN!

AND, AS THE TITANS' RESIDENT SHAPE-SHIFTER *LANDS*...

NEED A *ROAD MAP*, 'BORGY? OR IS SOMETHIN' *WRONG?*

YOU TELL THE *OTHERS* AND I SWEAR I'LL RIP OUT YOUR *HEART* --BUT YEAH, LOGAN, SOMETHIN'S *WRONG!*

THE *REST* OF YOU, EVEN GOLDIE-- YOU'RE USED TO THINGS ON A *COSMIC LEVEL*.

I'M *NOT*, AND MAN, EVERY SO OFTEN I GET A LITTLE *NERVOUS*, MEBBE EVEN A LITTLE *SCARED*.

TILL I MET YOU BIRDS I WASN'T ANY BIG-SHOT *SUPER-HERO*. AND NOW-- WELL, LIKE I SAY, IT TAKES SOME GETTIN' *USED TO*.

LEMME *TELL* YOU SOMETHING, VIC, IT'S A *STATE SECRET* KNOWN ONLY TO US OLD-TIME HEROES-- BUT SOMETIMES WE *ALL* GET SCARED.

EXCEPT *ME*, OF COURSE, I MEAN, I JUST GOT INTO THIS RACKET TO MEET *GIRLS!*

DON'T YOU *EVER* STOP WITH THE JOKES?

YEP, BUT THOSE ARE THE TIMES EVEN *I* CAN'T STAND MYSELF.

14

HER NAME IS *PRINCESS KORIAND'R*, NOW CALLED *STARFIRE*, AND SHE SOARS AHEAD WITHOUT CONCERN. TRAINED BY THE *WARLORDS OF OKAARA*, SHE SEEMS TO *THRIVE* ON BATTLE.

BUT *DICK GRAYSON*, KNOWN AS *ROBIN*, FINDS HIS THOUGHTS ARE ON TACTICS AND PLANNING. HIS FRIENDS ARE *POWERFUL*, BUT THEY ARE *UNDISCIPLINED!* HE WORRIES ABOUT WHAT IS TO COME.

AS *KID FLASH* RACES AHEAD, HE IS TORN WITH *DOUBTS*. HE HAD WANTED TO LIVE A NORMAL LIFE AS *WALLY WEST*, BUT HIS POWERS HAVE ALWAYS *PREVENTED* HIM FROM FINDING THE PEACE HE DESPERATELY DESIRES.

VICTOR STONE, TOO, HAS DOUBTS. HE HAD *HATED* BEING TURNED INTO THIS *CYBORG* MONSTROSITY, BUT NOW HE WORRIES THAT HE IS BEGINNING TO ENJOY THE *THOUSAND NEW SENSATIONS* HE FEELS.

LIKE *KORIAND'R*, *DONNA TROY*, *WONDER GIRL*, IS ALSO *CALM* AS SHE GLIDES AHEAD. BUT WHILE SHE DOES NOT *RELISH* BATTLE, THIS AMAZING AMAZON IS STILL READY TO MEET ANY *MENACE*.

BUT THE *CHANGELING*, *GARFIELD LOGAN*, FINDS A PAINFUL *KNOT* FORMING DEEP WITHIN HIS STOMACH. DESPITE HIS FANCIFUL FACADE, HE FRETS ABOUT HIS PLACE IN THE IMPENDING *BATTLE*.

AS WELL HE SHOULD. AHEAD OF THESE NEW TITANS, FLOATING HIGH ABOVE MANHATTAN, TRIGON GESTURES WITH AN ALMOST TOTAL *DISDAIN* FOR THE HUMAN *GNATS* SCRAMBLING IN FEAR FAR BELOW.

HOW *EASY* IT IS FOR HIM TO CREATE *TERROR* IN THEIR HEARTS. ALMOST *TOO* EASY, TRIGON THINKS. THESE ARE SPINELESS MAGGOTS WHO COWER WHEN SHOWN EVEN THE MOST *MINUTE* DISPLAY OF POWER.

THEY DO NOT DESERVE TO BE *TOYED* WITH, THEY SHOULD SIMPLY BE *ERADICATED--INSTANTLY!*

15

IT IS WITH A SICKENINGLY CASUAL AIR THAT TRIGON PLUNGES AHEAD. HE GIVES NO MORE THOUGHT TO THE DEVASTATING *CONSEQUENCES* OF HIS ACTIONS THAN YOU MIGHT GIVE TO THE STAMPING OUT OF AN ANT.

HE MERELY GESTURES AND THE GROUND BELOW HIM HEAVES. YET, SOMEHOW WE'RE SUPPOSED TO *DEFEAT* HIM--?

I FEAR RAVEN HAS GIVEN US AN IMPOSSIBLE *TASK!*

SKREEEE

SO, YOU ARE THE INSECTS MY DAUGHTER HAS SENT TO ATTACK ME?

YOU ARE PERSISTENT...

...BUT, ULTIMATELY, YOUR EFFORTS ARE *USELESS!*

TO ONE WHO HAS DECIMATED WORLDS, ONE WHO HAS RAVAGED GALAXIES--

--AND BROUGHT AN ENTIRE UNIVERSE TO ITS KNEES--

--THE PUNY POWERS YOU DISPLAY ONLY SERVE TO WHET MY APPETITE FOR DESTRUCTION!

MOOSE-HEAD AIN'T *KIDDIN'.* HE'S GOT MORE'N ENOUGH POWER TO *TRASH* US.

16

144

IN ATTACKING ME YOU PLAY A CHILDREN'S GAME--

--BUT I SHALL LET THE GAME RUN ON!

AND TEACH YOU WHAT IT MEANS TO FACE THE WRATH OF TRIGON!

HUNH? STARTING TO SPIN AGAINST MY WILL...

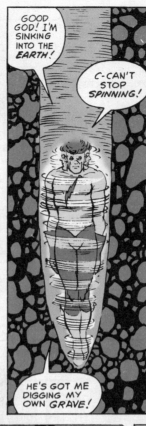

GOOD GOD! I'M SINKING INTO THE EARTH!

C-CAN'T STOP SPINNING!

HE'S GOT ME DIGGING MY OWN GRAVE!

CRIPES! HE TOOK OUT LOGAN AN' FLASHER WITHOUT EVEN BLINKIN'!

DON'T THINK A COUPLE BILLION DECIBELS A' SOUND'S GONNA MEAN MUCH TO HIM, BUT I GOTTA TRY--

MUST YOU?

A FRUITLESS EFFORT AGAINST ONE WHO CAN TURN YOUR POWERS AGAINST YOU!

BREEAAAMM

AGGHH! SOUND SCREAMIN' THROUGH MY SKULL!

TOO MUCH PAIN... GONNA BLACK OUT!

MEANWHILE...

RAVEN--? THIS TIME, STAY PUT! HALF THE TITANS ARE DOWN, AND I NEED HELP!

FOR ONCE, EXPLAIN WHAT'S GOING ON HERE?

FORCES BEYOND MY COMPREHENSION, ROBIN. BUT I HAVE RETURNED TO TELL YOU ALL IS NOT LOST.

THE COUNCIL OF AZARATH HAS HEARD MY PLEA. EVEN NOW THEY MEET TO DECIDE ON THEIR COURSE OF ACTION.

YOU KEEP TALKING ABOUT AZARATH AND COUNCILS. AND I STILL DON'T UNDERSTAND ONE BLESSED THING.

HOLD! THEY SUMMON ME BACK. A DECISION HAS BEEN REACHED.

WAIT, RAVEN! DON'T GO-- DON'T...

...GONE AGAIN...

...DAMN!

17

145

AN INSTANT IS ALL IT TAKES, AND, FOR RAVEN, THE NOISY BATTLEGROUND OF NEW YORK BECOMES THE CATHEDRALED SILENCE OF THE TEMPLE AZARATH...

...AND ROBIN'S PERPLEXED PRESENCE IS REPLACED WITH THE STOIC BEAUTY OF RAVEN'S MOTHER, ARELLA...

WELL? *TELL* ME, MOTHER. WHAT HAS THE COUNCIL *DECIDED?*

WE PERMITTED YOU TO *SPEAK* TO US, MY DEAR, BUT YOU KNEW THE *OUTCOME* BEFORE YOU LEFT.

BUT I HAD THOUGHT...BELIEVED I COULD CONVINCE YOU--

OUR *HOME WORLD* IS AT STAKE HERE, MOTHER. OUR WORLD... AND OUR *UNIVERSE.*

WE *TOLD* YOU, ARELLA. YOUR DAUGHTER WOULD NOT *LISTEN.* DESPITE ALL HER TRAINING AND STUDIES HERE, SHE NEVER TRULY *UNDERSTOOD* US.

WE *FLED* THE EARTH AND ITS VIOLENT WAYS MORE THAN NINE CENTURIES AGONE. WE ESTABLISHED AZARATH AS OUR HOME TO WORSHIP THE WAYS OF *PEACE.*

AND WE WILL NOT PERMIT YOU TO BRING EARTH'S *EVIL* TO OUR TEMPLE DOORS AGAIN. *BEGONE,* RAVEN -- YOU ARE NO LONGER *WELCOME* HERE.

NO!! I WILL NOT GO, MONKS. AND I WILL USE ALL THE *POWER* YOU HAVE GIVEN ME TO *RESIST* YOUR SENDING ME AWAY.

WHEN I WAS FIRST *BORN* HERE, YOU WANTED ME *SLAIN*-- BECAUSE YOU SENSED THE SEEDS OF *EVIL* WITHIN ME THAT I HAD INHERITED FROM MY FATHER, TRIGON.

PERHAPS YOU SHOULD HAVE *HAD* ME KILLED, BECAUSE AS I GREW I COULD NOT BE *CONTENT* WITH YOUR PASSIVE APPROACH TO FINDING PEACE.

THERE CANNOT BE *TRUE* PEACE SO LONG AS YOU PERMIT EVIL TO *EXIST.* AND EVIL *DOES* EXIST.

--EVIL IN ITS MOST *VILE* FORM, EVIL AT ITS MOST *DEADLY...* EVIL IN THE GUISE OF *TRIGON.* IF YOU FAIL TO USE YOUR POWERS TO *STOP* HIM, THEN YOU ARE ONLY *PROMOTING* THAT WHICH YOU PROFESS TO *DESPISE.*

THEY WILL NOT LISTEN TO YOU, DAUGHTER. THESE FOOLS ARE ONLY *COWARDS* WHO HIDE WITHIN THEIR PRAYERS!

18

THESE INSIGNIFICANT WORMS WOULD NOT EVEN RAISE ONE FINGER IN SELF-DEFENSE. BUT, YOU, ARELLA-- YOU WERE NOT ALWAYS THIS WAY.

THAT WAS BEFORE I CAME TO THE *TEMPLE*, BEFORE I TOOK *THEIR* DISCIPLINES AS *MINE*.

THUS RAVEN WAS BORN!

WHEN I MADE YOU MY BRIDE, YOU FOUGHT ME. YOU TRIED TO RESIST ME, AND YOU LOST!

WE DO NOT *FEAR* DEATH HERE, TRIGON, SO IF YOU MUST, DO YOUR *WORST*.

MY WORST, FAIR ARELLA, WOULD BE BEYOND THAT WHICH YOUR PUNY MIND COULD CONCEIVE.

BUT, HAVE NO FEAR-- YOU WILL DIE AS HAVE ALL MY BRIDES WHO HAVE PRECEDED YOU.

NO, TRIGON-- THEY MIGHT NOT FIGHT YOU, BUT I *WILL*.

IF MY MOTHER WON'T STAND BESIDE ME-- I WILL HAVE MY *FRIENDS*!

--AND SUMMON THOSE WHO WILL STAND *BESIDE* ME.

BEFORE ME NOW-- TITANS APPEAR!

OUTSIDE THIS TEMPLE MY POWERS ARE ONLY *EMPATHIC*, BUT HERE, STRENGTHENED BY AZARATH'S MYSTIC FORCES, I CAN SPREAD MY POWERS TO THE *BEYOND*--

HER MOTHER, ARELLA, TAUGHT HER TO AVOID STRUGGLE, TO EMBRACE PASSIVITY, YET TRIGON'S BLOOD HERITAGE HAD MADE HER *RESTLESS* WITHIN THESE TEMPLE WALLS; A WOLF AMONG THE SHEEP. FOR ALL HER LIFE THESE TWO PERSONAS HAVE STRUGGLED FOR *DOMINANCE*, AND NOW, AS SHE COMMITS HERSELF TO *FIGHT* THE BATTLE AHEAD, SHE IS SUDDENLY VERY MUCH *FRIGHTENED*, FOR SHE KNOWS WHICH SIDE HAS *WON*...

19

CLOUDS OF THICK EBON SMOKE BILLOW FORTH, THEN EXPLODE WITH LIGHT AND SOUND. AND, WHEN THE FURY FINALLY SUBSIDES...

YOU BROUGHT THEM *HERE*? BUT YOU *KNOW* THAT IS AGAINST OUR *CODES*!

THEY'RE *HERE*, MOTHER-- AND EMPATHICALLY I'VE LET THEM *UNDERSTAND* WHAT HAS HAPPENED.

RAVEN--? WE TRIED *SEARCHING* FOR YOU...

I SAID I WOULD *FIGHT* FOR THE EARTH, AND I *MEANT IT*!

...BUT AS SOON AS YOU *DISAPPEARED*, TRIGON TOOK OFF, LEFT US *BEHIND*.

MY DAUGHTER IS A FOOL! SHE WILL LEAD ME TO *AZARATH*!

"WE STOOD THERE, HELPLESS ...LOST...

"...THEN..."

MAN, DIDN'T THINK I'D EVER *FIND* YOU GUYS AGAIN. I THOUGHT TRIGON HAD *KILLED* YOU...

H-HE JUST *IGNORED* US...LIKE WE WERE *NOTHING*.

HOW DID YOU *FREE* YOURSELF, WALLY?

"FRANKLY, IT TOOK A WHILE TO *FIGURE OUT*. BUT I STARTED SPINNING AT AN EVEN *FASTER* RATE.

"CHANGING MY COURSE, ARCING BACK UP TO THE SURFACE AS TRIGON'S BLAST WORE OFF.

"BUT, WHEN I *GOT* TO THE SURFACE, I SAW TRIGON FLYING AWAY. I TRIED TO *FOLLOW*, MOVING FASTER TO KEEP UP WITH HIM.

"BUT, HE KEPT PULLING AWAY FROM ME...UNTIL HE FINALLY *DISAPPEARED*."

YET WE STAND TOGETHER, WITH YOU DARING TO *RESIST* THE POWER SUPREME.

BUT I WARN YOU, HUMANS, WHAT LITTLE PATIENCE I POSSESS IS QUICKLY WEARING THIN.

20

FOR AN ALL TOO BRIEF MOMENT, THERE IS *SILENCE*-- AS LONG BREATHS ARE DRAWN, AND MINDS ARE SET FOR ACTION. THE TITANS ARE PLAINLY WORRIED, PERHAPS EVEN *AFRAID*...

...BUT THERE IS NO FEAR IN *TRIGON'S* THOUGHTS.

FOR, HE KNOWS ONLY *ONE* HUMAN EMOTION -- TOTAL, ALL-CONSUMING *HATRED*!

WITH A SNARL TURNING HIS UPPER LIP, HE WAVES HIS STAFF BEFORE HIM AS IF TO SIGNAL THE BEGINNING OF BATTLE...

SKRAAK

MY FATHER SURRENDERED TO ONE ALIEN TYRANT, BUT I SWEAR, TRIGON, I WILL NOT DO THE *SAME*!

I'LL *DEFEND* MY NEW WORLD -- TO THE *DEATH*!

STARFIRE!!

YOU'LL GET YOUR CHANCE TO ATTACK, BUT WAIT TILL I GIVE THE SIGNAL!

REMEMBER WHAT I *SAID*, RICHARD--

YEAH, YEAH, WE KNOW, SO KNOCK OFF THE *SERMONS*.

BUT IF YOUR OLD MAN *WANTS* HIS FIGHT -- HE'S *GOT* ONE!

HE'S WAITING FOR OUR FIRST MOVE... SO *CONFIDENT*... SO *CERTAIN* THERE'S NOTHING WE CAN DO TO *STOP* HIM.

UH OH, HIS EYES ARE STARTIN' TO *GLOW*! SOMETHIN' TELLS ME THAT SPELLS *TROUBLE*!

WHY DO THEY *FIGHT*, RAVEN? DO THEY NOT REALIZE THE *FUTILITY* OF IT ALL?

THEY FIGHT BECAUSE THEY WANT TO *HELP*. THEY FIGHT SO OUR WORLD MAY CONTINUE TO LIVE IN *PEACE*!

ALL RIGHT, GUYS -- EVERYONE GET *READY*--

NOW!!

21

They attack with an astounding display of unrestrained power. They are somewhat *frightened*, true, for not one of them has ever before faced such an *overwhelming force*, but they channel that fright into *action*, and they wield their power as never they have before.

Hours ago, the Justice League of America *chastised* this group, called them children. But, even those venerable long time heroes would gasp in appreciative *awe* if they could but see these Titans wage a battle they know they are doomed to *lose*.

They rise to the *challenge* this interdimensional killer presents with impossible passion and skill. But, sadly, that is not *enough*.

Trigon has conquered a *universe*, and, as yet, the Titans are *not* enough to conquer *him*...

22

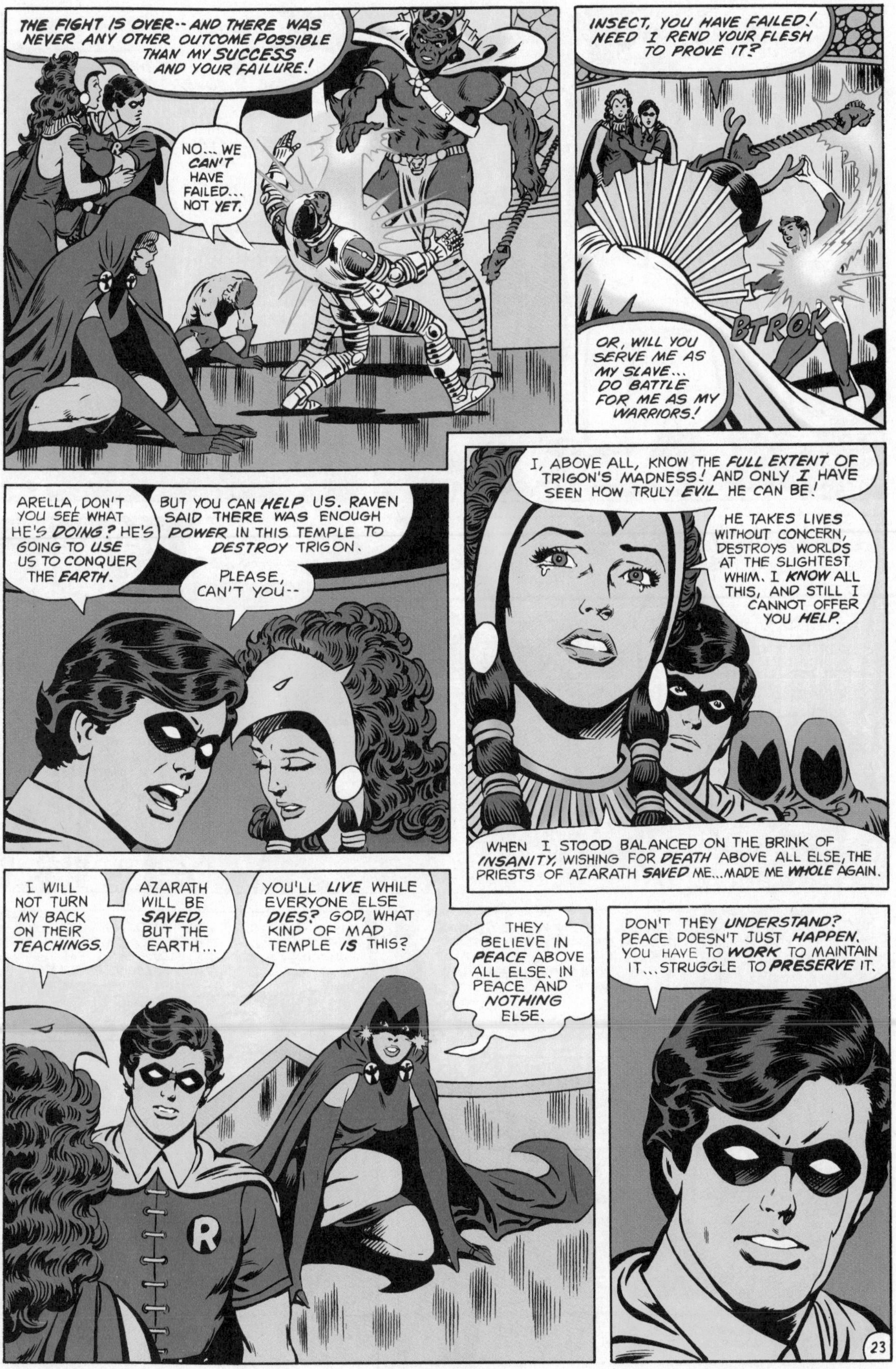

THE FIGHT IS OVER-- AND THERE WAS NEVER ANY OTHER OUTCOME POSSIBLE THAN MY SUCCESS AND YOUR FAILURE!
NO... WE CAN'T HAVE FAILED... NOT YET.
INSECT, YOU HAVE FAILED! NEED I REND YOUR FLESH TO PROVE IT?
BTROK
OR, WILL YOU SERVE ME AS MY SLAVE... DO BATTLE FOR ME AS MY WARRIORS!
ARELLA, DON'T YOU SEE WHAT HE'S DOING? HE'S GOING TO USE US TO CONQUER THE EARTH.
BUT YOU CAN HELP US. RAVEN SAID THERE WAS ENOUGH POWER IN THIS TEMPLE TO DESTROY TRIGON.
PLEASE, CAN'T YOU--
I, ABOVE ALL, KNOW THE FULL EXTENT OF TRIGON'S MADNESS! AND ONLY I HAVE SEEN HOW TRULY EVIL HE CAN BE!
HE TAKES LIVES WITHOUT CONCERN, DESTROYS WORLDS AT THE SLIGHTEST WHIM. I KNOW ALL THIS, AND STILL I CANNOT OFFER YOU HELP.
WHEN I STOOD BALANCED ON THE BRINK OF INSANITY, WISHING FOR DEATH ABOVE ALL ELSE, THE PRIESTS OF AZARATH SAVED ME...MADE ME WHOLE AGAIN.
I WILL NOT TURN MY BACK ON THEIR TEACHINGS.
AZARATH WILL BE SAVED, BUT THE EARTH...
YOU'LL LIVE WHILE EVERYONE ELSE DIES? GOD, WHAT KIND OF MAD TEMPLE IS THIS?
THEY BELIEVE IN PEACE ABOVE ALL ELSE. IN PEACE AND NOTHING ELSE.
DON'T THEY UNDERSTAND? PEACE DOESN'T JUST HAPPEN. YOU HAVE TO WORK TO MAINTAIN IT... STRUGGLE TO PRESERVE IT.
23

IT IS OVER NOW, ONLY THE POWERLESS STAND BEFORE ME-- WHILE THESE OTHERS LIE DEFEATED AT MY FEET.

SOME WOULD CALL THEM VALIANT FOES, BUT ALL I SEE ARE CONTEMPTIBLE FOOLS WHO WILL BE RETRAINED --

--SO THEIR POWERS MAY SERVE ME AS I DEMAND!

WAIT, TRIGON... LET ME SPEAK!

RAVEN, WHAT ARE YOU DOING?

TRIGON COULD HAVE SLAIN ME MANY TIMES, BUT HE NEVER DID.

I BELIEVE THERE IS SOMETHING...STILL SOME SPARK OF DECENCY WITHIN HIM THAT I CAN REACH... THAT I MIGHT PERSUADE.

FATHER, I CALL OUT TO YOU WITH A PROPOSITION.

YOU WANTED ME TO RULE AT YOUR SIDE, AND I WILL... I'LL STAND BESIDE YOU, BUT ONLY IN YOUR DIMENSION.

TAKE ME, TRIGON --BUT LEAVE THIS DIMENSION AND ITS TEEMING WORLDS ALONE!

GLADLY I WOULD SACRIFICE MYSELF!

YOU WOULD FORSAKE THIS PLANET? YOU WOULD COME WITH ME?

NO, RAVEN. YOU DON'T KNOW WHAT YOU'RE DOING!

RAVEN, LISTEN TO ME. I WAS ALSO A SACRIFICE TO SAVE A WORLD, AND BECAUSE OF THAT I KNOW THE TORTURES THAT AWAIT YOU.

DO NOT GO... THERE MUST BE ANOTHER WAY!

OOOHHH! MAN, I FEEL LIKE DUMBO JUST SAT ON MY HEAD. WHAT DID TRIGON HIT ME WITH?

IF ONLY THERE WAS ANOTHER WAY, KORIAND'R, BUT THERE IS NONE! MY HAPPINESS, MY LIFE, IS NOTHING IF I CAN GIVE IT TO SAVE A UNIVERSE.

CEASE ALL YOUR FIGHTING, MY FRIENDS. MY MIND IS MADE UP. I WILL DO AS MY FATHER BIDS.

24

THEN, DAUGHTER, I WILL ACCEPT YOUR OFFER.

GIVE ME YOUR HAND.... AND SWEAR TO LEAVE THIS DIMENSION BEHIND YOU, FOR YOU WILL NEVER AGAIN RETURN!

I WILL JOIN YOU, FATHER ... AND I GO...

...WILLINGLY...

STOP 'ER! WE CAN'T LET HER GO WITH THAT KILLER!

NO, CYBORG... WE MUSTN'T INTERFERE. I ALWAYS ACCUSED HER OF RUNNING FROM BATTLE. LORD, SHE'S PROBABLY THE BRAVEST OF US ALL!

IT'S TOO LATE, STAR! SHE'S GOIN' --LIKE SHE WAS NEVER TRULY HERE!

WE CAN STILL PREVENT THIS MADNESS! WE CAN STILL DESTROY TRIGON! RAVEN CANNOT KNOW WHAT TERRORS SHE IS SUBMITTING HERSELF TO.

NO! DON'T LET HER GO, BLAST IT! RAVEN, I DON'T WANT YOU AWAY FROM ME -- I WANT YOU HERE, I WANT YOU TO KNOW HOW MUCH I LO--

BUT, IT IS TOO LATE, KID FLASH. MUCH TOO LATE.

THEY ARE BOTH GONE NOW, ALREADY TRAVERS-ING THE DIMENSIONS, SOON TO LAND ON A WORLD THAT WILL MAKE HELL SEEM LIKE A PARADISE BY COMPARISON. SHE IS GONE BEFORE YOU CAN SAY THAT, DESPITE ALL THAT HAS HAPPENED, YOU STILL LOVE HER.

SO, INSTEAD, YOU STAND ALONGSIDE THE OTHERS. AS HELPLESS AS THEY ARE, BUT MUCH, MUCH SADDER. AND TEARS COME TO YOUR EYES, A THICK LUMP FORMS WITHIN YOUR THROAT, AND YOUR STOMACH FEELS AN EMPTINESS THAT WILL NOT PASS.

NEXT ISSUE: GEORGE PÉREZ RETURNS TO THE DRAWING BOARD AS THE TITANS FACE THEIR GREATEST BATTLE YET IN THE DARK, BROODING DIMENSION OF TRIGON THE TERRIBLE: BE HERE FOR

LAST KILL!

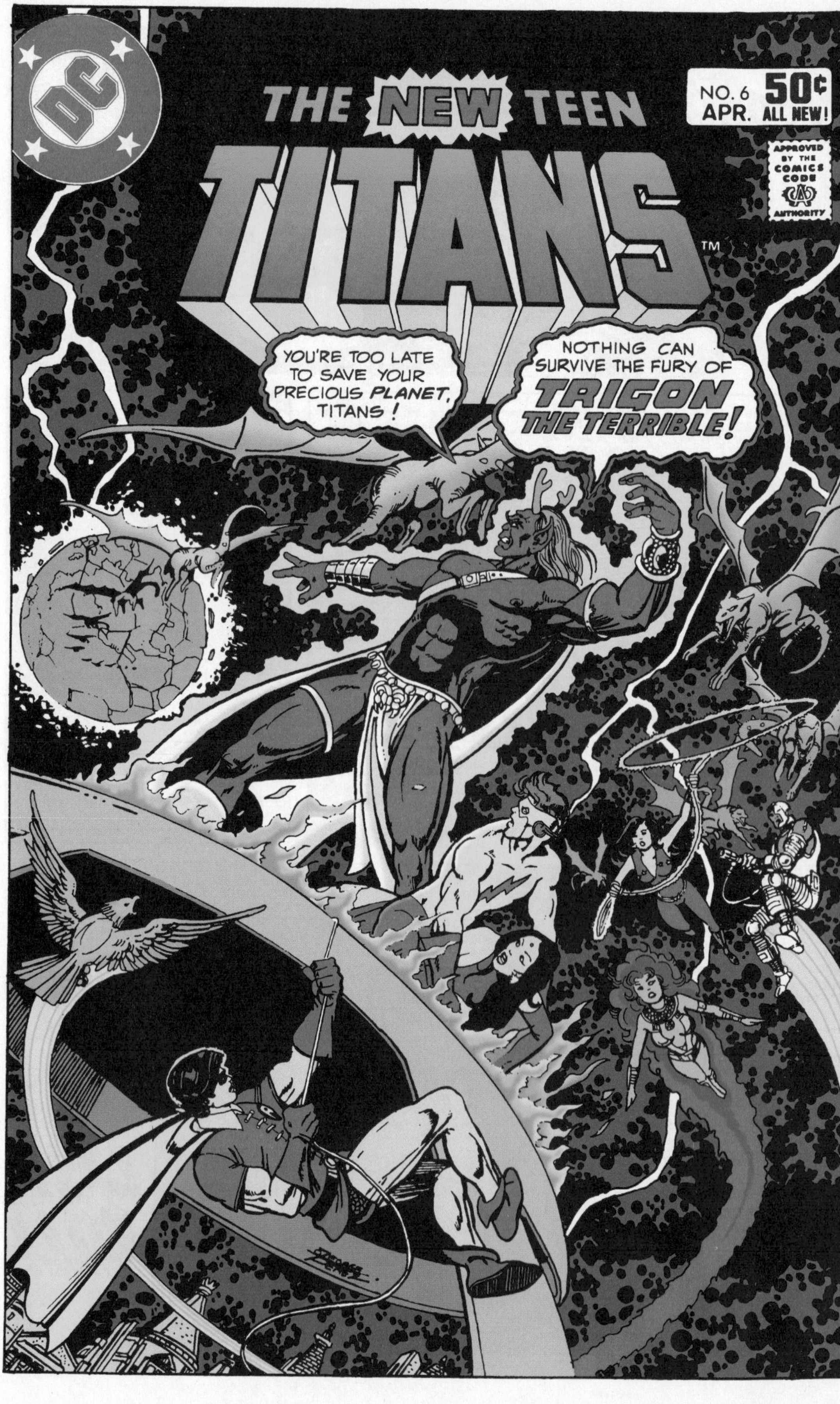
DC
THE NEW TEEN
TITANS
TM
NO. 6
APR.
50¢
ALL NEW!
APPROVED BY THE COMICS CODE AUTHORITY
YOU'RE TOO LATE TO SAVE YOUR PRECIOUS PLANET, TITANS!
NOTHING CAN SURVIVE THE FURY OF TRIGON THE TERRIBLE!

RAVEN TREMBLES AS TRIGON'S WORLD SUDDENLY APPEARS BEFORE HER LIKE SOME DARK, DREADED NIGHTMARE COME TO LIFE. SHE IS AN EMPATH, A "FEELER" OF PAINS, A "SENSER" OF EMOTIONS WHO HAS KNOWN ALL THE MYRIAD PASSIONS FROM UNBRIDLED JOY TO HEARTRENDING FEAR-- BUT THE SUDDEN COLD TERROR SHE SENSES HERE FRIGHTENS HER BEYOND ANY EMOTION SHE HAS EVER FELT BEFORE...

THIS IS HER FATHER'S PLANET, AND THE WORLD SHE WILL BE IMPRISONED ON FOR THE REST OF HER TORTURED LIFE.

PROLOGUE:

GOD SAVE US! TRIGON HAS RETURNED!

HAIL TRIGON!

HAIL TRIGON! HAIL THE MASTER!

THE NEW TEEN TITANS
™

THOSE PRATTLING *DOLTS* BELOW US ARE MY *CHATTEL!* THEY EXIST ONLY TO *OBEY* MY SLIGHTEST *WHIM!*

SHOULD THEY *ANNOY* YOU, SHOULD THEIR VERY PRESENCE PERTURB YOU, I WILL *DESTROY* THEM WHERE THEY STAND!

THEIR EYES ARE SO EMPTY OF *HOPE.* ALL I SENSE IN THEM IS *FEAR.*

WHAT MANNER OF *WORLD* HAS MY FATHER CREATED?

WOMAN, *SMILE* AT THE MASTER!

KEEP IN *LINE,* YOU SPINELESS MAGGOTS!

YOU ARE HERE TO WELCOME HOME THE *MASTER.* SING *PRAISES* TO HIM -- OR *DIE!*

YOU FAIL TO SPEAK, DAUGHTER. WHAT DO YOU *THINK* OF TRIGON'S WORLD?

TO DO *WHAT?* THEY SERVE NO PURPOSE OTHER THAN SERVING *ME.*

THERE IS NO *JOY* HERE, FATHER. NO *LOVE.* THESE PEOPLE ARE YOUR *SLAVES* -- AND THEY *FEAR* YOU.

THEY SHOULD BE SET *FREE!*

NOW, YOU SCUM, *SALUTE* THE MASTER AS HE PASSES!

IGNORE THEM, DAUGHTER. THEIR LIVES ARE AS *MEANINGLESS* TO US AS THE LIFE OF AN *INSECT.*

M-MOTHER... IS *HE* THE MASTER? H-HE'S A *MONSTER!*

SILENCE, RUDA... IF TRIGON *HEARS* YOU...

SHE CALLED ME A *MONSTER,* DID SHE?

MASTER, SHE DOESN'T KNOW WHAT SHE'S *SAYING.* SHE'S ONLY A *CHILD!*

AGE MEANS NOTHING TO *TRIGON.*

2

FROM THE MOMENT YOU ARE *BORN,* I DEMAND YOUR TOTAL *OBEDIENCE,* YOUR COMPLETE *SUBSERVIENCE.*

YOU ARE TO BE TAUGHT THAT I AM YOUR *GOD,* THAT I HOLD YOUR VERY *LIFE* IN MY HANDS.

AND YOU WILL *LEARN* TO VIEW ME WITH THE *RESPECT* I DEMAND.

GOD! WHAT IS HE *DOING* TO THE GIRL?

THE *DEATH STARE!*

MASTER, *PLEASE...* I *BEG* OF YOU... SHOW HER *MERCY!*

FATHER, I CAN SENSE THE *PAIN* YOU ARE CAUSING HER. STOP IT, FOR GOD'S SAKE-- *STOP IT!*

PLEASE, MASTER, ANYTHING YOU *WANT* FROM ME, I WILL *GIVE* YOU. TAKE MY LIFE... JUST PLEASE SPARE *HERS!*

TRIGON-- DON'T YOU *CARE* WHAT YOU ARE DOING TO HER? HER BLOOD-- IT *BOILS!*

TRIGON!?!

LESSONS MUST BE *TAUGHT.*

DISCIPLINE MUST BE *MAINTAINED!*

IT *WILL* BE MAINTAINED... WITHOUT HAVING TO *KILL* HER!

NO! HER DEATH WILL BE A *LESSON* FOR THE OTHERS.

FOR GOD'S SAKE, FATHER-- *STOP...* PLEASE STOP!

BUT SHE'S A *CHILD...* HER DEATH IS *IMMORAL.*

AND I CANNOT LET YOU DO THIS... NO MATTER *WHAT* YOU MIGHT DO TO *ME.*

PLEASE, IF YOU CAN *HELP* HER...

I CAN ONLY *TRY!*

MY POWERS ARE THOSE OF AN *EMPATH*-- THE POWER TO DRAW PAIN AWAY FROM THE *CHILD...*

...TO DRAW IT INTO ME!

3

AGGHH! AZAR, HELP ME... THE PAIN IS TOO GREAT...

GOD! GOD! MY SKIN BOILS... MY FLESH CRAWLING... SO VERY PAINFUL...

AGHHH...TOO MUCH...IT HURTS TOO MUCH...DON'T KNOW IF I CAN EXPEL THE PAIN...BUT I...MUST...

LEAVING ME SO WEAK...SO DRAINED. BUT...I AM WHOLE...

...AND THE CHILD STILL LIVES! TAKE HER AWAY NOW... TEACH HER, AND, ABOVE ALL, LOVE HER!

THANK YOU, THANK YOU!

A WASTED DISPLAY OF YOUR POWERS, RAVEN.

I STILL WILL NOT PERMIT ANYONE TO DISPUTE MY AUTHORITY.

RAVEN IS SPEECHLESS, AS SHE IS LED THROUGH THE GRIMY TEEMING STREETS TOWARD TRIGON'S INNER CASTLE-KEEP, SHE IS DRAINED, LOST, HELPLESS, AND UNABLE TO COPE WITH THE OVERWHELMING EVIL HER FATHER EMBODIES.

YOU DISAPPROVE, DAUGHTER. BUT, YOU WILL LEARN... YOU WILL LEARN.

NOT EVEN YOU!

FOOSH!

NO!

NOW, RAVEN, LET US GO TO MY CASTLE. THERE IS STILL MUCH OF MY WORLD YOU MUST SEE, MUCH YOU MUST KNOW!

GOD, MY GOD... MY GOD...

SHE WANTS TO FLEE, TO RACE BACK TO THE EARTH, BUT STAYING PRISONER HERE ON TRIGON'S WORLD WAS THE PLEDGE SHE MADE TO SAVE THE EARTH FROM TRIGON'S MURDEROUS WRATH. AND SO, TEARS STREAMING FROM HER STEEL-GRAY EYES, SHE PLODS HOPELESSLY ONWARD...

4

YOU ARE MY *DAUGHTER*, AND THEREFORE A *GOD* LIKE MYSELF, AND FAR *ABOVE* THE RABBLE WHOM WE COMMAND.

THEY ARE HARDLY WORTH OUR *ATTENTION*, LET ALONE OUR DISCUSSING THE *VALUE* OF THEIR LIVES.

SIRE, YOUR DARK HORDES HAVE RETURNED FROM XYNTHIA... THEY REPORT *UNREST*.

AND THE PROPER *PREPARATIONS* HAVE BEEN MADE?

INDEED, SIRE! THIS IS XYNTHIA'S *QUEEN*. WILL *SHE* SERVE YOU?

A *COMELY* WENCH, SOON TO BE THE *LAST* OF HER RACE, YES, PREPARE HER FOR *TONIGHT*. SHE WILL *DO*.

NOW THEN, GROOL, WHAT SEEMS TO BE THE *PROBLEM?*

THIS *PROCLAMATION*, MASTER.

THE XYNTHIANS DEMAND THAT YOUR DARK HORDES *LEAVE* THEIR PLANET IMMEDIATELY.

THEY FURTHER DEMAND THAT YOU PAY FOR THE *DAMAGE* YOUR HORDES HAVE ALREADY INFLICTED.

VERY WELL, GROOL, WE WILL ORDER MY DARKLINGS TO *DEPART*.

WHAT? YOU ARE GOING TO ALLOW THE XYNTHIANS TO MAKE *DEMANDS?*

OF COURSE NOT, GROOL. BUT I DO NOT WANT MY *ARMIES* TO DIE WITH XYNTHIA'S SCUM.

XYNTHIA.

FOOLS!

5

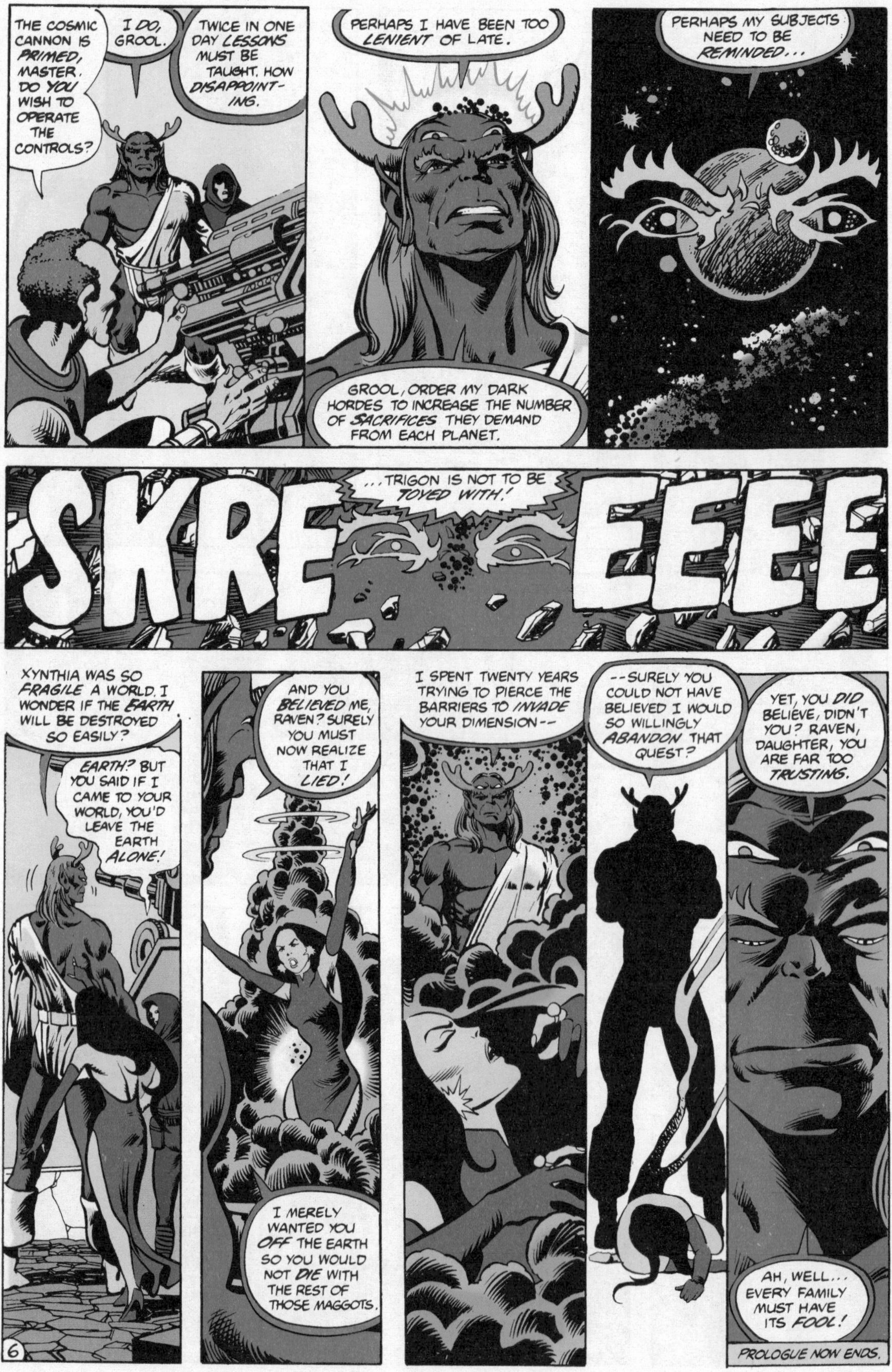
THE COSMIC CANNON IS PRIMED, MASTER. DO YOU WISH TO OPERATE THE CONTROLS?
I DO, GROOL.
TWICE IN ONE DAY LESSONS MUST BE TAUGHT. HOW DISAPPOINTING.
PERHAPS I HAVE BEEN TOO LENIENT OF LATE.
GROOL, ORDER MY DARK HORDES TO INCREASE THE NUMBER OF SACRIFICES THEY DEMAND FROM EACH PLANET.
PERHAPS MY SUBJECTS NEED TO BE REMINDED...
SKREEEEE
...TRIGON IS NOT TO BE TOYED WITH!
XYNTHIA WAS SO FRAGILE A WORLD. I WONDER IF THE EARTH WILL BE DESTROYED SO EASILY?
EARTH? BUT YOU SAID IF I CAME TO YOUR WORLD, YOU'D LEAVE THE EARTH ALONE!
6
AND YOU BELIEVED ME, RAVEN? SURELY YOU MUST NOW REALIZE THAT I LIED!
I MERELY WANTED YOU OFF THE EARTH SO YOU WOULD NOT DIE WITH THE REST OF THOSE MAGGOTS.
I SPENT TWENTY YEARS TRYING TO PIERCE THE BARRIERS TO INVADE YOUR DIMENSION--
--SURELY YOU COULD NOT HAVE BELIEVED I WOULD SO WILLINGLY ABANDON THAT QUEST?
YET, YOU DID BELIEVE, DIDN'T YOU? RAVEN, DAUGHTER, YOU ARE FAR TOO TRUSTING.
AH, WELL... EVERY FAMILY MUST HAVE ITS FOOL!
PROLOGUE NOW ENDS.

LAST KILL!

ELSEWHERE: THE TEMPLE AZARATH NOW STANDS IN RUIN, WRENCHED FROM ITS VERY FOUNDATIONS DURING TRIGON'S EARTHSHAKING BATTLE WITH THE TITANS...

SHE'S *GONE*...WITH THAT GRINNING *DEVIL.* AND WE LET HER GO!

TRIGON WAS NOT *INVINCIBLE*... WE COULD HAVE *DEFEATED* HIM. I FEEL *ASHAMED* ALLOWING RAVEN TO *GO* WITH HIM.

YOU KNOW WE HAD NO *CHOICE*, KID FLASH. IT WAS RAVEN'S OWN *DECISION.*

BUT WE DID OUR *BEST*, GOLDIE. LET'S FACE IT-- FIGHTIN' *TRIGON* ISN'T EXACTLY THE SAME AS TAKIN' ON THE *MUPPETS!*

YEAH, WE DID OUR *BEST,* ONLY OUR BEST WASN'T *GOOD ENOUGH.*

I GOT ME A SICK *FEELIN',* GREENIE... MEBBE WE TITANS JUST DON'T *MEASURE UP.*

NO! WE'RE GOOD, VERY GOOD, AND THERE'S NO *SHAME* IN LOSING TO SOMEONE *STRONGER.*

BUT WE'VE GOT TO *REGROUP,* RETHINK OUR *STRATEGY*... FIND THE BEST WAYS TO CHANNEL OUR *STRENGTHS.*

MARV WOLFMAN
and
GEORGE PÉREZ
co-creators
PABLO MARCOS
Guest inker
JOHN COSTANZA
letterer
JERRY SERPE
colorist
LEN WEIN
editor

7

WHY DO YOU *GRIEVE,* ARELLA? YOUR DAUGHTER, RAVEN, DID AS WE REQUIRED OF HER!

THOUGH SHE HAS ALWAYS *REBELLED* AGAINST US, IN THE END SHE *RETURNED* TO OUR TEACHINGS OF *PASSIVITY.*

BUT STILL, SHE IS *GONE...GONE* TO THE HELL THAT IS *TRIGON'S* WORLD.

AND I WILL *NEVER* SEE HER *AGAIN.*

ONCE SHE LEFT OUR TEMPLE TO SEEK OUTSIDE AID IN *COMBATTING* TRIGON, YOU KNEW SHE WOULD NOT BE PERMITTED TO *RETURN* TO AZARATH.

STILL, SHE IS MY *DAUGHTER* AND I MOURN HER *LOSS.*

IS THAT *ALL* YOU'RE GONNA DO? LEAVE RAVEN TO *ROT* ON TRIGON'S PLANET?

WE CAN STILL *SAVE* HER!

WE WILL *FIGHT* FOR HER LIFE.

THERE WILL BE NO FIGHTING. RAVEN SACRIFICED *HER* LIFE FOR THE LIFE OF THIS *WORLD.* IT IS *OVER.*

BULL! NO WAY IT'S OVER...NOT *YET!!*

DON'T *PUSH* IT, FLASH... AT LEAST NOT *HERE!*

WHA--? DON'T TELL ME YOU'RE GONNA LEAVE RAVEN *BEHIND?*

NO! BUT CAN'T YOU SEE THESE PEOPLE WON'T *HELP* US?

THEN, WE WILL *MAKE* THEM HELP US.

WE HAVE THE POWER TO DO WHATEVER WE *WANT!*

STARFIRE! *DON'T!*

BUT I *MUST,* ROBIN! *I* ABOVE ALL KNOW WHAT IT IS LIKE TO BE SOMEONE'S *PRISONER.*

I KNOW THE *DEGRADATIONS,* THE HORRORS THAT YOU FACE. AND I WILL NOT ALLOW *RAVEN* TO SUFFER THE WAY *I* SUFFERED THOSE SIX LONG YEARS AS A SLAVE OF THE *CITADEL!*

8

PLEASE, KORIAND'R, *DON'T!* WE CAN'T FORCE THESE PRIESTS TO GO AGAINST THEIR *BELIEFS.*

AND WE CANNOT ALLOW RAVEN TO *SUFFER* BY OUR *INACTION!*

MAYBE THERE'S *ANOTHER* WAY.

RAVEN SAID THE TEMPLE AZARATH NORMALLY EXISTED *BETWEEN* DIMENSIONS... AND THAT MEANS *YOU* HAVE THE POWER TO *TAKE* US WHERE WE WANT TO GO.

YOU DON'T HAVE TO VIOLATE YOUR *OATHS,* BUT WILL YOU JUST SHOW US WHAT TO *DO?*

NO, *LOOK* AT HIM, ROBIN. HE WON'T DO *ANYTHING* TO HELP US OR RAVEN.

FLASH...!

HE DOES NOT *UNDERSTAND,* BUT WE ARE USED TO SUCH IGNORANCE.

LONG AGO WE LEARNED THAT PASSIVITY BREEDS INNER *CONTENTMENT*--

--WHILE *VIOLENCE* ONLY BEGETS *MORE* VIOLENCE.

LOOK! WE ARE AT *PEACE* WITH OURSELVES WHILE YOU *SEETHE* WITH *ANGRY PASSIONS.*

SURE YOU'RE AT PEACE WITH YOURSELF, YOU DON'T CARE ABOUT ANYONE ELSE *BUT.*

MAN, YOU WERE GOING TO LET *TRIGON* TAKE OVER OUR WHOLE BLASTED *UNIVERSE* JUST SO YOU COULD PRESERVE YOUR BLASTED *INNER PEACE.*

MISTER, YOU *SICKEN* ME!

TO BE TOTALLY *PASSIVE* DOES NOT CREATE *PEACE* ...IT IS THE BREEDING GROUND FOR *SUBJUGATION!*

YOU TALK OF *SUBJUGATION*... OF *SLAVERY,* BUT WHAT DO YOU *KNOW* OF THE DESTRUCTION AND SLAVERY OF THE *MIND* AND *SOUL?*

LISTEN TO *MY* STORY, AND MAYHAP YOU WILL BETTER UNDERSTAND US *ALL!*

9

IT BEGAN TWENTY YEARS AGO. I WAS EIGHTEEN, CONFUSED, VERY *ALONE*, AND SEARCHING FOR *ANSWERS* TO QUESTIONS I COULDN'T EVEN VOICE.

"I REJECTED *RELIGION*, EMBRACED THE *OCCULT*. DON'T ASK ME *WHY*. IT JUST SEEMED *RIGHT*. GOD, HOW WRONG I WAS.

"PERHAPS OUT OF *BOREDOM*, OR PERHAPS LOOKING FOR SOME SORT OF *MIRACLE*, I JOINED A *SATANIC CULT*. THEN, ONE NIGHT...THERE WAS A *CEREMONY* AND I WAS OFFERED-UP AS THE *BRIDE OF SATAN*.

"THOUGH I CANNOT UNDER-STAND *WHY* NOW, I WENT ALONG WITH THEM... *WILLINGLY*. PERHAPS WHEN YOU ARE *DESPER-ATE*... ANYWAY, THEY BEGAN THEIR *CHANTS*, AND THE SKIES GREW *DARK*, THICK WITH THUNDER AND CRACKLING WITH LIGHTNING.

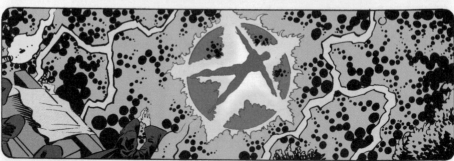

"AN *IMAGE* APPEARED, CERTAINLY NOT AN IMAGE OF *EVIL*. HE WAS *MAGNIFICENT*, THE LIVING EMBODIMENT OF SO MANY OF MY UNSPOKEN DREAMS. I REACHED UP TO HIM, TOOK HIS *HANDS*, AND HE *SPOKE* TO ME IN A DEEP, WARM VELVET VOICE...

"I CANNOT LIE. I LOVED HIM, CHERISHED HIM, WORSHIPPED HIM.

"AND, PERHAPS FOR THE FIRST TIME IN A LIFE FILLED WITH LONELINESS, I FELT LOVED, AND CARED FOR... AND WANTED.

"HE TOOK ME AS HIS BRIDE AND WE WERE MARRIED BY THE PRIESTS OF SATAN.

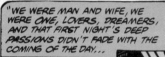

"WE WERE MAN AND WIFE, WE WERE ONE, LOVERS, DREAMERS, AND THAT FIRST NIGHT'S DEEP PASSIONS DIDN'T FADE WITH THE COMING OF THE DAY...

"...FOR EACH TIME I GAZED INTO THOSE SWEET, TENDER EYES, I FELT MORE AND MORE ENTHRALLED. ENTHRALLED! WHAT AN APT WORD!

"ENTHRALLED... I SHOULD HAVE KNOWN... I SHOULD HAVE GUESSED, BUT, FOOL THAT I WAS, I WANTED TO BELIEVE SOMEONE CARED.

"MY LOVER, THE ONE WHOM I THOUGHT WAS LIKE SOME GOD SENT DOWN TO EARTH TO SAVE ME--

"-- TURNED OUT TO BE EVIL INCARNATE!

"HE WAS VICIOUS, SAVAGE... THE MOST HIDEOUS CREATURE GOD COULD HAVE CREATED...IF INDEED HE WAS CREATED BY GOD AND NOT SATAN HIMSELF!

"TO HIM I WAS NOTHING, LESS THAN NOTHING. HE DID WHATEVER HE WANTED WITH ME.

"THEN, WHEN HE WAS DONE, HE CAST ME ASIDE LIKE SOME USELESS RAG!

"IT HURTS TO EVEN REMEMBER. THE PAIN ONCE MORE KNOTS MY STOMACH, AND THAT SICKNESS I FELT THEN RETURNS. THOSE WERE TERRIBLE, TERRIBLE DAYS!"

11

YOU MUST UNDERSTAND, MY MOTHER *ABANDONED* ME AT BIRTH—NOT EVEN KNOWING WHO MY *FATHER* WAS.

I BECAME A *WARD OF THE STATE,* SHUNTED FROM UNCARING FAMILY TO UNCARING FAMILY. I LONGED FOR LOVE...ANY LOVE, FOR SO VERY LONG.

AND WHEN I THOUGHT I HAD FOUND IT...

SHE EXHALES SADLY, THEN CONTINUES. "TRIGON BANISHED ME TO THE EARTH, AND I WATCHED THE CULT I HAD JOINED *DESTROYED* BEFORE MY EYES.

"SO AGAIN I WAS ALL *ALONE,* BUT THIS TIME WITH A *CHILD* GROWING WITHIN ME...

"...AND THE DREADED KNOWLEDGE THAT MY CHILD'S FATHER WAS *TRIGON* HIMSELF.

"I SOUGHT COUNSELING, BUT ALL STATE AGENCIES REJECTED ME.

"MY OWN FEARS? TRIGON? I DON'T HONESTLY KNOW.

"BUT NOTHING COULD *HELP* ME. THEN, AT LAST, I KNEW WHAT TO DO... FOR THE ONLY ANSWER SEEMED TO BE *DEATH.*

"I WAS SCARED, SO VERY SCARED AS I TOOK THESE SLEEPING PILLS, AND I LAY DOWN IN A DARK, DESERTED ALLEYWAY, WAITING FOR DEATH TO *CLAIM* ME...

"YOU WILL LAUGH, I'M SURE, BUT SUDDENLY THE DARKNESS SEEMED TO *LIFT...*

"THE AIR SEEMED TO *SHIMMER* IN THAT ALLEY THAT I HAD PICKED TO BE MY *DEATHBED...*

"THERE WAS AN UNEARTHLY *GLOW* THAT I THOUGHT WAS THE LIGHT OF *GOD* HIMSELF SHINING DOWN ON ME. AND, INSIDE THE LIGHT, THERE WAS THE FIGURE OF A *MAN...*

"HE TOUCHED ME...

...AND I TOOK HIS HAND.

"AND I WENT WITH HIM, BACK INTO THE LIGHT WHICH CLOSED EVEN AS I STEPPED THROUGH. I WAS LEAVING THE WORLD *BEHIND,* AND NEVER ONCE DID I THINK OF *LOOKING BACK.*

⑫

I WAS BROUGHT TO *AZARATH,* AND TAUGHT A NEW WAY OF LIFE, A WAY TO EXPUNGE ALL MY FEELINGS OF *HATE* AND *GREED,* AND ALL THE MORE BASIC *VIOLENT* EMOTIONS.

THE PRIESTS GAVE ME A NEW *LIFE,* AND NOT SINCE THE DAY I CAME HERE HAVE I EVER REGRETTED THAT COMING.

"A MORE *LOVELY* CHILD HAD NEVER GRACED THE WORLD.

"*LOVELY,* YET *FRIGHTENING.* FOR SHE AVOIDED THE PRIESTS... MORE COMFORTABLE IN *MEDITATION* THAN IN PRAYER.

"THOUGH SHE WAS RAISED IN THE *PEACE* OF *AZARATH...*

"... HER HERITAGE BOILED WITH THE *RAGE OF TRIGON.*"

AND WE ALL SENSED THAT DIFFERENCE. THE CHILD GREW AND REBELLED, AND CONSTANTLY *QUESTIONED* OUR REGULATIONS.

IT WAS INEVITABLE THAT ONE DAY SHE WOULD *LEAVE* US... AND ONCE YOU LEAVE THE TEMPLE AZARATH, YOU CAN NEVER *RETURN.*

THEY NURTURED ME, TAUGHT ME, AND NINE MONTHS LATER, *RAVEN* WAS *BORN.*

ENUFF OF THIS HISTORY LESSON. SO NOW WE KNOW HOW *ROTTEN* YER LIFE WAS-- WELL, WHAT DOES THAT HAFTA DO WITH *SAVIN'* RAVEN?

SHE'S STILL STUCK IN THAT OTHER DIMENSION... AN' WHATEVER *ELSE* SHE MAY HAVE DONE, LADY--

SHE'S STILL YER *KID!*

CYBORG, GETTING *ANGRY* WON'T HELP RAVEN.

OR MEBBE, WHEN YOU GET INVOLVED IN ALL THIS *COSMIC HOOHAH,* THINGS LIKE THAT DON'T MATTER NO MORE!

AND REMAINING CALM *WILL?* NO, ROBIN, THE TIME FOR WORDS HAS PASSED.

WE HAVE A *BATTLE* TO WAGE-- THE BATTLE FOR *RAVEN'S* LIFE!

I HAVE TO AGREE, ROB. WHILE WE DAWDLE HERE, RAVEN'S SUFFERING.

LISTEN, *I* WANT TO HELP HER AS MUCH AS *YOU* DO. BUT, WE STILL HAVE TO BE SHOWN THE WAY TO *RAVEN'S NEW WORLD.*

WILL YOU DO THAT MUCH FOR US? *WILL* YOU?

WE WILL OPEN THE *DOORWAY TO THE UNKNOWN. YOU* MUST DO THE REST.

BUT, I SWEAR, YOUR LUST FOR BATTLE WILL YET BE THE *UNDOING* OF YOU ALL!

13

WE HAD KNOWN OF TRIGON LONG BEFORE HE LEARNED OF OUR WORLD, FOR MORE THAN A CENTURY AGO WE MASTERED THE SECRETS OF *DIMENSIONAL TRAVEL.*

WE USED THOSE SECRETS TO TRANS-PORT OUR TEMPLE BETWEEN DIMENSIONS... AND THAT PATHWAY LIES BEHIND THAT *DOOR.*

OPEN THE DOOR, AND YOUR VOYAGE BEGINS, BUT I *WARN* YOU, IT IS STILL A PATH FRAUGHT WITH *DANGER.*

WE'LL *RISK* IT.

BUT NOT *ALONE,* ROBIN, I--I WILL JOIN YOU... AS YOUR *GUIDE.*

BUT, ARELLA, IF YOU *LEAVE,* YOU KNOW OUR *RULES...*

I KNOW, BUT CYBORG IS *CORRECT!* DESPITE ALL ELSE, RAVEN IS MY *DAUGHTER.*

X'HAL! ENDLESS *SPACE*... A GULF BETWEEN WORLDS!

AND YET WE CAN SOMEHOW *BREATHE* HERE...

IT'S SIMPLY *AWESOME!* STEPS LEADING BETWEEN ALL THE MANY DIMENSIONS.

STEPS MY *BUTT!* THESE THINGS ARE *MOVIN'!*

IF I DIDN'T KNOW BETTER, I'D SAY WE WERE ON SOME KINDA COSMIC *ESCALATOR!*

ONLY SOMEONE SHOULD'A WARNED ME TO TAKE SOME *DRAMAMINE!* I'M GETTIN' *AIRSICK!*

A PATHWAY BETWEEN *DIMENSIONS.* I NEVER SUSPECTED SUCH A THING *EXISTED!*

YOU LOOK *WORRIED,* DICK.

I *AM,* KORIAND'R. WE'RE ON OUR WAY TO FIGHT SOME-THING ALMOST *UNKNOWN*...SOME-THING *OBSCENE...*

I DON'T KNOW IF WE'RE UP TO IT YET...IF WE REALLY STAND A *CHANCE* AGAINST TRIGON.

14

AND THOUGH I WILL NOT *VIOLATE* MY TEACHINGS HERE, I CANNOT ALLOW HER TO BE *HARMED*.

THEN TAKE OUR LOVE *WITH* YOU, ARELLA, AND OUR PRAYERS, FOR NEVER AGAIN WILL WE *MEET*.

YOU *SURE* OF THIS? I MEAN, YOU'RE GIVING UP EVERYTHING YOU EVER WANTED.

NO, I'M NOT CERTAIN THIS IS THE *RIGHT* THING TO DO...

...BUT I AM SURE IT IS THE *ONLY* THING I CAN DO.

THEN, I WILL PRAY THAT YOU TREAD *CAREFULLY.*

AND MAY THE *PEACE* YOU HAVE COME TO KNOW HERE IN AZARATH BE WITH YOU *ALWAYS*.

WE'RE ALMOST *THERE*, ARELLA. HOW DO YOU *FEEL*?

THEN WHY ARE MY KNEES *SHAKING* SO MUCH THEY COULD *CHURN BUTTER*?

I'M STARTIN' T'FEEL BETTER ABOUT THIS, LOGAN. SOMETHIN' TELLS ME WE'RE GONNA *MAKE* IT.

PAINED. SO MANY BAD *MEMORIES* THAT I WOULD HAVE PREFERRED *FORGOTTEN* RETURN TO *HAUNT* ME NOW.

15

THE VOID IS WARM ABOUT THEM, BUT THERE IS A DARK CHILL RADIATING FROM THE GREAT CRIMSON PLANET THAT LOOMS AHEAD.

THEY ARE SILENT AS THEIR FEET TOUCH THE HARSH, ROCKY GROUND, AS THE COSMIC STAIRWAY BECOMES BROAD STEPS CARVED FROM MOUNTAIN STONE...

ARELLA SHUDDERS, TRYING TO SHAKE AWAY THE FEELING OF DREAD THAT SEEMS OMNIPRESENT. SHE SAYS NOTHING, HOPING THE OTHERS WILL NOT SENSE THAT WHICH SO WORRIES HER.

SO THIS IS TRIGON'S PLANET, HUH? NOT EXACTLY YOUR NEIGHBORHOOD HOLIDAY INN.

SO WHERE NOW?

PAL, IF I SEE THAT BIG, RED BOZO, BELIEVE ME YOU'LL KNOW.

BUT IF I SEE RAVEN, THEN I'M GONNA MOVE HEAVEN AND EARTH TO SAVE HER.

TRIGON HAS MANY CASTLES, YET I SENSE RAVEN'S PRESENCE IN THAT DIRECTION.

WE GO THERE.

LORD, EVEN AFTER ALL SHE DID TO ME, I STILL LOVE HER!

AND I WANT HER TO KNOW THAT BEFORE I LOSE HER AGAIN!

SOMETHIN' TELLS ME THIS IS IT! WE'RE GONNA HAFTA FIGHT FER EVERY INCH.

MAYBE NOT. WALLY, DO A SUPER-SPEED RECONNAISSANCE. IF YOU SEE TRIGON, GET BACK HERE FAST!

BUT THEN...

GR'AWLL

HOLY HANNAH-- WHAT?!?

16

170

MY DAUGHTER'S *FRIENDS*... SO YOU BRING THE BATTLE TO *MY* WORLD, EH?

NOT *YOU*, BIG RED-- THAT OVERGROWN *BENJY* THERE!

YET, YOU *BACK AWAY* FROM ME. YOU *FEAR* ME.

FANG *UPSETS* YOU, EH? VERY WELL, FANG-- *SIT!*

HOOBOY, WHAT DOES HE *EAT?* CYCLE 12?

I SEE ONLY *SIX* OF YOU. YET, YOU *BELIEVE* YOU CAN TOPPLE MY *EMPIRE?*

WE DON'T CARE ABOUT YOUR *EMPIRE*, TRIGON. ALL WE WANT IS *RAVEN!*

WE WANT HER *BACK*, AND WE'RE WILLING TO *FIGHT* FOR HER!

ARE YOU ALSO WILLING TO *DIE* FOR HER? FOR YOU *SHALL.*

JUST AS YOUR *WORLD* WILL DIE... FOR EVEN NOW MY *DARK HORDES* PREPARE FOR *BATTLE!*

THAT *DOES* IT, MISTER!

WE WEREN'T *READY* WHEN YOU FOUGHT US THAT *FIRST* TIME.

FOOLS!

WE DIDN'T HAVE ANYTHING TO REALLY *FIGHT* FOR. BUT *NOW*--

--WE FIGHT FOR THE *EARTH!*

TITANS-- HIT HIM!

17

AND, AS THE TITANS FALL *UNCONSCIOUS* TO THE GROUND...

MASTER! YOUR DAUGHTER HAS *ESCAPED* HER *CELL!*

ESCAPED? AND YOU WERE HER *GUARD!*

BUT, SIRE, THERE WAS *ANOTHER WOMAN...* SHE USED SOME SORT OF *SPELL...*

I AM NOT CON- CERNED WITH *WHY* YOU PERMITTED HER TO ESCAPE...

...THE FACT *EXISTS.* THAT *CONCERNS* ME...

...THAT, AND THE *INCOMPE- TENCE* OF MY *IMPERIAL GUARD!*

KRUNCH!

NYAAAGHH

FORTUNATELY, THAT IS A PROBLEM EASILY *CORRECTED!*

NOW, YOU OTHERS-- FIND MY *DAUGHTER,* BRING HER TO ME...

OR ALSO RISK AROUSING MY *WRATH!*

YES, MASTER, WE WILL *FIND* HER. WE *SWEAR!*

DO NOT SWEAR! *DO!*

THE ALLEYWAY IS DARK, AND FILLED WITH CRAWLING SHADOWS...

HERE, RAVEN... WE CAN *REST!*

JUST A MOMENT TO CATCH YOUR *BREATH.* THEN WE MUST *CONTINUE!*

MOTHER, YOU ALWAYS TOLD ME... WARNED ME OF HIS *EVIL.* BUT HOW COULD I HAVE POSSIBLY *IMAGINED* SUCH EVIL COULD *EXIST?*

IT *OVER- WHELMED* MY *EMPATHIC* SOUL... MADE ME *ILL* BEYOND MEASURE.

REST YOUR MIND, RAVEN. FORGET... TRY TO CALM YOUR THOUGHTS.

WE CAN ONLY *TRY* TO--

ARGGHHM

MY LORD, AZAR! THAT HORRIBLE *SCREAM...*

IT IS THE WAIL OF *TORTURED SOULS* ...CRYING OUT IN *AGONY!*

18

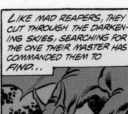

AYE, SOULS AND *MORE!* THE WORLD TURNS DEEP *SCARLET,* THE COLOR OF THICK RICH BLOOD, AS GREAT GRAY *DEMONS* SCREECH SKYWARD, VOMITING STREAMS OF *WILDFIRE...*

LIKE MAD REAPERS, THEY CUT THROUGH THE DARKENING SKIES, SEARCHING FOR THE ONE THEIR MASTER HAS COMMANDED THEM TO FIND...

NOTHING *STOPS* THEM. NOT MIGHTY STONE *BUILDINGS* NOR THE PLAINTIVE PLEAS OF THE THOUSANDS WHO *FALL* LIKE WHEAT BEFORE THE SCYTHE...

THEY'RE AFTER US, MOTHER... TRIGON WILL HAVE THEM DESTROY *EVERY-THING* UNTIL HE *FINDS* US.

AZAR! I FEEL ALL THOSE CRIES... ALL THAT *PAIN...*

WE CAN NOT STAND BY *ANY LONGER.* WE HAVE TO *STOP* THE SUFFERING WHILE WE *CAN!*

TRIGON, *HEAR* ME! I *CALL* TO YOU NOW!

I TURN MYSELF OVER TO YOU! JUST *STOP* THE SENSELESS *SLAUGHTER!*

THEN HOLD MY HAND AND *PRAY* WITH ME, RAVEN. FOR WHEN TRIGON COMES, WE WILL BE *BEYOND* PRAYER... BEYOND *HOPE...*

YOU PRAY FOR *BOTH* OF US... I CANNOT LET THE CARNAGE CONTINUE A MOMENT MORE.

IT IS *STOPPED,* DAUGHTER. AND I AM *HERE!*

TRIGON!

19

173

YES, ARELLA, MY ONE-TIME BRIDE!

AND NOW, BEFORE YOU TWO CAN *DELAY* MY OPERATIONS ANY LONGER...

NO, TRIGON... I WON'T ALLOW YOU TO *DESTROY* US!

WHAT? YOU DEFY YOUR SACRED OATH OF AZAR AND *RESIST* ME?

AND SO RAVEN *RUNS*, WHILE ARELLA STRAINS TO KEEP HER MYSTIC SHIELD BEFORE HER. BUT THEN, THE STRAIN *OVER-TAKES* HER. SHE FEELS HER-SELF WEAKEN, IF ONLY FOR A MOMENT...

I RETURNED TO YOUR WORLD TO SAVE RAVEN, AND I'LL DO ANYTHING TO PREVENT YOUR *DESTROYING* HER!

GO, RAVEN. FIND YOUR *FRIENDS*.. SEND THEM AGAINST TRIGON BEFORE IT'S *TOO LATE!*

BUT, WITH TRIGON, EVEN A *MOMENT* IS MUCH *TOO LONG.*

FIND THE *TITANS?* BUT *WHERE?*

TRIGON *DEFEATED* THEM, THEY COULD BE IN ANY OF HIS *DUNGEONS*...

...AND I CANNOT SEEM TO SEPARATE *THEIR* EMANATIONS FROM ALL THE *OTHERS* ON THIS-- *WHAT?*

HE HUNTED ME DOWN SO *SWIFTLY?* WHAT DID HE DO TO MY *MOTHER?*

CONCERN YOURSELF WITH WHAT I SHALL DO TO *YOU.*

YOU, MY ONLY *OFFSPRING* EVER TO SURVIVE TO *ADULT-HOOD.*

YOU, MY ONLY CHILD NOT TO BE *SLAIN* BY SOME LUNATIC PRO-TESTING MY RULE!

I WANT YOU *BESIDE* ME, DAUGHTER... TO *RULE* WITH ME.

NEVER! WHEN I FIRST *CAME* HERE I DID NOT REALIZE WHAT YOU WERE TRULY *LIKE.*

I COULD NO MORE STAND BESIDE *YOU* THAN I COULD STAND BESIDE *SATAN* HIMSELF!

TRIGON STARES INTO RAVEN'S GRIM-GRAY EYES REALIZING THAT SHE WOULD FIRST *KILL* HERSELF BEFORE SERVING HIM. HE DRAWS A LONG, DEEP BREATH BEFORE DECIDING WHAT TO DO *NEXT*...

BUT...

YOU MIGHT HAVE CONTROLLED *ME*, TRIGON, BUT YOU WILL NOT EXTEND YOUR EVIL TO MY *DAUGHTER!*

20

WHAT? I FEEL *WEAK*... BUT *HOW*--*WHO*--?

ARELLA! IT COULD ONLY BE *HER!* DAMN ME FOR NOT *SLAYING* HER WHEN FIRST WE *PARTED!*

MOTHER, BUT *HOW*--?

AZARATH TAUGHT ME *MANY* THINGS, RAVEN... HOW TO INCREASE MY EMPATHIC POWERS FROM SIMPLY DRAWING OUT *PAIN*...

...TO TAPPING THE VERY *CORE* OF THE SOUL ITSELF!

BUT, I CANNOT HOLD HIM FOR *LONG*. HE FIGHTS ME, *RESISTS* ME... AND HIS POWERS FAR *OVER-SHADOW* MINE!

GO, RAVEN-- HURRY TO YOUR *FRIENDS*. LET ME *GUIDE* YOU TO THEM NOW WHILE THERE STILL IS *TIME!*

TRIGON'S BREAST SEETHES WITH ANGER AS HE STRUGGLES AGAINST THE FORCES WHICH TRY TO OPPRESS HIM. THEN, AT LONG LAST...

GONE... *BOTH* OF THEM ARE *GONE* NOW!

I COULD HUNT THEM DOWN, *DESTROY* THEM-- BUT WHY *BOTHER?*

LET THEM *WASTE* THEIR TIME IN *HIDING*. FOR, WHILE THEY DO, I WILL MOVE MY *DARK HORDES* INTO *THEIR* DIMENSION--

"-- AND RULE *THEIR* UNIVERSE AS WELL!"

MEANWHILE...

AZAR BE PRAISED! THERE ARE MY *FRIENDS*, AND I SENSE THE SPARK OF *LIFE* STILL BURNING WITHIN THEM!

THEY *LIVE*... THEY *LIVE!!*

SILENTLY, SOLEMNLY, RAVEN REACHES FIRST FOR ROBIN, HER LONG FINGERS DRAWING FORTH HIS PAIN, THEN...

...RAVEN...MY *BELT*... LOCK-PICK... HURRY, PLEASE...

CALM YOURSELF, MY FRIEND...

FOR THIS KEY WILL NOT ONLY *FREE* OUR FELLOW TITANS--

--BUT FREE OUR *DIMENSION* FROM THE HORRORS OF TRIGON'S RULE!

21

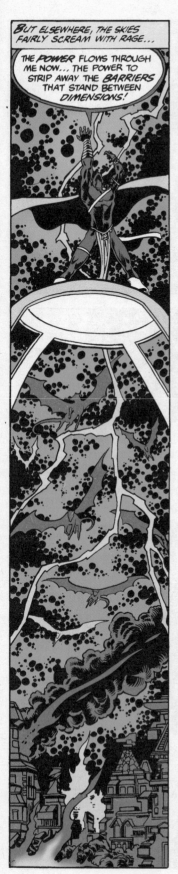

BUT ELSEWHERE, THE SKIES FAIRLY SCREAM WITH RAGE...

THE *POWER* FLOWS THROUGH ME NOW... THE POWER TO STRIP AWAY THE *BARRIERS* THAT STAND BETWEEN *DIMENSIONS!*

THE BARRIERS WILL *CRUMBLE!* THEY WILL *FALL!* AND WHEN I WALK THROUGH THEM AGAIN, THIS TIME MY DARK HORDES WILL *FOLLOW!*

FOR TWENTY YEARS I HAVE *AWAITED* THIS MOMENT!

BEHOLD! THE PLANET EARTH -- MY FIRST STEP IN THE CON-QUERING OF A *NEW DIMENSION!* IT STANDS LONELY, DEFENSELESS, FOR WHAT FEW *HEROES* THEY POSSESS WILL FIND THEM-SELVES HELPLESS TO PREVENT THEIR WORLD'S *DESTRUCTION!*

BUT...

MY FATHER IS *READY* TO BREAK THROUGH THE *DIMENSIONAL WALLS!*

HURRY, ALL OF YOU!

HE WAS *EXPECT-ING* US! WE'VE GOT *COMPANY!*

GRAWWL

LEMME HANDLE BOWSER!

SURE YER *UP* TO IT, LOGAN?

GRAWWLL

YEAH, WHAT'S A LITTLE *POOCH* TO A GUY WHO CAN *CHANGE SHAPES?*

HEY, LASSIE, WANNA HEAR ANY *SHAGGY DOG STORIES?*

NAH, DIDN'T *THINK* YOU WOULD!

22

THANK AZAR YOU'VE COME, RAVEN! TIME GROWS *TOO SHORT!*

RAVEN TOLD ME WHAT YOUR *PLAN* IS. YOU SURE IT'LL *WORK?*

IT *MUST,* WALLACE, IT'S OUR ONLY *HOPE!*

WE ADD *OUR* POWERS TO YOUR *OWN...*

...AND PRAY IT IS ENOUGH TO DO WHAT MUST BE *DONE!*

SUPPOSED TO START *SPINNING...* INCREASING MY INNER *VIBRATION-AL RATE...*

BUT, TO DO WHAT THEY *WANT,* I'VE GOT TO MOVE FASTER THAN I'VE EVER MOVED *BEFORE!*

WE'VE GOT TO *LINK* OUR POWERS TOGETHER.... A *SINGLE* EFFORT IS ALL THAT WILL *WORK!*

WHAT ARE WE *WAITIN'* FOR, ROBIN? TRIGON'S WITHIN OUR *GRASP!*

CYBORG, YOUR *INTERNAL POWER SUPPLY...* CAN IT BE HOOKED IN WITH *ANOTHER* POWER SOURCE?

THEN WE'LL LINK *YOU* WITH *STARFIRE...* FOCUS *HER* POWER THROUGH *YOU* AS WELL!

IF WE ATTACK *NOW,* WE'RE *DOOMED.* RAVEN SAID WE WOULD ONLY *DEFEAT* HIM BY WORKING AS *ONE!*

BELIEVE IT, SHORT-PANTS! I'M LIKE A LIVIN' POWER BATTERY!

WONDER GIRL, YOUR *MAGIC LASSO* IS LIKE WONDER WOMAN'S... IT CAN BE USED TO SAP TRIGON'S *WILL!*

GOTCHA, ROB... ALREADY *MOVING OUT!*

THIS WORKS ON *ORDINARY MORTALS...* BUT CAN IT POSSIBLY AFFECT *HIM?*

YOU BEGIN YOUR *ATTACK?* AND YOU DELAY MY *PLANS!*

I WILL NOT *PERMIT* SUCH EFFRONTERY!

23

YET... SUDDENLY I FEEL MY STRENGTH *FADING* AGAIN! ARELLA! IT MUST BE *HER!* DAMN THAT WOMAN!

TOGETHER WE ARE *WEAKENING* TRIGON... IT MAY YET BE POSSIBLE FOR WONDER GIRL TO FURTHER DAMPEN HIS *WILL!*

IT MUST *WORK,* DAUGHTER! IT *MUST!*

TEARS STREAM DOWN RAVEN'S FACE AS SHE DIGS DEEPER, EVER DEEPER TO HER OWN *SOUL.* THE PAIN ALMOST OVERWHELMS HER, BUT STILL SHE MUST TAP ALL HER EMPATHIC STRENGTH...

WE *WEAKEN* TRIGON WHILE FLASH WIELDS HIS INCREASED SUPER-SPEED TO RIP OPEN THE DOORWAY TO THE *NETHERVERSE!*

THANK HERA! THEIR PLAN IS *WORKING!*

MINERVA BE PRAISED! THERE'S THE *HOLE,* BUT TRIGON'S *RESISTING* ME!

ATTACKED ON ALL SIDES... MY POWER BEING *DRAINED!* STILL I SHALL RISE TO *DESTROY* YOU ALL!

WHAT ARE WE *WAITING* FOR, ROBIN?

I'LL TELL YOU WHEN TO *OPEN FIRE!*

SWEAT BEADS ROBIN'S FORE-HEAD AS HE COUNTS THE PRECIOUS MOMENTS. THIS MUST BE PERFECTLY *TIMED*... EVERYTHING MUST BE *COORDINATED* TO ATTACK TRIGON AT HIS *WEAKEST*...

ROBIN, I CAN NO LONGER FIGHT ON. DO IT, ROBIN-- DO IT *NOW!*

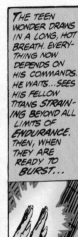

THE TEEN WONDER DRAWS IN A LONG, HOT BREATH. EVERYTHING NOW DEPENDS ON HIS COMMANDS. HE WAITS... SEES HIS FELLOW TITANS STRAINING BEYOND ALL LIMITS OF *ENDURANCE.* THEN, WHEN THEY ARE READY TO *BURST*...

NOW! FIRE!

IT IS A MIND-STAGGERING *SCREAM* WHICH SEEMINGLY SHATTERS THE VERY *SKIES* THEMSELVES. IT IS THE SCREAM OF *TOTAL MADNESS!* THE SCREAM OF *UTTER DEFEAT.*

SKR!

EEEEEE

BUT, IT ECHOES FOR ONLY ONE HEART-RENDING MOMENT...

2A

178

...FOR THE NEXT MOMENT, IT IS *GONE.*

IT *WORKED.* GREAT *ATHENA,* IT *WORKED!*

COULDN'T'A LASTED ANOTHER *SECOND.*

MAN, I'M TOTALLY *DRAINED!*

HOLD IT! ARELLA-- SHE'S HEADING TOWARD THE *DIMENSIONAL DOORWAY.*

HERA! WHAT IS SHE DOING?

THERE WAS NEVER ANY *OTHER* WAY, MY FRIENDS. I COULD NOT RETURN TO *AZARATH!*

THUS LET MY *SACRIFICE* BE FOR THE GOOD OF *ALL!*

WAIT, ARELLA-- *DON'T!*

BUT, ROBIN'S PLEA COMES *TOO LATE,* FOR EVEN AS THE *SLIM* FIGURE BRIDGES THE GULF BETWEEN DIMENSIONS, THE GIANT PORTAL EX- PLODES WITH IMPOSSIBLE *FURY...*

AND, IN AN INSTANT, IT EXISTS *NO MORE...*

MEANWHILE...

HOLEEE CRUD! YOU GUYS *FORGET* ABOUT ME?

IT TOOK *EVERY-* *THING* I HAD, BUT BOWSER'S DOWN FOR THE COUNT!

ONLY, I *PITY* WHOEVER THEY PICK AS HIS *KEEPER* WHEN HE FINALLY *WAKES UP!*

RAVEN, I DON'T UNDERSTAND...WHAT WAS ALL THAT *ABOUT?* WHY DID YOUR MOTHER--

IT WAS AS SHE *SAID,* SHE HAD NO OTHER *CHOICE.*

RAVEN *TOLD* ME ABOUT IT WHEN I *BROUGHT* HER HERE. TRIGON COULD'VE ESCAPED BACK THROUGH THAT *DI- MENSIONAL DOORWAY* IF SOMETHING DIDN'T BLOCK HIS *PATH.*

BUT NOW MY MOTHER *GUARDS* THE BRIDGE... AS SHE MUST FOR ALL *ETERNITY.*

SHE, WHO BELIEVED IN *PEACE,* MUST NOW BE FOREVER AT *WAR...*

...LEST *TRIGON* BE PERMITTED TO EVER BE *FREE* AGAIN!

AND SOMEWHERE, IN A DIMENSION *BEYOND TIME AND SPACE,* A *WAR* BEGINS THAT WILL NEVER SEE... AN *END.*

25

NEXT ISSUE: ASSAULT ON TITANS' TOWER!

IT'LL BE GOOD!

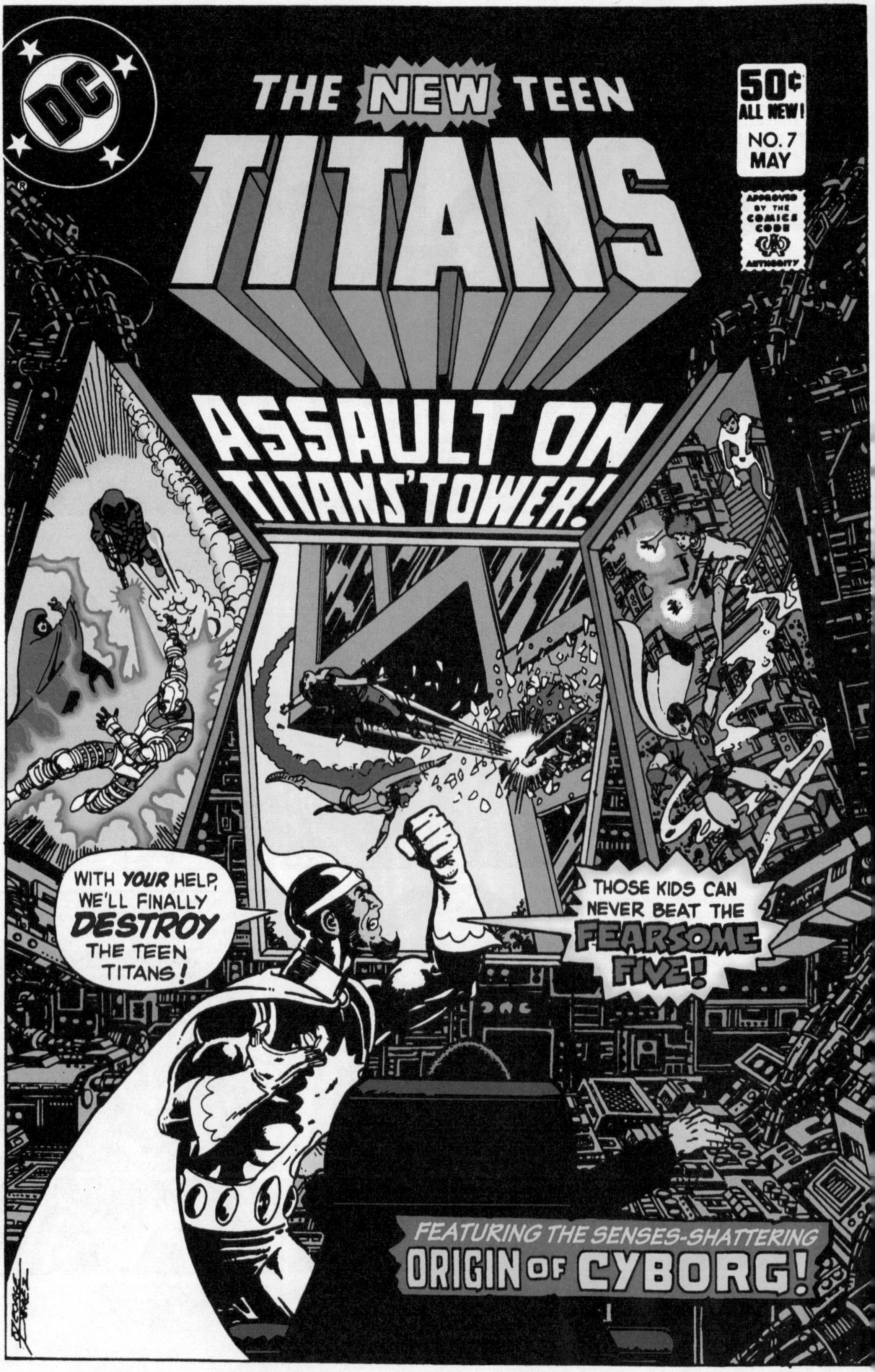
THE NEW TEEN
TITANS
50¢
ALL NEW!
NO. 7
MAY
APPROVED BY THE COMICS CODE AUTHORITY
ASSAULT ON TITANS' TOWER!
WITH YOUR HELP, WE'LL FINALLY DESTROY THE TEEN TITANS!
THOSE KIDS CAN NEVER BEAT THE FEARSOME FIVE!
FEATURING THE SENSES-SHATTERING
ORIGIN OF CYBORG!

THE NEW TEEN TITANS

ASSAULT ON TITANS' TOWER!

THE TEMPLE AZARATH, SOMEWHERE BEYOND EARTH...

NOW WATCH CAREFULLY. NOTHING UP MY SLEEVE, AND NEVER ONCE DO MY FINGERS LEAVE MY HANDS!

YET, WITH JUST THE MAGIC WORDS -- "LET'S-GET-THE-BLAZES-OUTTA-HERE" -- 'GAR THE GREAT' WILL REMOVE US FROM THIS COCKAMAMIE DIMENSION--

--AND *POOF* US RIGHT BACK *HOME* AGAIN!

WITH THE AID OF *ARELLA*, RAVEN'S MOTHER, THE TITANS HAVE DEFEATED AND BANISHED *TRIGON THE TERRIBLE*, HE WHO IS RAVEN'S DEMONIC FATHER. NOW, THE TITANS SOLEMNLY STAND IN THE *TEMPLE AZARATH* WHERE RAVEN WAS BORN, WAITING FOR THE TEMPLE MONKS TO RETURN THEM TO THE EARTH, MANY DIMENSIONS AWAY...

CREATED BY
MARV WOLFMAN
WRITER
GEORGE PÉREZ
PENCILLER

INKER:
ROMEO TANGHAL
LETTERER:
JOHN COSTANZA
COLORIST:
JOHN DRAKE

LEN WEIN
EDITOR

CENTRAL PARK, NEW YORK, SOMEWHERE ON EARTH (THOUGH NOBODY WANTS TO ADMIT IT)...

WELL--? WHERE'S THE *APPLAUSE*? OR BETTER STILL--WHERE'S THE *MONEY*? YOU KNOW WHAT THE *CAB FARE* IS FROM AZARATH TO HERE?

W-WALTER--?

I TOLD YOU WE SHOULD'A JOGGED *SOMEWHERE ELSE*. I *TOLD* YA!

HI THERE, WE'RE THE *TITANS*, SUPER HEROES, DO-GOODERS, AND BEATERS-OF-BAD-GUYS.

WE *ALSO* DO WEDDINGS AND BAR MITZVAHS!

YOU ALL RIGHT, RAVEN? IS THERE ANYTHING WE CAN DO FOR YOU?

SADLY, WONDER GIRL, THERE IS NOTHING *ANYONE* CAN DO. I HAVE NOWHERE TO GO NOW, NO PLACE TO CALL MY *HOME*.

HEYYY! YOU ARE ONE FIIIINE-LOOKIN' *MOMMA*...

THANK YOU. AND *YOU* ARE A FINE-LOOKING MOTHER *YOURSELF*.

C'MON, KORY, DON'T LET THAT CREEP *BUG YA*.

OH, GAR... HE WAS *CUTE*.

CUTE? OH YEAH... I *FORGOT*. YOU'RE STILL NEW HERE ON EARTH.

WELL, DON'T *WORRY*, GOLDIE, FROM NOW ON I'LL TEACH YA EVERYTHING YA GOTTA KNOW.

YOU'RE IN *MY* HANDS NOW.

I PREFER *DICK'S* HANDS, GAR.

FIGGERS.

YOU *DO* HAVE A PLACE TO STAY, RAVEN-- *TITANS' TOWER*.

YOU STILL OFFER ME *SANCTUARY*-- EVEN AFTER WHAT I'VE *DONE*?

I WOULD HAVE THOUGHT YOU WOULD *HATE* ME FOR THAT.

HATE? OH, *NO*, RAVEN.

MAYBE I STILL DON'T *UNDERSTAND* WHY YOU REFUSE TO *BATTLE* FOR WHAT YOU BELIEVE IN, BUT HATE--? YOU'RE A *FRIEND*.

YOU HELPED TO *FIND* ME...YOU SAVED ME FROM THE *GORDANIANS*...

KORIAND'R'S *RIGHT*. YOU BROUGHT US TOGETHER, AND, WELL, *I* AT LEAST *OWE* YOU FOR THAT.

SINCE I LEFT COLLEGE, MY LIFE HAS BEEN TURNED *IN-SIDE OUT*. BEING WITH THE TITANS HAS BEEN A *LIFESAVER*.

GEE, MA, THIS PARK IS REAL *DULL*!

ROBBIE'S ON TARGET, RAVE. ALL I HAD BEFORE WAS MY *BILLIONS* TA KEEP ME BUSY.

NOW LOOK AT ME. I SPEND MY DAYS *RISKIN' MY LIFE*.

WHO WOULD ASK FOR ANYTHING *MORE*?

I DUNNO. YOU AN' ME, WE NEVER REALLY *HIT IT OFF*. MEBBE WE NEVER *WILL*--

--'CAUSE I KEEP *REMEMBERIN'* HOW YOU KEPT *DISAPPEARIN'* ON US.

WE'VE BEEN FIGHTIN' TOGETHER, BUT I STILL DON'T KNOW WHAT YOUR *POWERS* ARE... WHAT YOU CAN *DO*.

GOTTA SAY THIS, BUT EVEN *NOW*, I STILL DON'T REALLY *TRUST* YOU.

2

HEY, HOLD ON... I JUST WANNA GET A *HOT DOG.* I'M *FAMISHED.*

GET ONE FER ME, TOO...WITH *EVERYTHIN'!*

MY *POWERS?* SIMPLY PUT, I AM AN *EMPATH.* I CAN *SENSE* PAIN AND EMOTIONS-- I CAN *DRAW YOUR* PAIN INTO *MY BODY--*

--AND PLAY OFF YOUR *EMOTIONS...* TO CREATE IMAGES WITHIN YOUR MIND.

I ALSO POSSESS AN ELEMENTARY *PRECOGNITIVE* POWER...WHICH AT TIMES ALLOWS ME TO SENSE THE *FUTURE.*

AND THEN, OF COURSE-- THERE IS MY *SOUL SELF...*

HEY, LISTEN, I DON'T WANT TO *INTERRUPT,* BUT I'VE GOT SOMETHING TO SAY THAT JUST WON'T *WAIT.*

YOU SEEM *CONFUSED...* YOUR EMOTIONS INFLAMED. ARE YOU *ANGRY* WITH ME, WALLACE?

NO, WELL...I THOUGHT SO AT FIRST, BUT REALLY, I'M ANGRY AT *MYSELF.*

I THOUGHT I *LOVED* YOU, RAVEN-- THEN I LEARNED HOW YOU PUT THAT THOUGHT IN MY HEAD. AND *NOW...*

NOW, ALL I AM IS *CONFUSED.*

YOU GOTTA UNDERSTAND, I NEVER *WANTED* TO BE A HERO, NEVER ASKED TO BECOME ONE. IT JUST *HAPPENED!* ALL I EVER REALLY WANTED WAS TO GO TO SCHOOL, GROW UP, MAYBE GET *MARRIED* AND HAVE KIDS...

I NEVER WANTED TO BE *SPECIAL.* ANYWAY, I HAVE TO *THINK...* DECIDE WHAT'S BEST FOR ME. AND I CAN'T DO IT *HERE...*

I HAVE TO GO HOME, TO *BLUE VALLEY...* AND MY *PARENTS.* YOU *FOLLOW* ME?

I CERTAINLY *DO,* WALLY. MY ANSWER'S HERE... I HOPE YOU'LL FIND *YOURS* SOMEWHERE!

I HOPE SO, *TOO,* ROBBY-- BECAUSE I'M BEING TORN IN *TWO* DIRECTIONS AT ONCE...

LORD, I NEED TIME *ALONE.*

YOU KNOW, WHEN I *GOT* THESE POWERS, I WISH I HAD GOTTEN SOME *WISDOM* AS WELL...

BUT, SEEING AS I *DIDN'T...* I'VE JUST GOT TO SIT AND THINK...JUST LIKE ALL THOSE *OTHER* KIDS OUT THERE--

ALL WITH TOO MANY *PROBLEMS...* AND TOO FEW *ANSWERS.*

BUT, AS KID FLASH RACES HOMEWARD, TO THE WEST OF NEW YORK, ON THE JERSEY PALISADES...

C'MON, DR. LIGHT. WE'RE TOGETHER--SO WHAT *NOW?* WHO DO WE *ROB?*

PATIENCE, DEAR SHIMMER.

I HAVE LEARNED THAT *FIVE* IS THE *OPTIMUM* NUMBER FOR SUCCESS IN OUR BUSINESS, AND, AT PRESENT, THE FEARSOME FIVE IS *ONE SHY* OF THAT OPTIMUM.

WE NEED ANOTHER *MEMBER* BEFORE WE CAN--

...HELP ME, LIGHT... PLEASE... HELP ME...

BY THE DARK LIGHT--*PSIMON?*

APPEARING IN MY LIGHT-SHAFT... BUT YOU'RE *DEAD!* TRIGON *KILLED* YOU!

...NO...HE *BANISHED* ME TO ANOTHER DIMENSION... PLEASE, LIGHT, *FREE* ME...

FAT *CHANCE,* FILTH, YOU TRIED TO *KILL* US!

FREE HIM AND I'LL USE MY *MATTER-TRANSMUTING* POWERS TO TURN HIM INTO *PAPER*-- LIKE MY *CHAIR.*

NAH, GIVE 'IM TA *MAMMOTH* -- LEMME *CRUSH* 'IM!

YOU HEARD THE *CONSENSUS* -- YOU'RE *OUTTA LUCK.*

NO...PLEASE LISTEN TO ME...TRIGON *CONTROLLED* ME...TURNED ME *AGAINST* YOU...

FREE ME NOW... I SWEAR I'LL BE YOUR *LOYAL* PARTNER...

FERGET IT. I DON'T *TRUST* THAT GUY!

BARAN, M'BOY, YOU AN' YER SISTER SELINDA AIN'T *THINKIN'* RIGHT, LISSEN TA *GIZMO.*

WE COULD USE THAT DOME-HEAD'S PSIONIC POWERS, AN' IF HE GETS OUTTA HAND--

--YOU ALREADY SAID *YOU* COULD DESTROY 'IM. AS FER ME--

STA'NG

WELL, I GOT PLENTY OF HOMEMADE DOODADS STRONG ENUFF TA *BLAST* THAT BOZO RIGHT BACK WHERE HE *CAME* FROM.

SEE WHAT I *MEAN?*

YOU'RE *IN,* PSIMON-- ONLY HOW DO WE *FREE* YOU?

THERE IS A *CERTAIN DEVICE...* FOLLOW MY *INSTRUCTIONS...*

④

AND MOMENTS LATER...

LISSEN, LIGHT--I STILL DON'T TRUST THAT FREAK, SO LEMME DO SOME TINKERIN' WITH THAT MACHINE HE TOLD US ABOUT-- JUST IN CASE.

GIZMO, MY DIMINUTIVE FRIEND, MY SENTIMENTS EXACTLY.

A LITTLE INSURANCE WOULD NOT HURT OUR PARTNERSHIP, WOULD IT?

I STILL DON'T LIKE THIS, LIGHT--BREAKING INTO TITANS' TOWER, I TOLD YOU WHEN WE FIRST MET--

--I'M A THIEF, NOT A HERO-FIGHTER. I WANT CASH, AND THAT'S ALL!

SHIMMER, YOU SHALL SOON HAVE MORE CASH THAN EVEN YOUR GREEDY MIND COULD CONCEIVE--

--BUT WE HAVE PRIORITIES, AND RESCUING OUR DIMENSION-LOST MEMBER SEEMS TO BE THE FIRST OF THEM.

DOOR'S LOCKED, BUT THAT DON'T MATTER NONE.

THERE AIN'T NO DOOR BUILT--

--THAT MAMMOTH CAN'T BUST THROUGH!

NOT BAD, BIG FELLA. EVER THINK OF HIRIN' YERSELF OUT AS A HOUSE-WRECKER?

KRUNCH!

PHASE ONE IS COMPLETE; NOW FOR PHASE TWO--

BUT FIRST--LET ME PROJECT SOME SENSOR LIGHTS. WHEN ONE FINDS WHAT WE CAME HERE FOR--

BUT, HIDING DEEP WITHIN TITANS' TOWER...

--IT WILL INSTANTLY REPORT BACK TO ME.

THIS WASN'T SUPPOSED TO HAPPEN... NO ONE WAS SUPPOSED TO FIND ME, NOT UNTIL THE REASON THAT I BUILT THIS TOWER HAD FULLY COME TO PASS.

BUT THEY-- THEY WILL FIND ME...

...AND THEN RUIN ALL THAT I HAVE TRIED SO DESPERATELY TO CREATE HERE!

5

BUT, AS THE FEARSOME FIVE MAKE THEIR WAY UP THROUGH THE *LABYRINTH* THAT IS TITANS' TOWER...

LOOKS LIKE WE GOT HOME JUST *IN TIME*, GUYS. COMPANY'S COME CALLING--

INTRUDERS *HERE*, IN OUR *HOME*? BUT *WHY*--?

"OUR HOME"? C'MON, GOLDIE, THIS AIN'T *OUR* HOME. WE DIDN'T BUILD IT, AN' FER ALL WE KNOW--IT COULD BE SOME SORT'A *DEATH TRAP!*

THEN PERMIT ME TO *INVESTI-GATE...*

IN AN INSTANT SHE IS GONE, DISAPPEARING WITHIN THE FOLDS OF THE DARK SMOKE THAT SEEMS TO CARRY HER OFF INTO OBLIVION...

...BUT WHICH ACTUALLY RE-APPEARS DEEP WITHIN THE WALLS OF *TITANS' TOWER...*

I HAVE BEEN BANISHED FROM THE TEMPLE AZARATH, MY MOTHER FACES AN ETERNAL BATTLE WITH MY FATHER WITHIN THE LAND OF LIMBO, BUT NO LONGER DO I FEEL *ALONE...*

DESPITE ALL I HAVE *DONE* TO THEM, THESE TITANS STILL *TRUST* ME, STILL *WELCOME* ME AS ONE OF THEIR OWN--

--AND STILL CALL ME THEIR *FRIEND.* BY AZAR, I CANNOT LET THEM DOWN *NOW!*

I SENSE DARKNESS... FEAR AND HATRED... AN AWESOME *EVIL...* CLOSING IN ON ME.

NO MATTER WHAT PERIL I FACE, I MUST LIVE UP TO THAT FRIEND-SHIP... BE WORTHY OF THEIR TRUST OR--*HOLD!*

AZAR PROTECT ME-- I'M BEING *ATTACKED!*

PROBING LIGHTS... ENCIRCLING ME... DRAINING ME... CANNOT *ESCAPE*--

I CAN BARELY STAND, LET ALONE *RESIST...* CAN BARELY THINK, LET ALONE PLAN ANY COUNTER-ATTACK--

BUT THE OTHERS--THEY MUST BE *WARNED*-- MUST BE *PROTECTED...*

UNNHHHH! ONLY MY *SOUL-SELF* CAN HELP THEM NOW!

THE FIRST TITAN HAS BEEN *DOWNED...* I TOLD YOU MY CONSTRICTING LIGHT BEAMS WOULD DO THE JOB, EH, MY FRIEND?

YEAH, BUT WHAT ABOUT THAT *SHADOW-* THING THAT LEFT HER BODY...

MERELY LIGHT WITHOUT SUBSTANCE... AND WHAT LIGHT CAN BOTHER THE *MASTER OF LIGHT*--?

I DUNNO, YOU TRUST THEM LITTLE *BEAMS* TOO MUCH. ME, I ONLY TRUST WHAT I CAN *BUILD.*

'CAUSE WHEN I *BUILD* 'EM, I BUILD 'EM TO *KILL!*

6

BUT... UP THERE-- THE WITCH'S *SOUL-SELF!*

CYBORG, WHEN ARE YOU GOING TO *STOP* CALLING RAVEN A *WITCH?*

WHEN SHE PROVES SHE *AIN'T*... AN' *MEBBE* NOT EVEN *THEN!*

UH-OH, I DON'T LIKE THE LOOK OF THAT. SOMETHIN'S GOTTA BE *WRONG!*

SO WHAT ARE WE *WAITIN'* FOR? IF THERE'S SOME-THIN' INSIDE THE TOWER--

--LET'S *FIND* IT!!

NO, CYBORG-- *WAIT!*

FORGET IT, SHORT-PANTS, I'M *FED UP* WITH WAITIN'--FED UP WITH YOU ORDERIN' ME AROUND. NOTHIN' STOPPIN' ME *NOW!*

SINCE WHEN AM *I* CON-SIDERED NOTHING?

HUNH?

THAT AIN'T *FAIR.* GET THIS MAGIC LASSO *OFF 'A* ME.

I WILL WHEN YOU'RE READY TO STOP ACTING LIKE A *BULL IN A CHINA SHOP.*.

GRRRR... OKAY... *OKAY*...!

CYBORG, FIRST RULE OF THUMB-- *LOOK* BEFORE YOU RUN. YOU SEE THAT HINGE-LIKE *DEVICE* ON THE DOOR? WATCH...

BLAMMMO!

HOLLEEEE!

MAYBE *NEXT* TIME YOU WON'T RACE AHEAD?

NEXT TIME? YOU'RE EXPECTING A NEXT TIME? *SHEEESH!*

STARFIRE, IF YOU PLEASE...

I WOULD *LOVE* TO, ROBIN.

JUST A SMALL BLAST OF MY *STARBOLT POWER*...

SKREEAMMM!

AWRIGHT, TITANS-- LET'S *MOVE OUT!*

THERE'RE OBVIOUSLY *CREEPS* WAITIN' HERE, SO LET'S *FIND* 'EM--

--AN' LET'S *SMASH* 'EM!

CYBORG NEVER *LEARNS...* HE JUST SMASHES HIS WAY THROUGH *EVERYTHING.* BUT IF THERE'S SOMETHING *WRONG,* THERE'RE VERY FEW *OTHERS* I'D WANT MORE AT MY SIDE.

LOOK THERE-- IT'S RAVEN'S *BODY!*

SOMETHING'S HERE, I CAN *SMELL* IT... WAITING FOR US TO MAKE A WRONG MOVE. AND IT'S UP TO *ME* AS THE TITANS' *LEADER* TO MAKE SURE WE *DON'T!*

A MOMENT LATER, AS THE EBON SHADOW SEEMS TO *MERGE* WITH THE FALLEN FIGURE OF THE YOUNG SORCERESS...

I...WAS *ATTACKED...* NO TIME TO SEE WHO WAS THERE.

BUT I SENSED THE PRESENCE OF *SEVERAL* ATTACKERS ...I SENSED TERRIBLE *POWER* AS WELL.

BEWARE, MY FRIENDS-- THERE IS *DANGER* AFOOT.

YOU THINKING WHAT *I'M* THINKING, PAL?

YOU *GOT* IT... WE'VE GOT TO *SEARCH* THIS PLACE...

...ONLY TROUBLE IS THERE COULD BE TUNNELS, PASSAGES, HALLS WE DON'T EVEN *KNOW* ABOUT.

DON'T *WORRY* ABOUT IT, LEGS. I THOUGHT I REMEMBERED SEEIN' *THIS* HERE.

TAKE A LOOK-SEE.

THE *BLUE-PRINTS!* CYBORG, YOU'RE NOT *HALF* AS CRAZY AS YOU *PRETEND* TO BE.

I KNOW. BUT I GOT AN *IMAGE* TO MAINTAIN!

8

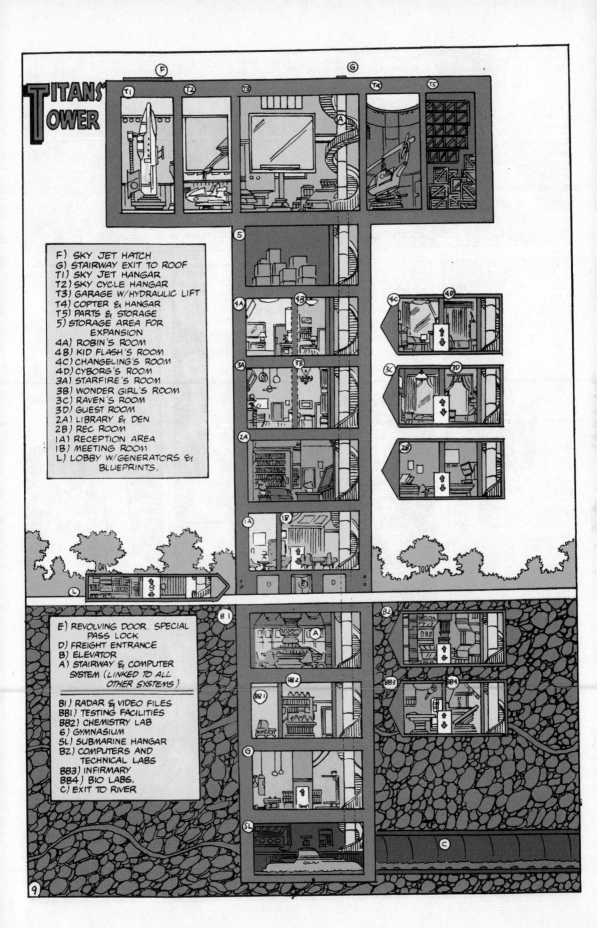

TITANS' TOWER

F) SKY JET HATCH
G) STAIRWAY EXIT TO ROOF
T1) SKY JET HANGAR
T2) SKY CYCLE HANGAR
T3) GARAGE W/HYDRAULIC LIFT
T4) COPTER & HANGAR
T5) PARTS & STORAGE
5) STORAGE AREA FOR
   EXPANSION
4A) ROBIN'S ROOM
4B) KID FLASH'S ROOM
4C) CHANGELING'S ROOM
4D) CYBORG'S ROOM
3A) STARFIRE'S ROOM
3B) WONDER GIRL'S ROOM
3C) RAVEN'S ROOM
3D) GUEST ROOM
2A) LIBRARY & DEN
2B) REC ROOM
1A) RECEPTION AREA
1B) MEETING ROOM
L) LOBBY W/GENERATORS &
   BLUEPRINTS.

E) REVOLVING DOOR. SPECIAL
   PASS LOCK
D) FREIGHT ENTRANCE
B) ELEVATOR
A) STAIRWAY & COMPUTER
   SYSTEM (LINKED TO ALL
   OTHER SYSTEMS)

B1) RADAR & VIDEO FILES
BB1) TESTING FACILITIES
BB2) CHEMISTRY LAB
6) GYMNASIUM
SL) SUBMARINE HANGAR
B2) COMPUTERS AND
   TECHNICAL LABS
BB3) INFIRMARY
BB4) BIO LABS.
C) EXIT TO RIVER

THIS ALL SEEMS SO *SILLY.* WE SHOULD BE GOING *AFTER* THEM.

TRUST ME, KORIAND'R, WE *WILL.* CYBORG--?

YEAH, THIS PLACE IS AN *ARSENAL.* AN' RIGHT NOW, IT'S UNDER *THEIR* CONTROL-- WHOEVER *THEY* ARE.

WELL, WE CAN'T WAIT TO BE *ATTACKED.* I VOTE WITH KORIAND'R--

BUT FIRST WE MUST *PREPARE.* I SENSE THEIR POWER IS *GREATER* THAN OURS.

MEANWHILE...

WAIT! WAIT! WAIT! THAT'S ALL I EVER *HEAR.* I'M GETTIN' *FED UP* WITH ALL THIS WAITIN'!

I WANNA BLAST ME SOME *TITANS!*

C'MON, LIGHT, THIS GUARD-DUTY'S DRIVIN' ME BATTY. WHEN DO WE TAKE OFF THE *KID GLOVES?*

ONE MOMENT, GIZMO. NOW, MY FRIEND, WE'VE USED YOUR *DIMENSIONAL TRANSMITTER* TO LOCATE OUR FINAL *MEMBER--!*

WILL YOU *BRING* HIM TO US, OR MUST I USE MY *LIGHT POWERS* TO STRIP AWAY THE VERY *FLESH* FROM YOUR BONES?

PLEASE, CAN'T YOU *UNDER-STAND* ME?

THE TRANSMITTER'S ALREADY CAUSED *ONE MUTILATION... ONE DEATH...* I DARE NOT RISK USING IT *AGAIN.*

FERGET IT, LIGHT. LEMME USE MY LITTLE *MIND-TAPPER* HERE, IT'LL GET WHAT WE *WANT* OUTTA HIM--

--COURSE, IT'LL ALSO BURN OUT HIS *BRAINS,* BUT *WHAT THE HEY,* RIGHT?

WELL, YOU'VE *HEARD* WHAT MY *SHORT* FRIEND HERE HAS PREPARED FOR YOU.

WILL YOU *COOPERATE--?*

OR, WILL YOU SUFFER THE *CONSEQUENCES?*

BUT, IMMEDIATELY OUTSIDE THE STORAGE FACILITIES...

I TELL YOU, THEIR EMANATIONS COME FROM *WITHIN*... POWERFUL FORCES THAT--*HOLD!*

CYBORG, DO NOT ASK ME *HOW*, BUT SOMEHOW THIS RELATES TO YOU...

THEN STEP ASIDE, WITCH, AN' LEMME *THROUGH!*

BUT...

NO... STAND BACK... THEY COME TO *US*... INCREDIBLE *FORCE WAVES* DISINTEGRATING THE STORAGE ROOM *DOOR*--

K-RAMM

CURSE ME FOR A *FOOL!* I SHOULD HAVE REALIZED WHO OUR INVADERS WERE ALL ALONG--

BUT YA *BLEW* IT, LADY-- AN' THAT'S WHY THE *FEARSOME FIVE* IS GONNA TRAMPLE YOU ALL BUT GOOD!

YOU? I'VE BEEN *ITCHIN'* TA GET MY HANDS ON YER SCRAWNY NECK, RUNT--

WELL, YA *AIN'T*, BIG-SHOT--

KREEEEEEE

AGGHHH!

--NOT UNLESS YA KNOW HOW TA BREAK FREE OF MY *NEURAL DISRUPTOR!*

YOU ONLY GOT *SECONDS*, TIN-MAN... SECONDS BEFORE MY LITTLE *GIZMO* BLOWS OUT ALL YER CIRCUITS!

SEEYA IN THE *JUNK-PILE*, JERK! HA! HA! HA!

VICTOR?!?

M-MY INSIDES! THEY'RE *BURNIN'* UP...

THE PAIN HAS CAUSED HIM TO *BLACK OUT*. HE CANNOT HEAR ME.

BUT, I CAN FEEL HIS PAIN... TERRIBLE TO TOUCH... IT SCREAMS OUT AT ME...

HORRIBLE PAIN... AZAR HELP ME NOW, HIS BODY *SHRINKS* AT MY TOUCH. H-HE'S *DYING!*

BUT, I WILL NOT *LET* HIM DIE!

HE GAVE ME THE *HELP* I NEEDED, I CANNOT *FORSAKE* HIM NOW...

BUT HIS PAIN... IT FLOWS THROUGH ME... INTO ME... *TERRIBLE*... ALMOST BEYOND ANY PAIN I HAVE EVER ABSORBED BEFORE...

M-MUST HOLD IT A MOMENT MORE ...A SECOND MORE. *NOW!* NOW IT CAN BE *EXPELLED!*

WILL HE... *YES*... HIS EYES OPEN...

HUH? WHA-- WHA' *HIT* ME? WHAT HAPPENED? *RAVEN?* THEN IT *WASN'T* A NIGHTMARE?

11

YOU WERE IN *PAIN*, VICTOR... I USED MY EMPATHIC POWERS TO DRAW THAT PAIN *AWAY* FROM YOU.

EVEN THOUGH I CALLED YOU A *WITCH*? EVEN THOUGH I NEVER *TRUSTED* YOU?

YET, YOU *HELPED* ME IN MY STRUGGLE AGAINST *TRIGON*.

VICTOR, PLEASE *BELIEVE* IN ME... PLEASE *TRUST* ME.

TRUST? YEAH... MEBBE I CAN... TRUST A *WITCH*!

BUT THIS TIME CYBORG SAYS IT WITH A *SMILE*...

WHILE...

I HEAR YOU'VE BEEN *LOOKING* FOR US, ROBIN.

SHIMMER? THEN THE *FEARSOME FIVE* ARE OUR FOES?

YOU'RE *BRIGHT*, ROBIN, AND SINCE YOU *REMEMBER* ME, YOU'LL ALSO REMEMBER MY *MATTER-TRANSMUTING POWERS*.

HOLY--! SHE TURNED THE STAIRWAY-- INTO GAS!!

POISONOUS GAS, ENOUGH TO *KILL* YOU WHERE YOU STAND!

LORD, HOPE I CAN HOLD MY BREATH... SOMER-SAULT TO THE *LANDING*--

I'VE GOT AN *AIR-BREATHER* IN MY UTILITY BELT... IF I CAN *GET* TO IT IN TIME...

BUT, EVEN AS THE ACROBATIC ACE LANDS ON THE FLOOR BELOW...

NOT *NICE*, RED, DEFINITELY A *TEN* ON THE STINKY SCALE!

SHRINK!

WHAT?!?

WELL, WHATTAYA KNOW? IT TOOK ONE JACKASS TO GIVE *ANOTHER* JACKASS A BUTT ON THE *BUTT*!

CHANGELING...

I KNOW... NO *JOKES*, RIGHT?

WRONG! THANKS... REALLY, JUST *THANKS*.

AND, IN THE SECOND FLOOR RECREATION ROOM...

DAMES? I DON'T LIKE BEATIN' UP ON *BROADS*--

BUT, IF I GOTTA, I *GOTTA*!

SKOTCHH!

WONDER GIRL, LEAVE THIS WALKING MOUNTAIN TO *ME*.

MY *PLEASURE*, KORIAND'R.

12

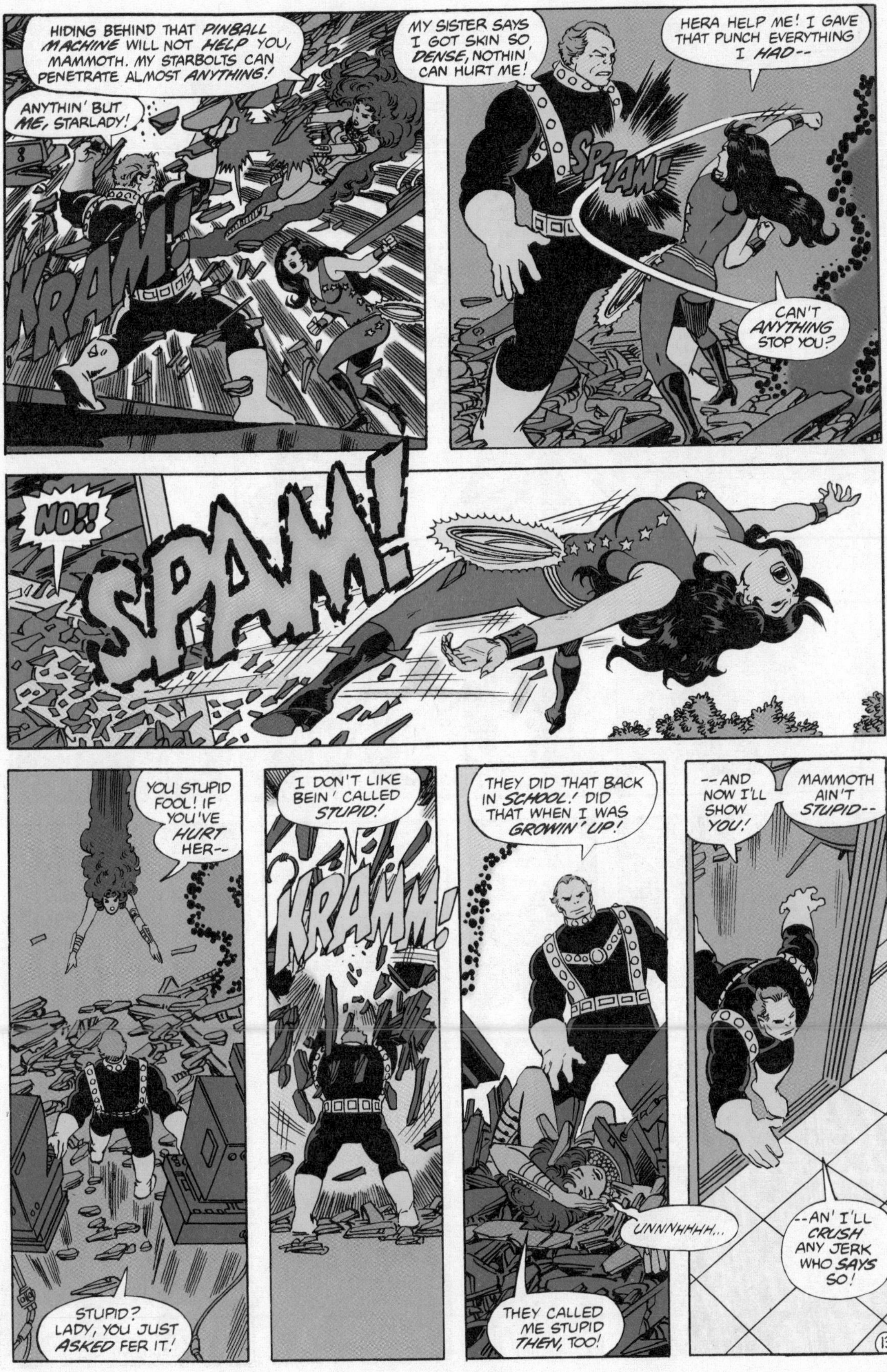
HIDING BEHIND THAT PINBALL MACHINE WILL NOT HELP YOU, MAMMOTH. MY STARBOLTS CAN PENETRATE ALMOST ANYTHING!
ANYTHIN' BUT ME, STARLADY!
KRAM!
MY SISTER SAYS I GOT SKIN SO DENSE, NOTHIN' CAN HURT ME!
HERA HELP ME! I GAVE THAT PUNCH EVERYTHING I HAD--
SPTAM!
CAN'T ANYTHING STOP YOU?
NO!!
SPAM!
YOU STUPID FOOL! IF YOU'VE HURT HER--
STUPID? LADY, YOU JUST ASKED FER IT!
I DON'T LIKE BEIN' CALLED STUPID!
KRAMM!
THEY DID THAT BACK IN SCHOOL! DID THAT WHEN I WAS GROWIN' UP!
UNNNHHHH...
THEY CALLED ME STUPID THEN, TOO!
--AND NOW I'LL SHOW YOU!
MAMMOTH AIN'T STUPID--
--AN' I'LL CRUSH ANY JERK WHO SAYS SO!
13

WONDER GIRL IS *DOWN*, STARFIRE KNOCKED *BREATHLESS*, AND THINGS AREN'T ALL *ROSY* IN THE BELOW-GROUND GYMNASIUM EITHER...

HEY, GREENIE, WATCH THE *BIRDIE!*

SPAM

MMMMM

MY *EYES!* I-I CAN'T *SEE?!!*

THIS ISN'T GOING WELL... THEY'VE GOT THEIR MOVES DOWN PAT-- PLANNED THIS ATTACK TO THE LAST *DETAIL...*

BUT *DR. LIGHT* ISN'T HERE WITH THE *OTHERS*-- AND THAT MEANS THESE GUYS WERE SENT TO RUN *INTERFERENCE...*

TO KEEP US BUSY WHILE LIGHT DOES-- *WHAT?!?*

LISTEN TO ME, GIZMO, YOU'VE GOT *YOUR* WEAPONS, BUT I'VE GOT MINE. THIS IS A *STALEMATE...*

HOW D'YA EXPECT TA *FIGHT*--

--WHEN YER ALL *TIED UP*--

--AN' *DROWNIN'* IN YER *PLAYPOOL* TA BOOT?

THOSE STEEL BANDS... CRUSH-ING ME... CAN'T *BREATHE...*

DON'T MAKE ME LAUGH, KID--

SPLOOSH!

BUT, JUST THEN...

WHERE'S *ROBIN?* I HEARD HIS CRY!

SKREEEE!

THE *STAR-BROAD*--? THAT BIG JERK MAMMOTH WAS SUPPOSED TA *TAKE CARE* OF YOU!

HE *FAILED* JUST AS *YOU'LL* FAIL-- *WAIT!*

ROBIN-- IN THE *POOL*--!

SO HELP ME, DWARF, IF YOU'VE *KILLED* HIM, MY STARBOLTS WILL BLAST YOU FROM HERE TO *TAMARAN!*

PLEASE, X'HAL-- LET ROBIN *LIVE...*

H-HE'S *STRUGGLING,* SLIPPING HIS HANDS *FREE...*

GIVEN TIME, HE COULD *ESCAPE,* BUT THERE'S *NO* TIME... NO TIME AT *ALL!*

14

CRIPES! SHE'S BLASTIN' OFF HIS *BANDS*... SHE'LL BE COMIN' AFTER *ME* NEXT.

WELL, LET *LIGHT* WORRY 'BOUT 'EM-- I GOT MY *OWN* LIFE TA LOOK OUT AFTER.

GOTTA *RUN*... GET *OUTTA* HERE--

POW

SHORTY... ...YOU JUST GOT *DONE* RUNNIN'!

GOLDIE, SHORT-PANTS *OKAY*?

HIS BREATHING IS *SHALLOW*... HIS HEARTBEAT *SLOW*...

VICTOR, HE NEEDS *HELP*!

R-RAVEN--? THANK X'HAL! YOU'LL *HELP* HIM, WON'T YOU? *PLEASE*?

YOU WON'T LET ROBIN *DIE*...

HE WILL NOT DIE, *KORIAND'R*, BELIEVE ME.

THERE IS VERY LITTLE WATER IN HIS LUNGS... HE SUFFERS MOSTLY FROM *SHOCK*...

HIS TRAINING *SAVED* HIM... GAVE HIM *STRENGTH*...

WOWEEE, MY HEAD FEELS LIKE *TRIGON* SAT ON-- *HEY*! WHAT'S GOIN' ON?

IT'S ROBIN, GOLDIE HADDA FISH 'IM OUTTA THE *POOL*.

"HAD TO"? DOES THAT MEAN HE'S--?

HIS PAIN FLOWS INTO *ME*... HIS SUFFERING BECOMES MY *OWN*...

THERE IS MUCH *AGONY*... SO MUCH-- *WAIT*... THE PAIN BEGINS TO *PASS*...

BY AZAR! HE RISES... HE RISES!

RAVEN, YOU *DID* IT! YOU'RE ALIVE, DICK--*ALIVE*!!

Y-YOU *SAVED* ME, RAVEN--?

NO, MY FRIEND... YOUR *STRENGTH* SAVED YOU...

I MERELY AIDED IN YOUR *RECOVERY*.

15

BUT, THE MOMENT OF REJOICING COMES TO A SUDDEN, SHOCKING END JUST INSTANTS LATER, AS...

MY HEAD-- AGGHH!

WHAT IN BLAZES-- EVERYTHIN' GROWIN' *BLACK*!!

WE'RE BEING ATTACKED... FROM *INSIDE OUR HEADS*-- BUT *HOW?*

I SHOULDN'T'VE *ASKED*-- IT COULD ONLY HAVE BEEN--

PSIMON? IT'S THAT PSIONIC *CREEP!*

FERGET THAT DOME-HEADED BOZO--

WHAT'S MY *FATHER* DOIN' WITH THEM?

YER *ONE* OF THEM, AREN'T YOU? YOU *SIDED* WITH 'EM?

QUITE *RELUCTANTLY*, I ASSURE YOU.

MAMMOTH, YOUR SISTER HAS BEEN *HURT*. SEE TO HER.

HURT? WHO HURT *SELINDA?*

TELL ME WHO *HURT* HER AN' I'LL *DEMOLISH* 'IM!

SELINDA... Y-YOU *OKAY?*

I WILL *LIVE*, BARAN. I WAS ONLY *BRUISED!*

FERGET HER, JUST WHY ARE *YOU* HERE AFTER I TOLD YOU THAT I NEVER WANTED TA *SEE* YOU AGAIN?

PLEASE, VICTOR, YOU MUST *UNDERSTAND*... WHEN I CAME HERE... WHEN I BUILT THIS *TOWER* FOR YOU--

YOU BUILT THIS CATASTROPHE? NO *WONDER* I HATED IT.

OH, VICTOR... I BUILT IT FOR *YOU*... FOR YOUR *FRIENDS*.

THIS LITTLE FAMILY SQUABBLE HAS ITS CHARMS, BUT I'M AFRAID WE HAVE *BETTER* THINGS TO DO THAN *LISTEN* ANY LONGER.

MY FRIENDS *FREED* ME, WHICH IS ALL THEY *WANTED*. NOW, IF YOU WILL PERMIT US TO *LEAVE*...

16

THEY ARE *STUNNED*, THESE TITANS ARE. PSIMON'S WORDS ARE NOT TO BE *BELIEVED*. THESE FEARSOME FIVE HAVE INVADED THEIR HEADQUARTERS, BATTLED THEM, AND NOW THEY SIMPLY WISH TO FREELY LEAVE? THOUGHTS AND PLANS RACE THROUGH THE TITANS' *MINDS*...

STARFIRE:

HOW TO ATTACK?

CHANGELING:

WHAT TO DO FIRST?

CYBORG:

WHO TO GO AFTER?

RAVEN:

HOW TO PREVENT NEEDLESS DEATH?

ROBIN:

THE NEXT MOVE... WHAT IS IT?

BUT, BEFORE ANYONE CAN REACT...

PSIMON, NO ONE'S GOING *ANYWHERE*-- NOT UNTIL THE TITANS ARE *THROUGH* WITH YOU!

BY THE DARK LIGHT-- *WHAT?*

BLESS MY *BOOTIES*...

...WHAT'S RED AND YELLOW AND *GORGEOUS* ALL OVER?

THE SAME ONE WHO'S GONNA TURN YOU *BLACK-AND-BLUE-AND-RED* ALL OVER-- IF YOU DON'T CUT OUT THOSE *CHAUVINIST REMARKS!*

SPOILSPORT!

ROBIN IS INDEED THEIR *LEADER*, FOR, WHILE THE OTHERS STILL STAND IN SILENT *SHOCK*...

STARFIRE, GET *PSIMON*, FAST. HE'S THE *GREATEST* DANGER!

LOVE TO, ROBBY. WHATEVER YOU WANT, YOU'VE *GOT!*

SKREEEEE

A *COLD*, HARSH DEATH-LIKE *GRIN* CROSSES STARFIRE'S LOVELY FACE AS SHE UNLEASHES HER DEADLY STARBOLTS. SHE *CRAVES* VIOLENCE, DOES THIS ALIEN WARRIOR. AND THAT LOVE FOR BLOOD CHILLS ROBIN TO THE MARROW.

17

AS PSIMON TUMBLES TO THE GROUND, STUNNED BY THE FEROCITY OF STARFIRE'S BLAST, THE OTHERS CONTINUE THEIR OPPRESSIVE ONSLAUGHT...

UNHH! H-HE'S TOO BLASTED STRONG... HIS GRIP--UN-BREAKABLE... CAN'T FREE MYSELF BY FIGHTING BACK...

...ONLY CHANCE... HAVE TO SUCKER HIM--

BAH! LOOK AT 'ER, LIGHT! SHE'S GIVIN' UP! I GOT HER BEAT!

DON'T STOP 'TIL SHE'S DOWN--I TELL YOU SHE'S STRONGER THAN--EH?

MAMMOTH, BEHIND YOU--

AHH, LET'S SEE NOW, YOU'RE STARFIRE, AREN'T YOU?

WELL, MY GOLDEN LOVELY, YOU WON'T HARM MY MOUN-TAINOUS FRIEND THE WAY YOU DID POOR PSIMON.

A LITTLE LIGHT BLAST WILL SEE TO THAT!

HOW WRONG CAN YOU GET, BRIGHT-EYES?

WE TITANS AREN'T DOWN TILL WE'RE OUT--

--AND YOU BOZOS HAVEN'T GOT A PRAYER OF DOING THAT!

WHUMP

SOMEONE-- HELP ME!

KEEP YOUR PANTS ON, LIGHT. I'LL GET TO YOU AFTER I FINISH OFF THIS LITTLE TRAMP!

C'MON, GIRLIE... JUST WATCH AS ONE TOUCH TRANSMUTES THIS WALL INTO A SOLID STEEL COFFIN--

--ONE FITTED JUST FOR YOU!

MAKE THAT COFFIN YOUR SIZE, SHIMMER. I DON'T INTEND TO LOSE THIS FIGHT.

BUT YOU WILL, GIRLIE--OH, I SWEAR YOU WILL! AND I WILL SO ENJOY WATCHING THE STEEL RE-FORM ABOUT YOU--

KEEP BLABBERIN', RED--GIMME TIME TA SET UP A RELAY CABLE--SHOOT MY INTERNAL POWER RIGHT INTO THIS WALL YOU'RE TOUCHIN'...

AND, WHEN EVERYTHIN'S SET--

--I TURN ON THE JUICE!

WH--WHAT??

SK RA KLE

NOT *BAD*, DIMWIT--YOU ACTUALLY BEAT UP A *LITTLE GIRL*.

WHAT'S *NEXT*, GRANITE-HEAD? PUNCHING OUT *OLD LADIES* AND *CRIPPLES*?

C'MON, C'MON, LESSEE WHAT YOU DO WITH A *REAL* MACHO GUY.

OKAY, JERK! I'M *READY*!

I'M *HERE*, PUNCH *ME* OUT. I *DARE* YA. C'MON --DO YOUR *WORST*!

HUH? WHAT'D YA *DO*? I--I CAN'T *SEE*? WHERE ARE YOU?

RIGHT *HERE*, UGLY...MAKIN' LIKE A *JELLY FISH*. C'MON, I TRIPLE DARE YA TA PUNCH ME *NOW*.

KEEP IT UP, GAR...JUST GIVE ME ANOTHER SECOND OR TWO TO GET BACK MY *STRENGTH*.

WHAT I'M *PLANNING* ISN'T EXACTLY ACCORDING TO *HOYLE*--

--BUT THE WAY *I* SEE IT, THIS ISN'T A *GAME*!

WHOOOM!

THIS IS *WAR*... AND WE'VE GOT TO *WIN*!

GREAT HERA! I USED ALL MY AMAZON *STRENGTH*... ALL MY POWER, AND HE'S STILL *STANDING*.

NO WAY, WONDY-- LOOKIT HIS *EYES*. THEY'RE EVEN EMPTIER THAN *NORMAL*!

TIMMBEERR!

WATCH OUT-- HE'S GONNA...

OH, NO... NOOOOOOO!!

MEANWHILE...

SKOOSH!

AH, SO IT'S *YOU*, ROBIN-- YOU WHO ARE ABOUT TO *FALL*! I HAVE TO ADMIT, I *PREFER* IT THIS WAY!

YOU ARE THE TITANS' *LINK* WITH THE *JUSTICE LEAGUE*-- AND TRUTHFULLY, I WOULD PREFER DESTROYING *THEM*, IF I HAD MY WAY...

BUT YOU KNOW WHAT THEY SAY ABOUT *BEGGARS* AND *CHOOSERS*, EH?

SORRY, LIGHT, BUT AS NEAR AS I CAN TELL, IT'S *YOU* WHO ARE ABOUT TO FALL.

YOU SEE, SINCE I *JOINED* THE TITANS, I'VE GOT *NEW* SUPER-POWERS!

19

COME OFF IT, KID. IF YOU EXPECT ME TO *BELIEVE*-- UHHHH!

AS A CERTAIN *FRIEND* OF MINE SAID-- "NEVER ONCE DO MY *FINGERS* LEAVE MY *HANDS*"!

WH-WHA-WHAT'RE YOU *DOIN'*?

JUST A LITTLE *HAND-PLAY*...

...AND IT'S A *BLACKOUT* FOR DOCTOR LIGHT!

THAT WAS *WONDER-FUL*, BUT HOW DID YOU *DO* IT?

UNNHHHHH!!

I DON'T *CARE* HOW-- JUST GIVE ME A *NICKEL* FOR THAT LITTLE SPEECH BACK THERE.

I *COPYRIGHTED* IT WHILE YOU WEREN'T LOOKING!

C'MON, ROB-- SPILL THE BEANS... WHAT'S THE *SECRET*?

SHEESH! THIS JOKER'S GONNA SLEEP FER A *MONTH!* WHAT DID YOU *DO*?

IT'S REALLY *EASY*, VIC. I SIMPLY PALMED A *SLEEP-GAS* CAPSULE FROM MY UTILITY BELT...

...WAVED IT UNDER HIS CROOKED LITTLE *NOSE*--

--AND HE WAS OUT LIKE A--

DON'T *SAY* IT, ROBIN-- DON'T *DARE* SAY IT!

MR. LOGAN, *I* WAS SPOUTING ONE-LINERS EVEN *BEFORE* YOU TURNED GREEN WITH ENVY.

OUR FRIEND HERE WAS OUT LIKE A... *LIGHT!*

HE SAID IT. I *WARNED* HIM, AND HE STILL *SAID* IT!

H-HE DOESN'T *LOOK* AT ME. WHEN OUR EYES MEET, HE *TURNS AWAY*. WHY WON'T HE LISTEN? WHY CAN'T HE *BELIEVE*?

TALK TO HIM, SILAS STONE... *TELL* HIM WHAT YOU HAVE REFUSED TO SAY.

YOU *KNOW*?

AND *UNDERSTAND*.

THEN... VICTOR, PLEASE, EVEN IF YOU WON'T *BELIEVE* ME... *LISTEN* TO ME. LET ME *TALK*...

TALK...

...ALL MY LIFE ALL YOU'VE EVER DONE IS *TALK*. SORRY, BUT I'VE GOT NOTHING LEFT TO TALK *ABOUT*.

THE POLICE COPTER RISES FROM THE SMALL ISLAND, ITS CARGO OF FIVE PRISONERS SECURE.

THERE WILL SOON BE A TRIAL, A CONVICTION, THEN IMPRISONMENT.

FOR NOW, AT LEAST, THE THREAT OF THE FEARSOME FIVE IS OVER.

EPILOGUE

BUT, AS THE WHOOPING OF THE HELICOPTER BLADES FADES INTO THE DISTANCE...

...THE TITANS FIND THEMSELVES SHROUDED WITH AN AWKWARD SILENCE.

THEN...

DR. STONE, YOU SAID YOU BUILT THE TOWER...BUT WHY DIDN'T YOU TELL US? WHY THE MYSTERY?

WITH AGE, ROBIN, THERE DOES NOT ALWAYS COME WISDOM. I WAS FOOLISH, PERHAPS HOPEFUL... PERHAPS...SHAMEFUL.

SINCE THE ACCIDENT...VICTOR AND I...WE HAVEN'T TALKED...BUT, I WATCHED HIM GROW ANGRY...BITTER, EVEN DANGEROUS.

THEN YOU PEOPLE CAME INTO HIS LIFE, AND FOR THE FIRST TIME IN SO VERY LONG, I SAW THAT HE WAS HAPPY.

HE SEEMED TO BELONG...AND I DIDN'T WANT THAT TO END FOR HIM.

FROM MY PATENTS... MY INVENTIONS, I HAD MONEY... I USED IT TO BUILD YOUR TOWER...TO GIVE YOU A HEADQUARTERS...TO GIVE VICTOR A HOME.

YOU WERE BUYIN' ME FRIENDS. THAT'S WHAT IT COMES DOWN TO. DAMN IT, DAD-- YOU ALWAYS THOUGHT YOU COULD BUY ANYTHIN' YOUR SCIENCE COULDN'T MAKE.

AN' WHAT DID YOU GET FOR IT ALL? YOU KILLED MY MOM, TURNED ME INTO THIS STEEL-ALLOY FREAK-SHOW!

VICTOR, I'VE TRIED TO EXPLAIN...

AN' I SAID FERGET IT. I'M SICK TO DEATH OF YOUR EXPLAININ'!

VICTOR, WITHIN YOU I SENSE SO MUCH FRUSTRATION AND ANGER.

PERHAPS, AT LAST, THE TIME HAS COME FOR THE TRUTH TO EASE YOUR PAIN.

YOU SAID BEFORE YOU TRUST ME. IF SO...

VICTOR STONE DRAWS IN A COLD BREATH, HIS TEETH GNASH IN DISGUST, BUT THIS TIME HE DOESN'T TURN AWAY.

QUIETLY, ALMOST ON THE VERGE OF TEARS, HE SIMPLY NODS.

21

I GUESS IT WAS A MISTAKE, VICTOR-- BELIEVING YOU WOULD BE INTERESTED IN *SCIENCE*, BUT YOU KNEW HOW YOUR MOTHER AND I HAD *HOPED*...

HOPED, I THINK, EVEN AFTER WE KNEW *BETTER*.

"YOU WERE NEVER COMFORTABLE IN THE LAB...NOT EVEN AS A CHILD. IT WAS ONLY OUTSIDE THAT YOU SEEMED TO COME ALIVE.

"SCIENCE, NO... YOU WERE AN ATHLETE, AND THAT SEEMED TO CONSUME YOU.

"MAYBE I SHOULD HAVE ENCOURAGED YOUR ATHLETICS...

"MAYBE, IF I HAD, THINGS WOULD HAVE BEEN DIFFERENT. BUT, BECAUSE I DIDN'T, I ALWAYS KNEW HOW YOU RESENTED ME.

"YOUR MOTHER WAS MY *ASSISTANT*, AND TOGETHER -- WE WERE EXPLORERS... VOYAGERS TO THE UNKNOWN.

"IT WAS OUR DREAM... TO SHATTER THE BARRIERS BETWEEN THE KNOWN DIMENSIONS.

"A DREAM I NEVER THOUGHT WOULD COME TO PASS. BUT, ON THAT CURSED DAY, MY DREAM... GOD, MY DREAM BECAME A NIGHTMARE.

"A LIFETIME OF WORK ACHIEVED, YOUR MOTHER AND I EMBRACED, HER HAND RESTED ON THE COMPUTER CONSOLE... BUT ONLY FOR A MOMENT...

"BUT THAT INSTANT WAS *ENOUGH*. ELINORE HAD ACCIDENTALLY RELEASED MICROWAVES INTO THAT OTHER DIMENSION... AND THAT THING SOMEHOW USED THEM...

"IT MERGED WITH THE MICROWAVES, TRAVELED ON THEM, AND SHATTERED THE SCREEN IN OUR LAB.

"AND THAT IS WHEN YOU CAME IN..."

MOM, IS IT ALL RIGHT IF I GO--

MOM?!?

"HOW CAN I TELL YOU WHAT IT WAS LIKE? ELINORE WAS CLOSEST TO THE SCREEN... CLOSEST TO THAT... THING...

"--IT TOOK HER...THAT DAMNED EVIL THING TOOK HER AND DESTROYED HER!

"AND THEN ...IT TURNED TO *VICTOR*...

D-DAD...?

22

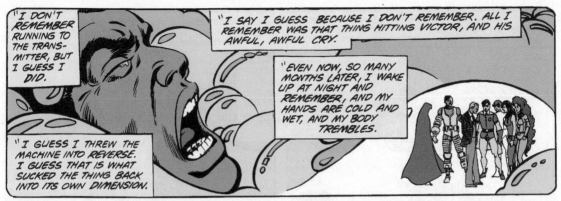

"I DON'T REMEMBER RUNNING TO THE TRANSMITTER, BUT I GUESS I DID.

"I SAY I GUESS BECAUSE I DON'T REMEMBER. ALL I REMEMBER WAS THAT THING HITTING VICTOR, AND HIS AWFUL, AWFUL CRY.

"EVEN NOW, SO MANY MONTHS LATER, I WAKE UP AT NIGHT AND REMEMBER, AND MY HANDS ARE COLD AND WET, AND MY BODY TREMBLES.

"I GUESS I THREW THE MACHINE INTO REVERSE. I GUESS THAT IS WHAT SUCKED THE THING BACK INTO ITS OWN DIMENSION.

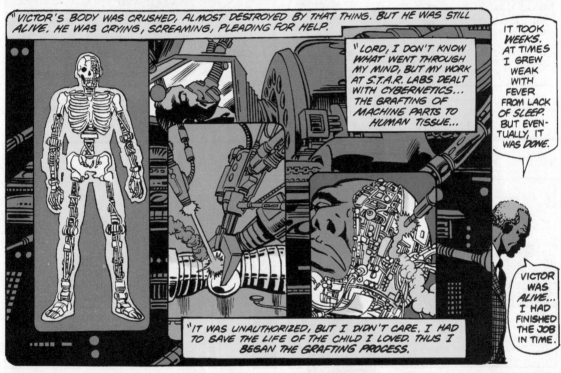

"VICTOR'S BODY WAS CRUSHED, ALMOST DESTROYED BY THAT THING. BUT HE WAS STILL ALIVE. HE WAS CRYING, SCREAMING, PLEADING FOR HELP.

"LORD, I DON'T KNOW WHAT WENT THROUGH MY MIND, BUT MY WORK AT S.T.A.R. LABS DEALT WITH CYBERNETICS... THE GRAFTING OF MACHINE PARTS TO HUMAN TISSUE...

IT TOOK WEEKS. AT TIMES I GREW WEAK WITH FEVER FROM LACK OF SLEEP. BUT EVENTUALLY, IT WAS DONE.

VICTOR WAS ALIVE... I HAD FINISHED THE JOB IN TIME.

"IT WAS UNAUTHORIZED, BUT I DIDN'T CARE. I HAD TO SAVE THE LIFE OF THE CHILD I LOVED. THUS I BEGAN THE GRAFTING PROCESS.

"IN TIME"? IT TIME FOR WHAT?

THAT THING... SOMEHOW ITS RADIATION POISONED ME. I WAS SLOWLY DYING -- BUT I COULDN'T DIE... NOT UNTIL I KNEW YOU WOULD LIVE.

OH, GOD -- YOU NEVER TOLD ME. I DIDN'T KNOW. AND ALL THIS TIME...

I...I HATE MYSELF!!

DON'T, VICTOR... PLEASE DON'T HATE. IT IS SO USELESS, SO WASTEFUL.

HATE ONLY CONSUMES... DESTROYS YOU PIECE BY PIECE. PLEASE DON'T LET IT DESTROY YOU.

OH, MY SWEET GOD...DAD...DAD...

...WE'VE GOT A LOT OF CATCHING UP TO DO...

23

THEY LEAVE THEN, FOR THERE IS MUCH THAT NEEDS BE DONE. SO MANY MEMORIES THAT MUST BE SHARED.

ON HYDRAULIC LEGS, VICTOR LEAPS ACROSS THE CITY, BLOCKS BLURRING PAST WITH EVERY INCREDIBLE JUMP.

ONCE THERE WAS BITTERNESS, BUT THAT IS FORGOTTEN. HATE IS FORGOTTEN. SORROW AND SELF-PITY, FORGOTTEN, TOO.

BUT, SOON THE MAN WHO IS A SUPER-HERO IS FORGOTTEN. ONLY VICTOR STONE AND SILAS STONE COUNT NOW.

NOW THERE IS ONLY THE TWO OF THEM, AND THE TAPESTRY OF FUTURE MEMORIES IS WHAT COUNTS... THE MEMORIES OF A FATHER AND HIS SON.

TOGETHER THEY SHARE THE PASSING WEEKS AS THEY NEVER HAD BEFORE.

ALONE, TALKING LISTENING... ALL THE HUMAN NEEDS THAT THERE WAS NEVER TIME FOR IN THE PAST... ALL THAT SO MANY PEOPLE WANT AND NEVER GRASP.

NOTHING IS PUT OFF BECAUSE OF TIME, NOTHING SHOVED ASIDE BECAUSE ONE IS TOO BUSY AND THE OTHER BUSIER STILL.

TWO MONTHS GO BY. ALL TOO SHORT A TIME TO CREATE A LOVE AND A BOND WHERE NONE HAD EXISTED BEFORE. YET, NOW IT EXISTS.

THEY ACCEPT THE IMPENDING TRAGEDY WHICH CANNOT BE FORGOTTEN. THEY ACCEPT ALL THOSE YEARS THEY HAD MISSED, ALL THE GROWING-UP THAT CANNOT BE RECAPTURED...

THEY ACCEPT ALL OF THAT, BUT IT CANNOT SPOIL WHAT IS NOW. THEY WON'T LET IT SOUR WHAT HAS BECOME SO SWEET.

24

ANOTHER MONTH PASSES, AND NOW SILAS STONE IS FRAIL. NOW HE IS BEDRIDDEN, AWAITING THE WARM SHADOWS OF THE ENDLESS NIGHT...

IT CAN'T BE *LONG* NOW, VICTOR... I'M SO SORRY, SO VERY SORRY.

DAD... *DAD...?*

...I...I WISH THERE WAS SOMETHING... SOME LAST THING FOR ME TO GIVE YOU, VICTOR, BUT...THERE'S NOTHING... *NOTHING.*

YOU ALREADY GAVE ME *EVERYTHING,* DAD.

YOU GAVE ME *LIFE...* YOU GAVE ME *REASON...* YOU GAVE ME *LOVE.*

AND I GAVE YOU NOTHING BUT *DISAPPOINTMENT...*

OH, VICTOR, NEVER *THAT,* NEVER DISAPPOINTMENT. YOUR MOTHER AND I WERE ALWAYS SO *PROUD* OF YOU.

EVERYTHING YOU EVER *DID...* FROM THAT BASEBALL TROPHY... I STILL CRY WHEN I SEE IT.

WE ALWAYS LOVED YOU, CARED FOR YOU, WANTED SO MUCH FOR YOU...

BUT, IN THE END, VICTOR, *HAPPINESS* IS ALL THAT REALLY MATTERS. PLEASE, BE HAPPY...BE HAPPY *ALWAYS...*

VICTOR TREMBLES AS THE AGED HAND GROWS COLD. HE TREMBLES AS THE MAN HE DID NOT UNDERSTAND FOR ALL TOO LONG IS FINALLY REUNITED WITH THE WOMAN HE LOVES.

IN PASSING, THIS MAN GIVES VICTOR MEMORIES WHICH SHALL GUIDE HIM FOR AS LONG AS HE LIVES.

AND THIS MAN THAT VICTOR CAME TO LOVE SO LATE, THIS MAN WHO GAVE ALL OF HIMSELF, IN PASSING GIVES ONE THING MORE THAT WILL BE CHERISHED ABOVE ALL ELSE.

25

NEXT ISSUE: THE HUMAN DRAMA CONTINUES AS WE REVEAL... *A DAY IN THE LIVES...!*

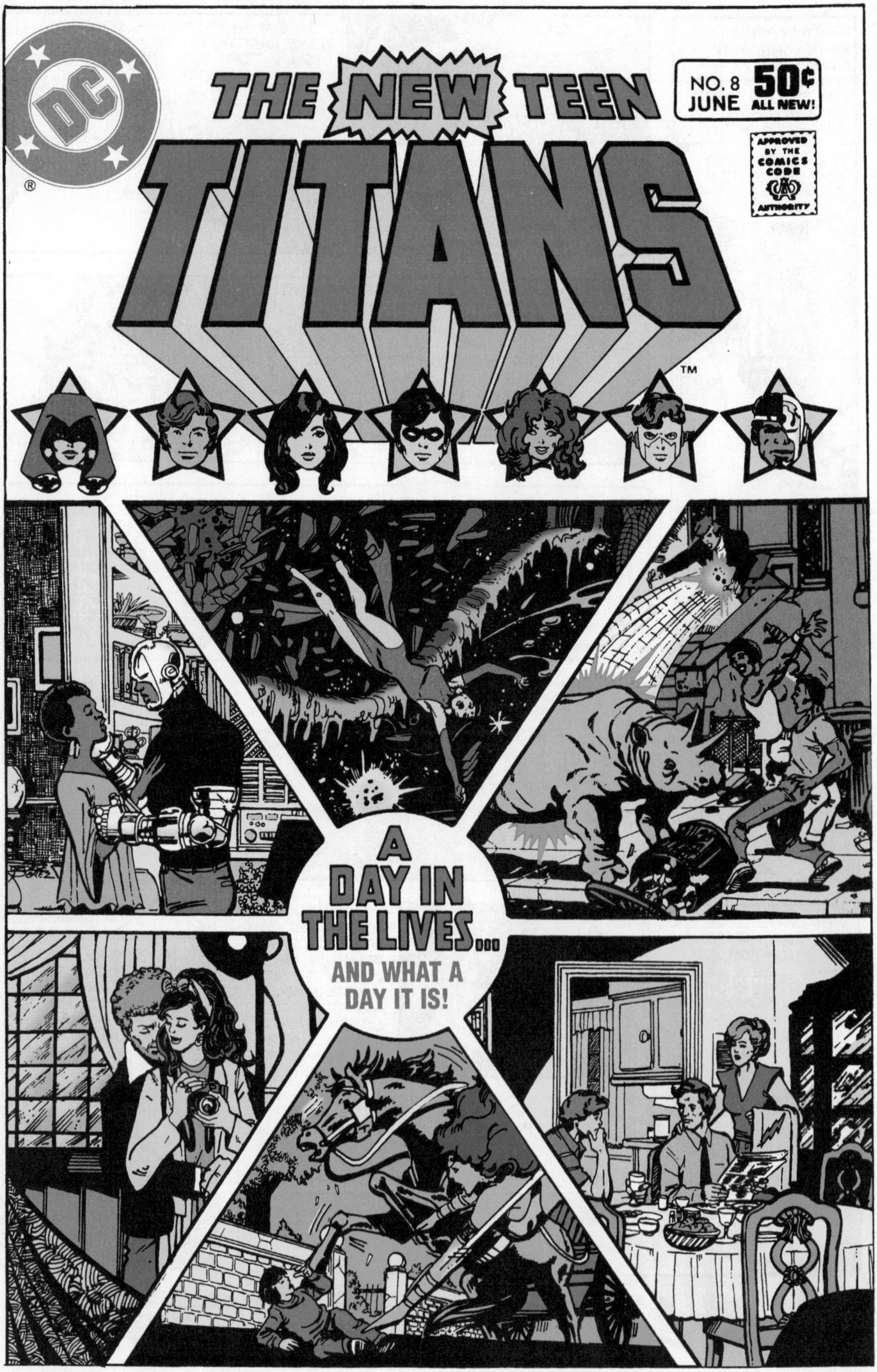
THE NEW TEEN
TITANS
NO. 8
JUNE
50¢
ALL NEW!
APPROVED BY THE COMICS CODE AUTHORITY
A DAY IN THE LIVES...
AND WHAT A DAY IT IS!

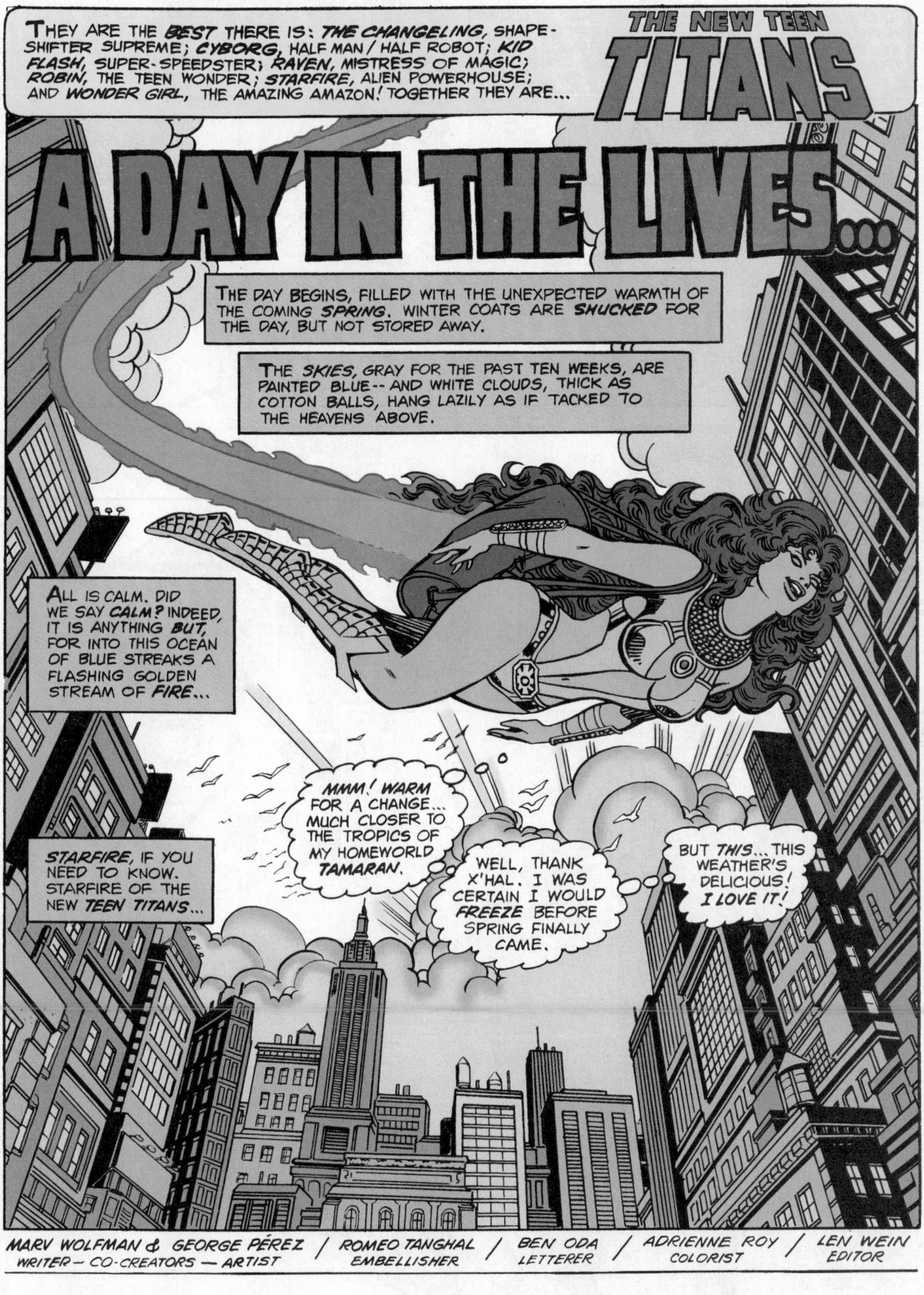
THEY ARE THE BEST THERE IS: THE CHANGELING, SHAPE-SHIFTER SUPREME; CYBORG, HALF MAN / HALF ROBOT; KID FLASH, SUPER-SPEEDSTER; RAVEN, MISTRESS OF MAGIC; ROBIN, THE TEEN WONDER; STARFIRE, ALIEN POWERHOUSE; AND WONDER GIRL, THE AMAZING AMAZON! TOGETHER THEY ARE...
THE NEW TEEN TITANS
A DAY IN THE LIVES...
THE DAY BEGINS, FILLED WITH THE UNEXPECTED WARMTH OF THE COMING SPRING. WINTER COATS ARE SHUCKED FOR THE DAY, BUT NOT STORED AWAY.
THE SKIES, GRAY FOR THE PAST TEN WEEKS, ARE PAINTED BLUE-- AND WHITE CLOUDS, THICK AS COTTON BALLS, HANG LAZILY AS IF TACKED TO THE HEAVENS ABOVE.
ALL IS CALM. DID WE SAY CALM? INDEED, IT IS ANYTHING BUT, FOR INTO THIS OCEAN OF BLUE STREAKS A FLASHING GOLDEN STREAM OF FIRE...
STARFIRE, IF YOU NEED TO KNOW. STARFIRE OF THE NEW TEEN TITANS...
MMM! WARM FOR A CHANGE... MUCH CLOSER TO THE TROPICS OF MY HOMEWORLD TAMARAN.
WELL, THANK X'HAL. I WAS CERTAIN I WOULD FREEZE BEFORE SPRING FINALLY CAME.
BUT THIS... THIS WEATHER'S DELICIOUS! I LOVE IT!

MARV WOLFMAN & GEORGE PÉREZ WRITER — CO-CREATORS — ARTIST / ROMEO TANGHAL EMBELLISHER / BEN ODA LETTERER / ADRIENNE ROY COLORIST / LEN WEIN EDITOR

OH, HOW I'D LOVE TO JUST *FLY*, FEELING THE WARM WINDS HOLDING ME, RUSHING PAST ME...

...BUT I PROMISED DONNA THAT I'D *MEET* HER FOR AN EARLY *LUNCH*.

AND, FRANKLY, IT'S ABOUT TIME I *EXPLORED* THIS CITY I NOW LIVE IN.

THIS IS A *GOOD* WORLD, I THINK. I'M GLAD TO *BE* HERE.

SO AWESOME, SO *MASSIVE* WHEN COMPARED WITH TAMARAN. SO VERY *CROWDED*, BUT SO FILLED WITH LIFE AND *BEAUTY*.

THOUGH SO MANY OF ITS CUSTOMS STILL *ELUDE* ME.

DONNA AND I ARE *FRIENDS*, YET BEFORE I SEE HER I AM SUPPOSED TO DRESS *DIFFERENTLY* THAN I AM NOW.

SO *VERY* CONFUSING.

THE SILVER FOX ADVERTISING AGENCY...

OKAY, OKAY... JEANIE, A LITTLE TO THE *RIGHT*, PLEASE. SANDY, ARCH THAT *HIP*.

PERFECT, JUST *PERFECT*...

UHHH, CANDY, TRY TO STAND *STILL*, WILL YOU, PLEASE?

OH, YEAH, SURE, MISS TROY. LIKE, Y'KNOW, I'M RILLY *TRYIN'*, BUT...

...WELL, IT'S JUST SO *HARD*, LIKE, I MEAN... KEEPIN' STILL IS SUCH A *DRAG*.

AND I'M *NOT* SUPPOSED TO CALL HER *WONDER GIRL*... YET, WHILE FIGHTING, I CAN'T CALL HER *DONNA*. SO *CONFUSING*.

YES, CANDY, I KNOW HOW *HARD* IT IS, BUT THAT'S WHY THEY PAY YOU THE *BIG BUCKS*.

=SIGH=

2

TELL YOU WHAT, CANDY, WHY DON'T YOU TRY TO *THINK* OF SOMETHING...

CANDY!! I TOLD YOU TO GET RID OF THAT *GUM!*

GEE, LIKE HOW CAN I *THINK* WITHOUT GUM? I MEAN, WOW, GUM-- IT SORT OF SOOTHES MY *KARMA*, IF Y'KNOW WHAT I MEAN.

AND WE CERTAINLY WOULDN'T WANT ANY RUFFLED *KARMAS*, NOW, WOULD WE?

OH, FOR CRYING OUT LOUD, LET'S *TAKE FIVE*, EVERYONE.

MADDY, GET ME AN *ASPIRIN*, WILL YOU?

IN FACT, MAKE IT A *DOUBLE!*

'EY, WHAT'SA *THEES?* THESE'A *PICTURES*, THEY MAKE'A MY CANDY LOOK'A SO SKINNY LIKE'A *SPAGETT'!*

MR. DELEVI, AS I WAS SAYING, CANDY IS, WELL, *WRONG* FOR THIS AD.

'EY, *YOU*, YOU'A TELLIN' *ME*, SERGIO DELEVI, HE DON'TA KNOW A *BEAUTY* WHEN HE SEES'A ONE?

IT'S'A THESE'A PICTURES, THEY *STINK!*

LISTEN HERE, MR. DELEVI, *YOU MAY* KNOW JEANS, BUT *I* KNOW PHOTOGRAPHY. YOU WANT THIS AD DONE *RIGHT*, GET THAT SQUIRMING FLAKE *OUT* OF HERE.

SHE MAY STROKE YOUR MASCULINE *EGO*, BUT AS A MODEL, *SHE'S* THE ONE WHO *STINKS.*

WHAT'S'A THIS? YOU GONNA LET THAT'A LITTLE GIRL INSULT'A MY *CANDY?*

MR. DELEVI, I'D *TRUST* DONNA IF I WERE YOU. SHE'S *YOUNG*, BUT SHE HAS THIS CLASSIC SENSE OF *BEAUTY*... OF *COMPOSITION*...

CARL, *CALL* ME WHEN YOU WORK THIS OUT!

YOU HAVE MY *SERVICE NUMBER.*

CONFUSION RUNS RAMPANT. BUT JUST WHEN IT'S ALL ABOUT TO *HIT THE FAN*...

HI, DONNA. AM I LATE FOR *LUNCH?*

WH-WHAT?

3

I SURE HOPE I DIDN'T INTERRUPT ANYTHING *IMPORTANT*.

BUT I GOT HERE AS SOON AS I *COULD*.

MAMMA MIA.

SHE'S'A *BEAUTY*, SHE'S'A *PERFECT*! SHE'S'A MY "*GOLDEN JEANS'A*" GIRL COME TO *LIFE*.

GOSH, SERGIO, BUT YOU SAID *I* WAS YOUR "*GOLDEN JEANS*" GIRL, DIDN'T YA?

AH, CANDY, MY LOVE... THE GIRL, DONNA, SHE'S'A *RIGHT*. YOU ARE'A *SPAGETT*! BUT THIS'A ONE-- SHE'S'A *PRIME FILLET*! MMMMM!

DONNA, LET ME GET *BACK* TO YOU, THIS IS GETTING *COMPLICATED*.

YEAH, I COULD USE SOME *FRESH AIR* ABOUT NOW. SEE YA *LATER*.

HOPE I DIDN'T CREATE ANY *PROBLEMS*, DONNA.

NOTHING I CAN'T *HANDLE*, KORY.

DONNA, THAT "*GOLDEN JEANS*" GIRL HE WAS TALKING ABOUT. WHAT *IS* IT?

GOOD MORNING, MISS TROY. YOUR PARTY'S *WAITING*.

THANKS, MAX.

BELIEVE ME, KORY, YOU DON'T WANT TO GET *INVOLVED*. IT'S, WELL...

DONNA, I'M OVER *HERE*!

AH, THERE'S MY *DATE*. C'MON, I'LL *INTRODUCE* YOU.

KORY, THIS IS *TERRY LONG*. TERRY, I'D LIKE YOU TO MEET...

DON'T *TELL* ME, HONEY. YOU'RE *KORIAND'R*, RIGHT?

DONNA'S TOLD ME ALL *ABOUT* YOU. YOU'RE AS *LOVELY* AS SHE SAID.

4

THE MID-MORNING SUN CASTS A SHIMMERING AURA OVER THE FACE OF TITANS' TOWER, A TEN-STORY SKYSCRAPER JUST OFF MANHATTAN'S EAST COAST...

YOU SURE YOU'LL BE *ALL RIGHT*, RAVEN?

I AM *CERTAIN*, RICHARD. I HAVE A *HOME* HERE NOW...

...AND I'VE SPOKEN TO *WALLACE*... ABOUT *US*, ABOUT *MANY* THINGS.

HE HAS CONVINCED ME THAT IT WOULD BE WISE NOW TO *LEARN* ABOUT YOUR PEOPLE AND THIS *CITY*...

BEING SHUNTED AWAY FOR SO MANY YEARS IN THE *TEMPLE AZARATH* HAS NOT PREPARED ME FOR THIS OUTSIDE *WORLD*.

WELL, THERE ARE *MANY* WAYS TO LEARN THINGS, RAVEN, BUT I'M SURE YOU'LL PICK WHAT'S BEST FOR *YOU*.

LISSEN, I'M KIND'A *LATE*... HAVE A SHOW AT THE *CIRCUS* I'M WORKING WITH NOW, THEN BACK TO *GOTHAM* TONIGHT...

SO I'LL SEE YOU AT THE NEXT *TITANS' MEETING*... IN ABOUT A *WEEK*.

TAKE CARE, RICHARD... AND *THANK YOU*.

AS THE SKYCYCLE SLIDES WESTWARD AWAY FROM NEW YORK CITY...

BETWEEN THE TITANS AND THE CIRCUS, I HAVEN'T HAD A REST IN *WEEKS*.

SURE COULD USE A *BREAK*... JUST TO GET MY *HEAD* TOGETHER.

MAN, I HOPE REJOINING THAT BIG TOP IS A GOOD *IDEA*.

BACK IN THE TITANS' TOWER...

WALLACE IS *RIGHT*, THERE IS *MUCH* I NEED TO *LEARN*.

1:05.

BUT, THIS *MANHATTAN UNIVERSITY* WALLACE SUGGESTED--?

STILL, IT *IS* A PLACE FOR LEARNING. VERY *WELL* THEN--

-- I SHALL LET MY SOUL-SELF *EXPLORE* THIS SCHOOL... SEE WHAT THERE IS TO *SEE*.

AND ONLY *THEN* SHALL I MAKE MY FINAL *DECISION*!

LIKE SOME GREAT GRIM *SHADOW*, RAVEN'S ASTRAL SELF RISES FROM THE MEDITATING FIGURE...

⑤

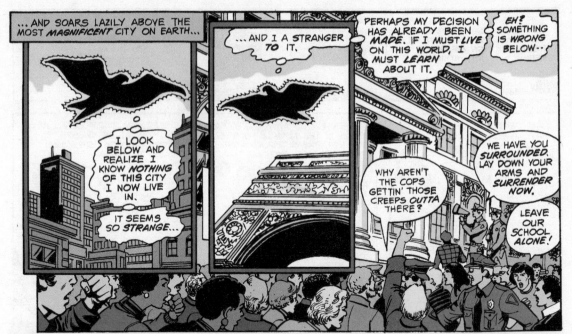

...AND SOARS LAZILY ABOVE THE MOST *MAGNIFICENT* CITY ON EARTH...

I LOOK BELOW AND REALIZE I KNOW *NOTHING* OF THIS CITY I NOW LIVE IN.

IT SEEMS SO *STRANGE*...

...AND I A STRANGER *TO* IT.

PERHAPS MY DECISION HAS ALREADY BEEN *MADE*. IF I MUST *LIVE* ON THIS WORLD, I MUST *LEARN* ABOUT IT.

EH? SOMETHING IS *WRONG* BELOW--

WHY AREN'T THE COPS GETTIN' THOSE CREEPS *OUTTA* THERE?

WE HAVE YOU *SURROUNDED*. LAY DOWN YOUR ARMS AND *SURRENDER* NOW.

LEAVE OUR SCHOOL *ALONE!*

I HEAR THEY'VE GOT A *BOMB!*

THIS IS NOT *RIGHT!* WE'RE THE *REVOLUTIONARIES*. THOSE KIDS ARE SUPPOSED TO SIDE WITH *US*.

PERHAPS THEY DO NOT *WANT* OUR REVOLUTION, *EH?* BUT IT DOES NOT *MATTER*.

THE BOMBS ARE *PLANTED*. THIS SCHOOL WILL *FALL*, AND OUR POINT WILL BE *MADE*.

THERE IS *NEVER* A POINT TO *VIOLENCE*.

MIKEL--? WH-WHAT *IS* THAT THING?

MIKEL?!?

--AND I WILL NOT PERMIT YOU TO CALLOUSLY *DESTROY* THIS WHICH IS SO *VALUABLE*.

BLAMM

6

212

BUT RAVEN IS *SILENT* AS HER LONG EBON CAPE *ENCIRCLES* THE FRIGHTENED TERRORIST. THE BLACKNESS OF SPACE SEEMS TO BURN WITHIN THE FOLDS OF HER SILKEN CLOAK...

SHE STANDS A SOMBER *SHADOW*...

WHILE, IN TITANS' TOWER, RAVEN'S *HUMAN* FORM SUDDENLY REALIZES THE *TIME*...

HER *SOUL-SELF* CANNOT BE *SEPARATED* FROM HER BODY FOR MORE THAN *FIVE SHORT MINUTES*...

FIFTY-EIGHT SECONDS REMAIN BEFORE AN UNSPEAKABLE *HORROR* WILL TRANSPIRE...

FIFTY-EIGHT SECONDS TO DO WHAT *MUST* BE DONE.

I AM NOT A *THING* --

I AM A *CONSCIENCE*, A HOPE, A PRAYER FOR UNDER-STANDING.

BUT, I HAVE *SEEN* SUCH PRAYERS ARE NOT *UNIVERSAL*, AND THUS I DO WHAT I CAN.

BUT THERE ARE DESTRUCTIVE *WEAPONS* HERE, AND THEY *MUST* BE DESTROYED IN TURN BEFORE INNOCENT PEOPLE ARE *HARMED*...

THE SECOND TERRORIST *FALLS.* HE IS *UNCONSCIOUS*, THOUGH NOT HARMED...

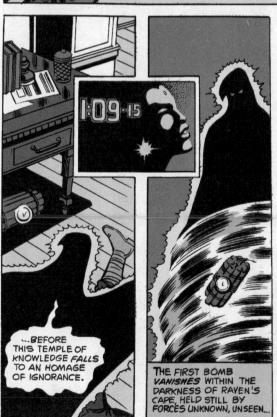

...BEFORE THIS TEMPLE OF KNOWLEDGE *FALLS* TO AN HOMAGE OF IGNORANCE.

THE FIRST BOMB *VANISHES* WITHIN THE DARKNESS OF RAVEN'S CAPE, HELD STILL BY FORCES UNKNOWN, UNSEEN...

...AS A SLEEK, BLACK *WRAITH* CUTS THROUGH THE UNIVERSITY'S HALLOWED HALLS...

RAVEN FEARS THE *HORRORS* THAT WILL COME IF SHE IS NOT *SUCCESSFUL*...

...AS SHE EQUALLY FEARS WHAT HORRORS MAY COME TO *HER* IF THAT SUCCESS TAKES EVEN A MOMENT *TOO LONG.*

THIRTY SECONDS REMAIN AS THE *SECOND* BOMB IS ENVELOPED BY THE GREAT EBON CLOAK...

7

I SENSE THE *FINAL BOMB*-- *GREAT AZAR!* ONE LAST *MADMAN*, BUT HE HOLDS *HOSTAGES!*

ARNIE-- L-LOOK! WHAT *IS* IT?

WHAT IN MARY'S NAME--? WHAT *ARE* YOU?

BUT RAVEN DOES NOT *ANSWER* THE RHETOR-ICAL QUESTIONS...

...KNOWING HOW *SHORT* TIME NOW IS...

INDEED, SHE MOVES WITH LIGHTNING-LIKE *SPEED*...

...REALIZING THAT, ONCE THE FIVE MINUTES ARE PAST, SHE WILL BE SUBJECTED TO *TERRORS* BEYOND ANY HUMAN COMPREHENSION...

BUT NOW THERE IS NO *FEAR* IN RAVEN'S MIND. INDEED, THERE IS ONLY AN INCREDIBLE *CALM* AS SHE RISES FROM THE VAST SCHOOL GROUNDS...

1:09:45

1:09:47

1:09:49

1:09:51

THE HUDSON RIVER IS TO THE *WEST*, AND SHE HOVERS ABOVE IT FOR JUST A LINGERING MOMENT...

1:09:53

1:09:55

BEFORE...

SKROOOM

ONLY *NOW* DOES THE FEAR BECOME *KEEN* IN HER MIND AS SHE ARCS ACROSS THE CITY BACK TOWARD TITANS' TOWER AND HER *HUMAN* SELF...

1:09:57

1:09:59

HER SOUL-SELF *STRAINS* WITH FRANTIC *TENSION*...

ONE SECOND REMAINS. THE TOWER LOOMS BEFORE HER...

1:10:00

ONE BRIEF *SECOND*...

ONE SECOND *TOO LATE.*

NO!

8

AN INTERLUDE...

GRAN'PA, THEY'RE REALLY GIVIN' 'WAY FREE TOYS? REALLY?

IT CERTAINLY DOES APPEAR TO BE THE CASE, JEREMY.

EXCUSE ME, SIR. I AM JEREMY THORNTON, AND I RECEIVED THIS INVITATION...?

AH, YES, MR. THORNTON-- THE FREE PUPPET. OH YES, HOLD ON, PLEASE.

IT IS FREE THEN? BUT WHY?

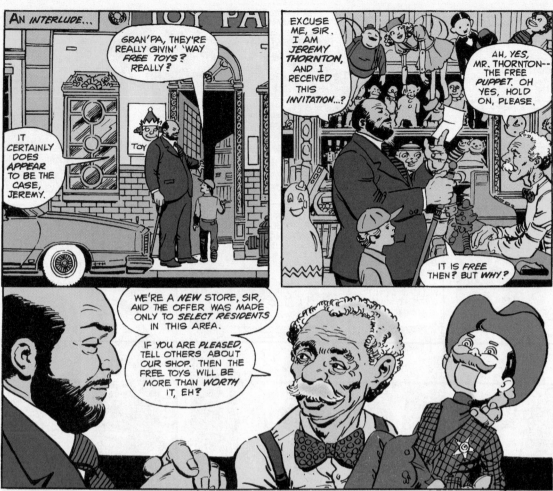

WE'RE A NEW STORE, SIR, AND THE OFFER WAS MADE ONLY TO SELECT RESIDENTS IN THIS AREA.

IF YOU ARE PLEASED, TELL OTHERS ABOUT OUR SHOP. THEN THE FREE TOYS WILL BE MORE THAN WORTH IT, EH?

WELL, YOUNG JEREMY SEEMS TAKEN BY IT.

IT'S REALLY FOR ME? NO FOOLIN'?

OH, YES, IT IS FOR YOU, CHILD. ENJOY IT.

BUT, ENJOYING THIS TENDER SCENE FROM A LONG DISTANCE...

WOW! THIS IS GREAT! WOW!

MASTER...

THERE HAS BEEN A PICKUP IN SHOP #3.

GOOD, GOOD. WHO WAS THE CUSTOMER?

JEREMY THORNTON OF DAYTON INDUSTRIES.

HE IS THE THIRD ONE, MASTER.

IT SEEMS THAT EVERYTHING IS GOING ACCORDING TO PLAN.

END OF INTERLUDE.

9

ELEVENTH AVENUE AND 44TH STREET IS NOT THE FIRST STOP ON THE NEW YORK TOUR BUS ROUTE. JUST BLOCKS AWAY FROM THE GLITTERING LIGHTS OF BROADWAY IT IS A DIRTY, FILTH-RIDDEN REMINDER THAT RICHES AND SQUALOR EXIST SIDE BY SIDE EVEN IN THE *GREATEST* METROPOLIS...

MOVING INTO YOUR *FATHER'S* APARTMENT?

NAH, THIS IS *MY* PLACE, LOGAN. I'M STAYING *PUT.*

BUT YOU DON'T *HAVE* TO LIVE HERE NOW. WITH THE MONEY FROM YOUR DAD'S *PATENTS...*

DON'T *HAVE* TO. BUT I *WANT* TO.

SO, YOU KNOW WHAT YOU'RE GONNA DO *NOW,* VIC?

YET, THIS POVERTY-TORN DISTRICT OF DESPAIR IS THE HOME AS WELL OF *VICTOR STONE,* ALSO KNOWN AS *CYBORG* OF THE NEW TEEN TITANS...

WHEN DAD DIED, SOMETHIN' *HAPPENED* TO ME. Y'KNOW, I *HATED* BEIN' THIS TIN-PLATED *MONSTER* HE TURNED ME INTO. WELL, I DON'T HATE IT *ANY-MORE.*

DON'T REALLY HATE *ANYTHIN'* ANYMORE.

BUT I GOTTA START REBUILDIN' MY *LIFE* NOW. FIGGER OUT WHAT I'M GONNA DO WITH MYSELF.

BRINGG!

AW, WHO'S CALLIN' *NOW?* PROBABLY SOMEONE TRYIN' TO *SELL* ME SOMETHIN'.

YEAH, *VIC STONE* HERE. WHO *IS* IT?

OOHHH ... LOGAN, IT'S FOR *YOU.*

SOME GUY WHO TALKS THROUGH HIS *NOSE.*

AHH, THE EVER-PRESENT *VERNON QUESTOR,* MY STEP-FATHER'S *BUSINESS MANAGER...*

YEAH, WHAT *IS* IT, QUESTOR? THIS IS *GAR LOGAN.*

LISSEN, IF THIS IS ABOUT SIGNING SOME MORE *STUPID PAPERS,* WELL, YOU CAN --

BUT, IN THE HAMPTONS ESTATE OF *STEVE DAYTON,* THE FIFTH RICHEST MAN IN THE WORLD...

MR. LOGAN, I ASSURE YOU THIS IS AN *EMERGENCY,* ONE THAT REQUIRES YOUR PERSONAL *ATTENTION.*

IT'S ABSOLUTELY *AWFUL,* MR. LOGAN. *SOREN WINSLOW* WAS JUST *SHOT TO DEATH,* SIR.

THAT MAKES *TWO* BOARD MEMBERS OF DAYTON INDUSTRIES IN *TWO DAYS,* SIR.

I FEAR, SIR, THAT SOMETHING IS VERY MUCH *AFOUL!*

10

OKAY, *OKAY*, I'LL GET RIGHT BACK HOME. JUST KEEP YOUR *SOCKS* ON. OKAY?

OH, MR. LOGAN, WHAT SHOULD WE *DO?* I'M IN A POSITIVE *DITHER* OVER THIS.

IF ONLY MR. DAYTON *HIMSELF* WERE HERE... BUT WE DON'T EVEN *KNOW* WHERE HE IS.

GOTTA *RUN*, VIC -- OR QUESTOR'LL *SHOOT* HIMSELF. I'M *NEEDED* BACK HOME.

HOME? I'VE SEEN *COUNTRIES* SMALLER'N YOUR PLACE.

I KNOW. MY BATHROOM AND KITCHEN ARE IN DIFFERENT *TIME ZONES.*

BUT, DIRECTLY OUTSIDE VIC STONE'S APARTMENT HOUSE...

MAN-O-MAN, *LOOKSEE* HERE. A *MEEEEN MACHINE.*

THERE'S GOTTA BE *FOUR HUNDRED* HORSES' RUNNIN' THIS BABY.

RUFFIE, THAT MAKES *200* HORSES *EACH*, AND I CAN CERTAINLY *LIVE* WITH *THAT.*

EARL, UMMM, EARL, PLEASE, EARL -- TELL ME I'M *SEEIN'* THINGS, EARL.

SEEIN' THINGS? YOU TURKEY, WHAT YOU MEAN --

-- OH *CRIPES!*

GONNA STEAL MY *CAR*, HUH? JOKERS, YOU MADE A *BIGGGG* MISTAKE!

LAST GUY WHO TRIED THAT... WELL, THEY'RE STILL PICKIN' *RHINO-HORN* DUST OUTTA HIS *BEHIND!*

WATCHING, VIC STONE *SMILES*, AND THE SMILE FEELS *GOOD.*

IT HAS BEEN SO LONG... *TOO* LONG.

HE **WALKS** THEN, UPTOWN FOR A WHILE, THINKING, WONDERING, DECIDING. THEN...

MARCY **LIVES** HERE...

...AND I HAVEN'T **SEEN** HER SINCE THE **ACCIDENT**.

USED TO BE REAL **CLOSE**, BUT THOSE DAYS **SEEM** LIKE THEY WERE CENTURIES IN THE **PAST**.

SHE'S PROBABLY GOT HERSELF A **NEW** GUY, BUT, MAYBE...

TIMIDLY, VIC STONE KNOCKS ON THE APARTMENT **DOOR**. A FEW SECONDS PASS SLOWLY BY, THEN...

WHO IS--? V-VICTOR?

YEAH, **HI**, MARCY. HOW **ARE** YOU?

B-BUT, I I THOUGHT, I HEARD... I MEAN, YOUR **ACCIDENT**. I THOUGHT IT WAS **SERIOUS**.

IT **WAS**. SO, HOW **ARE** YOU? DIDN'T **SAY**.

OKAY, I... YEAH, I'M **OKAY**.

VICTOR, I'M REALLY **SORRY** I NEVER CALLED. IT'S JUST-- VICTOR? YOUR ARM...

THEN, WHAT I HEARD... IT'S **TRUE**.

WHY **DIDN'T** YOU CALL, MARCY? I MEAN, IT WAS REAL **SERIOUS** BETWEEN US, AND THEN...

AFTER I HEARD WHAT **HAPPENED**, I... AND MY **PARENTS**, WELL THEY DIDN'T WANT--

WHAT **ABOUT** YOUR PARENTS, MARCY? WHAT DID **THEY** SAY?

Y-YOUR **FACE**!! VICTOR, MY GOD, OH, MY **GOD**.

VICTOR, PLEASE **UNDERSTAND**... MY MOM SAID SHE **SAW** YOU ON THE STREET... SHE TOLD ME SHE DIDN'T WANT ME TO EVER **SEE** YOU AGAIN.

WHY DID YOU **COME BACK** HERE, VICTOR? DIDN'T YOU KNOW THINGS COULDN'T BE THE **SAME** AGAIN?

GOD, VICTOR... WHY DIDN'T YOU JUST **DIE**, OR--

12

NO, I DON'T *MEAN* THAT. PLEASE, I REALLY DIDN'T *MEAN* IT, VICTOR.

IT'S JUST THAT I DIDN'T EXPECT TO EVER *SEE* YOU AGAIN...

VICTOR...?

DON'T HAFTA *EXPLAIN* YOURSELF, MARCY. I UNDERSTAND.

YOU *DON'T*, VICTOR... BUT MY PARENTS... I MEAN, WHILE I'M *LIVING* WITH THEM, I HAVE TO *LISTEN* TO THEM... *DON'T* I?

LOOK, I SAID IT'S *OKAY.* I'M NOT ANGRY.

GUESS I REALLY CAN'T GET TOO ANGRY AT *ANYTHING* NOW. I *KNOW* WHAT I AM, AND I EVEN LEARNED TO *LIVE* WITH IT.

IF YOU'VE GOT PROBLEMS *LOOKING* AT ME, IF YOUR PARENTS GOT PROBLEMS, WELL, THAT'S *YOUR* HANG-UPS, NOT *MINE.*

I'M NOT GONNA DESTROY MY LIFE BY BEIN' *BITTER.*

SEE YA AROUND, MARCY. OR BETTER YET, MAYBE I *WON'T.*

IF THAT DON'T BEAT *ALL.*

WOULD'VE EXPECTED THAT GARBAGE FROM ANYONE ELSE *BUT.*

GUESS I'VE BEEN HANGIN' 'ROUND THE *TITANS* SO MUCH THAT I FORGOT HOW *DIFFERENT* I REALLY AM.

I MEAN I ORIGINALLY JOINED 'EM JUST TO BE A FREAK *AMONGST* THE FREAKS.

BUT NOW I GOTTA REMEMBER I LIVE IN THE *REAL WORLD,* TOO. MY WHOLE LIFE CAN'T BE SPENT PLAYIN' *SUPER-HERO.*

CAN'T GO BACK TO BEIN' AN *ATHLETE,* EITHER... NOT WHEN I CAN RUN, JUMP, AN' PLAY BETTER'N *ANYONE!*

SO, WHAT'S *LEFT?* WHAT DO I *DO* WITH THE REST OF MY LIFE?

BONG!

HUH?

WHAT IN BLAZES? OHHH.

UHHH, MISTER...

YEAH? WHAT DO YOU WANT, KID?

MY BALL...

...please...?

YER BALL?

YER BALL?

AGAIN HE LAUGHS, A DEEP, PLEASANT LAUGH.

SURE, KID...

HIT ONE TO RIGHT FIELD FOR ME, HUH?

M-MISTER... YOUR HAND....!

NUTS! HE'S GONNA SCREAM. MUST THINK I'M SOME KIND'A MONSTER!

WOW, IT'S REAL NEAT. I WISH THEY GAVE ME ONE LIKE THAT.

BUT...

I MEAN, ALL THEY GAVE ME WAS THIS REG'LAR ONE.

HUH? I DON'T GET IT.

MY HAND. IT'S A PROS... PROSMETIC ...WELL, YOU KNOW...

A PROSTHETIC.... AN ARTIFICIAL ARM.

JOHNNY? WHAT'S TAKING YOU SO LONG? AND HAVEN'T I TOLD YOU NOT TO BOTHER-- OHHHH.

IT'S OKAY, MISS SIMMS. HE'S JUST LIKE US. HE'S GOT A PROS... A NEW HAND, TOO.

ONLY HIS IS REAL SHINY, AN' REAL NEAT.

SOMEONE PINCH ME AN' WAKE ME UP!

14

I SEE WHAT YOU *MEAN*. BUT YOU STILL SHOULDN'T BOTHER *STRANGERS*.

SO, WHO'S A *STRANGER?* MY NAME'S *VIC STONE.*

AND I'M *SARAH SIMMS*, THEIR *TEACHER*.

TEACHER? I DON'T *GET* IT.

ALL THESE KIDS GO TO A *SPECIAL SCHOOL*. THEY *ALL* HAVE PROSTHETICS OF *ONE* SORT OR ANOTHER.

AND THEY'RE OUT HERE, WELL, TO *RELEARN* THINGS... TO SHOW THEM THEY CAN LEAD A *FULL LIFE* AGAIN.

SOME OF THEM WEREN'T *SURE* BEFORE.

BUT NOW, THEY'RE LEARNING, ALMOST *FORGETTING* THEIR PROBLEMS.

MISS SIMMS, C'N HE *PLAY* WITH US? C'N HE, C'N HE?

KIDS, HE'S PROBABLY VERY *BUSY*, AND...

BUSY? MISS SIMMS, SOMEHOW I DON'T THINK I GOT ANYTHIN' MORE *IMPORTANT* TO DO THAN PLAY SOME *BALL*.

MAN, NEVER THOUGHT I'D SAY *THAT* AGAIN.

SO YOU SIT DOWN AN' *RELAX*.

ME? I'M ABOUT TO HAVE SOME *LONG OVERDUE FUN!*

C'MON, YOU CRUMMY KIDS -- LAST ONE TO THE DIAMOND'S A LOUSY *IMPERIAL STORMTROOPER!*

ELSEWHERE...

FIRST *DARKNESS*. THICKER AND DEEPER THAN THE BLACKEST *BLACK*. THEN, SUDDENLY MAD COLORS, SWIRLING, WHIRLING, WRENCHING FORMS AND SHAPES. COLD, THEN HOT, THEN *COLD* AGAIN.

IT IS *INSANITY* GONE ONE FURTHER STEP *INSANE*.

NO!

15

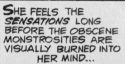

SHE FEELS THE *SENSATIONS* LONG BEFORE THE OBSCENE MONSTROSITIES ARE VISUALLY BURNED INTO HER MIND...

COLD CARESSES HER WITH FEARSOME, FRIGID FINGERS, PULLING AT HER, CLUTCHING AT HER, TUGGING HER DOWN, DOWN, EVER *DOWN*...

SHE *RESISTS*, FIGHTING, CLAWING, BUT THE SENSATIONS ARE *EVERYWHERE* AND THEY PRESS SO *HEAVILY* UPON HER WRITHING FLESH...

COLD SO KEEN, SO PAINFUL, IT IS LIKE AN ARCTIC HOARFROST.

SHE DIVES LOW TO *AVOID* THE OMNIPRESENT ICY HANDS...

BUT, THE COLD ABRUPTLY *ENDS*.

HEAT FROM DEEP WITHIN GROUND THAT HAD NOT EXISTED EVEN A MOMENT BEFORE SUDDENLY RUSHES UP TO *BLANKET* HER. HER SKIN HARDENS, TENSES AS BOILING WATERS HOLD HER IN AN INESCAPABLE GRIP.

AGAIN SHE IS BROUGHT DOWN TUMBLING WILDLY TOWARD THE GREAT FRANGIBLE GLASS-LIKE *MEMBRANE* WHICH FLOATS CALMLY IN THE DIMENSIONAL SEAS SO VERY FAR BELOW...

SHE TRIES RESISTING, BUT ANY FIGHT IS *USELESS* NOW.

16

IN A MOMENT SHE IS PULLED THROUGH, SHATTERING THE BOUNDS OF REALITIES...

AND, AS SHE IS DRAWN ALONG, PUSHED FURTHER INTO THE *DEPTHS*, RHYTHMIC PULSES OF HEAT THEN COLD THEN *HEAT* AGAIN LURE HER ON HER HEADLONG PLUNGE...

UNCONSCIOUSNESS PHASES IN AND OUT AS SHE IS HELPLESSLY DRAGGED ALONG BY THE OTHERDIMENSIONAL *UNDERTOW.*

THE FIRST SENSATIONS *FADE* NOW, HER JANGLED THOUGHTS RETURN AS SHE SPIES THE SWIRLING *WIND-TUNNEL* DRAWING HER DEEPER, EVER DEEPER TOWARD SOME PHANTOM *LIGHT* SO VERY FAR AWAY.

FOR THE FIRST TIME IN THESE BOTH PAINFUL AND PLEASURABLE MOMENTS, RAVEN CAN THINK...

IS *THIS* WHAT OCCURS WHEN I EXCEED THAT FIVE-MINUTE *LIMIT?*

I'VE BEEN THRUST INTO A *WORLD GONE MAD* --OR...

NO! THIS IS ANOTHER DIMENSION, ONE TRYING TO DESTROY MY *SOUL*....

...PREVENTING ME FROM REJOINING MY *HUMAN SELF!*

BUT I MUST RE-FORM OR BE LOST *FOREVER* IN THIS ETERNAL *INSANITY!*

SHE CONTINUES FLOATING DOWN TOWARD THE WARM NIMBUS OF BURNING ENERGY.

(17)

THE AFTERNOON SUN WARMS THE LENGTH AND BREADTH OF *BLUE VALLEY*, BASKING THE SMALL MID-WESTERN TOWN IN A GOLDEN HALO OF LIGHT.

...I DON'T *KNOW*, DAD, I JUST WISH I *DID*.

BUT, THE TRANQUILITY OF THIS PICTURESQUE SCENE IS AT ODDS WITH THE RAGING TURMOIL IN THE BREAST OF ONE WALLY WEST...

I *ENJOY* BEING A SUPER-HERO, I *DO*... ...BUT I REALLY WANT TO GO TO *COLLEGE*.

I WISH I COULD *HELP* YOU, SON, BUT THIS HAS GOT TO BE *YOUR* CHOICE.

IS THERE A WAY YOU CAN DO *BOTH*?

OF *COURSE* THERE IS, YES. BUT I DON'T *KNOW* IF I SHOULD DO BOTH.

BLAST IT, DAD. OTHER KIDS DON'T HAVE THESE PROBLEMS. THEY GO TO SCHOOL, GO OUT ON DATES, THEY HAVE *REAL* LIVES.

BUT NOT *ME*, NO SIR, I'M NOT THAT *LUCKY*. I DIDN'T *ASK* TO BE SPECIAL--

DIDN'T *ASK* TO HAVE LIGHTNING SPILL ALL THOSE *CHEMICALS* OVER ME...

...CHANGING ME, GIVING ME THE POWER OF *SUPER-SPEED*...

...THE SAME WAY *BARRY ALLEN* WAS TURNED INTO *THE FLASH*.

I'M *DIFFERENT*, AND I DIDN'T WANT TO BE.

DIFFERENT ISN'T *BAD*, SON. DON'T *THINK* OF IT THAT WAY.

HONEY, I CLEANED YOUR *COSTUME*. WHERE DO YOU WANT IT?

I'LL TAKE IT, MOM. AND MOM-- WHAT DO *YOU* THINK?

I MEAN, ABOUT *ME*... AND *KID FLASH*?

WHAT DO I THINK, HONEY? YOU DON'T TELL ME *EVERYTHING* ABOUT WHAT YOU DO, AND MAYBE THAT'S FOR THE *BEST*.

BUT, I DO *WORRY* ABOUT YOU. ABOUT WHAT YOU DO.

18

YOUR POWERS GIVE YOU AN AWFUL LOT OF *RESPONSIBILITY* FOR SOMEONE YOUR AGE...

BUT I'VE ALSO SEEN THE WAY THEY'VE *MATURED* YOU. THE BOYS WHO WERE YOUR *FRIENDS* YEARS AGO--THEY SEEM SO MUCH *YOUNGER* THAN YOU.

I MISS THE FACT YOU'RE NO LONGER A *LITTLE BOY*. BUT YOU'VE BECOME A GOOD MAN...

...AND I'M SO VERY *PROUD* OF THAT.

I *TRY* TO DO RIGHT, BUT LATELY I'M NOT EVEN SURE WHAT RIGHT *IS*.

SON, YOU DON'T HAVE TO MAKE YOUR DECISIONS *NOW*. YOU'RE JUST STARTING OUT. YOU STILL HAVE TIME TO HAVE *DREAMS*.

I WISH I KNEW WHAT TO *DO*.

I WANTED TO GO TO *EUROPE* WHEN I WAS YOUR AGE, MAYBE EVEN *LIVE* THERE.

BUT THE WAR TOOK ME *AWAY*, AND I HAD TO GET A *JOB* WHEN I RETURNED HOME. THEN YOUR MOTHER AND I GOT *MARRIED*.

WHAT I'M SAYING, SON, IS--*REALIZE* YOUR DREAMS, DO WHAT YOU FEEL INSIDE YOU IS *RIGHT*, AND WE'LL *BACK* YOU ALL THE WAY.

AND NOW, IF YOU DON'T MIND, HOW ABOUT *DINNER*? I'M STARVING.

I HAD A *HUNCH* YOU WERE UPSET, HONEY, SO I ROASTED YOUR *FAVORITE*...

...WITH *CHESTNUT DRESSING* AND FRESH *CRANBERRY* AS WELL.

AW, YOU DIDN'T HAVE TO, MOM.

SHHHH! DON'T *KNOCK* IT. I LOVE TURKEY.

AHEM, THERE'S THE LITTLE MATTER OF *CARVING* THIS BIRD NOW.

BUT I'M RATHER *BUSHED*. YOU DO IT FOR ME, SON.

BUT YOU ALWAYS CARVE THE TURKEY. IT'S A *TRADITION*.

THE *TRADITION* IS FOR THE CARVING TO BE DONE BY THE *MAN OF THE HOUSE*...

...SON!

AND THE SUN CONTINUES TO SHINE OVER BLUE VALLEY...

THE UNDULAT-ING LIGHT BATHES RAVEN'S GLOWING BODY WITH AN AURA OF BURNING *FISSION* AS SHE REACHES DEEP INTO HER SELF TOWARD THE CENTER OF HER BEING.

SHE HAS LEARNED TO *CONTROL* HER EVERY THOUGHT, TO USE HER MIND TO DRAW FORTH FROM ITS DARKEST RECESSES WHATEVER IS NOW NEEDED.

THE PAST MINUTES HAVE BEEN FILLED WITH *FEAR*, BUT SHE FORCES HERSELF *CALM*, FORCES THE INTRUDING TERRORS TO BE *BANISHED* FROM HER THOUGHTS.

BUT...

IMAGES, DARK AND TERRIBLE-- THEY SEEK TO *SHATTER* MY FORCED *TRANQUILITY.*

I *UNDERSTAND* IT NOW--I UNDERSTAND IT *ALL!*

MY SOUL AND BODY ARE *APART*... AND THESE DEMONS, THE DEMONS THAT LIVE IN US ALL-- THEY SEEK TO FURTHER *SEPARATE* MY SELVES!

TO PLUNGE ME EVER DEEPER INTO MY OWN *DESPAIR!*

BUT, I WILL NOT LET THEM *SUCCEED!*

I CAN *CONQUER* WHAT I AM... CONQUER MY OWN *FEARS*... CONQUER THE VERY *FORCES* WITHIN ME THAT SEEK TO TEAR ME *ASUNDER!*

I CAN CONQUER THEM *ALL*-- AND I WILL EMERGE *TRIUMPHANT!*

AND, IN AN INSTANT, ALL IS *GONE.*

20

I...AM BACK IN *TITANS' TOWER*... MY SOUL-SELF AND I ARE *WHOLE* AGAIN.

BUT, ALL THE *OTHERS* FROM THE TEMPLE AZARATH-- THEY WARNED ME THERE WAS NO *ESCAPE* FROM THE TERRORS I'D BEHOLD IF MY BODY AND SOUL WERE *SEPARATED* FOR TOO LONG.

THE *OTHERS*--? OF COURSE! THEIR VERY *PHILOSOPHY* PREVENTS THEM FROM *RESISTING*. THEY WERE *INCAPABLE* OF FIGHTING FOR THEIR OWN LIVES. BUT *I*--

I *FOUGHT!* I *RESISTED!* I CARED *TOO* MUCH FOR LIFE TO THROW IT AWAY.

THUS WHERE *THEY* FAILED, I *SUCCEEDED!*

I'VE CONQUERED THAT *FINAL BOUNDARY*. NEVER AGAIN SHALL I FEAR ITS COLD EMBRACE.

SHE STANDS TALL AND PROUD, FOR SHE HAS FACED THE METTLE OF HER COURAGE, AND SHE IS PLEASED WITH WHAT SHE HAS SEEN.

"*PERFECT! GREAT! JUST GREAT! ANOTHER* ONE NOW! YEAH... JUST *RIGHT!* PERFECT! NOW, TURN...HEAD BACK!

"*PERFECT, JUST PERFECT! GREAT! TURN AGAIN! HEAD BACK NOW. RIGHT! PERFECT! ABSOLUTELY GREAT!*"

21

I DON'T KNOW ABOUT *YOU*, DONNA, BUT I'M *ENJOYING* THIS.

I'LL *REMEMBER* THAT, TERRY. NEXT TIME I BRING ALONG A *BLINDFOLD*!

OKAY, KORY, THAT'S A *WRAP*!

I'LL SHOW THESE TO *CARL* WHEN THEY'RE DEVELOPED!

SHE'D MAKE A GREAT *MODEL*, DONNA.

OKAY, OKAY, JUST PULL THOSE *EYES* BACK IN, WILLYA?

YOU'RE MY GUY, AND DON'T YOU *FORGET* IT.

WELL, EXCUUUUUSE ME!

THAT'S *BETTER*!

YOU NEVER SAID ANYTHING ABOUT TERRY *BEFORE*, DONNA. WHEN DID YOU TWO *MEET*?

ABOUT A *YEAR* AGO, RIGHT AFTER MY *DIVORCE*!

AND MEETING DONNA WAS THE *GREATEST* THING THAT EVER *HAPPENED* TO ME.

I BET YOU SAY THAT TO *ALL* THE GIRLS WHO MADLY *LOVE* YOU.

I MUST SAY THIS HAS BEEN AN *ENJOYABLE* DAY... THE FIRST REALLY GOOD DAY I'VE HAD HERE ON EARTH SINCE... OOOPS! WAS I SUPPOSED TO SAY THAT, DONNA?

IT'S OKAY, KORIAND'R... TERRY *KNOWS*.

IT CERTAINLY SET ME *BACK* A LITTLE WHEN DONNA TOLD ME WHO SHE *WAS*.

BUT THEN I FIGURED, IF SHE'S A *WONDER* GIRL, I MUST BE SOME KIND OF WONDER GUY.

AND NOW, KORY, SINCE DONNA AND I HAVE A *DINNER* AND LATE NIGHT *DATE*...

IT'S BEEN A REAL *PLEASURE*.

YOU *TOO*, KORY. LISTEN, DON'T *WAIT* UP FOR ME, OKAY?

'BYE, HAVE A GOOD TIME.

H...HE KISSED MY HAND?

I DON'T KNOW *WHY*...

...BUT I CERTAINLY *ENJOYED* IT.

22

DONNA IS LUCKY TO HAVE FOUND SUCH A *NICE MAN.* I HOPE I--

HMMM. THOSE *BIRDS*... THEY SEEM SO CARE-FREE AND HAPPY.

WELL, I HAVE NOTHING *ELSE* TO DO TONIGHT...

...AND DONNA DID SAY I SHOULD *ENJOY* MYSELF...

I'VE GOT MY *STARFIRE* COSTUME RIGHT HERE, SO...

O NEWS DAI
E 21-8 ALIE
UPSET IMP

OOOHHH! FREE AT LAST, FREE TO *FLY,* FREE TO *BREATHE.* I *LOVE* IT!

THE AIR IS GETTING *COOLER,* BUT IT'S STILL SO *DELIGHTFUL.*

I *LOVE* BEING HERE. THIS *EARTH,* IT'S ALMOST AS MUCH A *PARADISE* AS HOME.

HOME--? *THIS* IS MY HOME NOW!

KORIAND'R ...OF THE PLANET *EARTH!*

I LOVE IT... I *LOVE* IT!

AND *YOU,* MY LITTLE WINGED FRIENDS, I HOPE *YOU* LOVE IT AS WELL!

23

SHE RISES HIGH INTO THE AIR, TURNING, CIRCLING, LETTING THE COOL NIGHT AIR *REFRESH* HER...

BUT, THE UNBRIDLED JOY OF TOTAL FREEDOM DOES NOT LAST *LONG*, FOR...

OH, NO-- *TROUBLE* ON THE *GROUND!*

THAT HORSE AND CARRIAGE SEEMS TO HAVE *BROKEN FREE,* AND--

THAT *CHILD*... JUST *LYING* THERE. THERE'S NO WAY TO GET HIM *OUT* OF THE WAY IN TIME.

X'HAL! HE'LL BE *CRUSHED!*

CAN'T REACH THE *CHILD*, BUT MY STARBOLTS CAN STILL STOP THE *HORSE*.

HAVE TO *TEMPER* MY BLAST... ENOUGH TO ONLY *STUN* THE HORSE BUT NOT ENOUGH TO *HARM* HIM.

AHHH... THERE ...THE BOY IS *SAFE*, AND ONCE MORE ALL IS *WELL*.

IT IS GROWING *DARK*. ANOTHER DAY IS *OVER*, AND I HAVE NOTHING *MORE* TO DO THAN--

OR, MAYBE I *DO* HAVE SOMETHING TO DO.

I WONDER WHAT *DICK* IS UP TO TONIGHT?

MMMMMM!

GOTHAM CITY HOME OF TH 100 MILL

THE DAY *ENDS* AS IT *BEGAN*, FILLED WITH *WARMTH*, AND BRIMMING WITH *HOPE*.

24

EPILOGUE:

A TWINKLING PANORAMA OF STARS CLOAKS MANHATTAN IN AN ALMOST PERFECT NIGHT.

JEREMY, TIME FOR *BED.*

YOUR *PARENTS* WILL BE HOME TOMORROW, AND I HAVE MY *WORK* TO KEEP ME BUSY.

G'NITE, GRAN'PA. I WISH I COULD *STAY* WITH YOU *MORE* I REALLY *LIKE* IT.

AND I LOVE *HAVING* YOU HERE, JEREMY. NOW, GO TO *SLEEP.*

UNHHH, I'M GETTING A BIT *TOO OLD* TO KEEP UP WITH THAT YOUNGSTER.

MY *BACK!* CERTAINLY COULD USE A NICE WARM *BATH*...

...AFTER I GET THESE *REPORTS* OUT OF THE WAY.

"PROJECT: PROMETHIUM" ...I'LL BE HAPPY WHEN *THIS* IS DONE-- EH?

JEREMY! IS THAT *YOU* OUT THERE?

I *TOLD* YOU, JEREMY-- NOTHING MORE TO *DRINK*--

OH, MY GOODNESS...

MY *GOD!*

BANG!!!!!

AHAHAHAHA...

THE BEGINNING OF PROJECT: PROMETHIUM, AND POSSIBLY THE END OF THE NEW TEEN TITANS.

NEXT ISSUE: **PERIL OF THE PUPPETEER!**

231

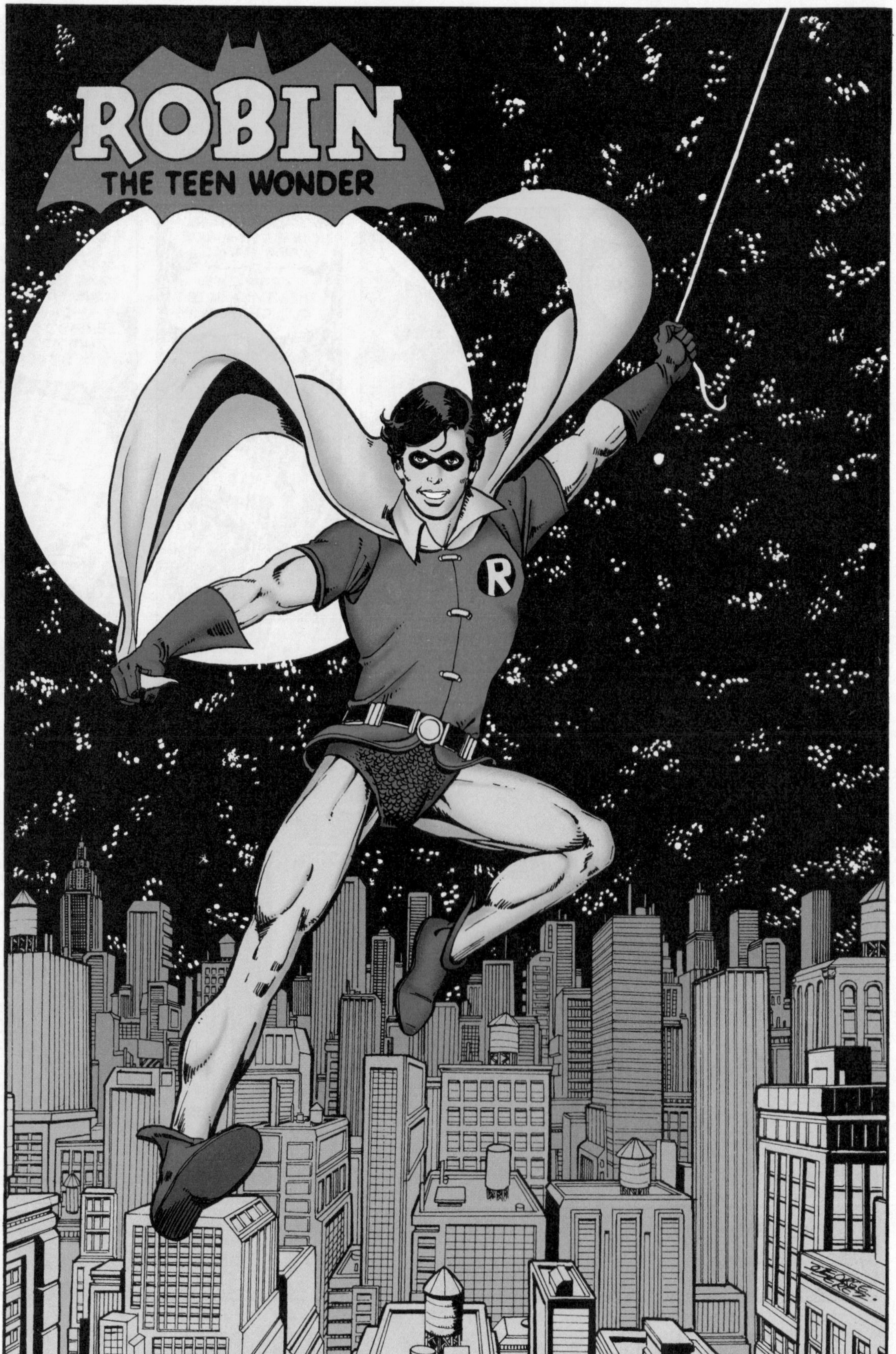
ROBIN
THE TEEN WONDER
™

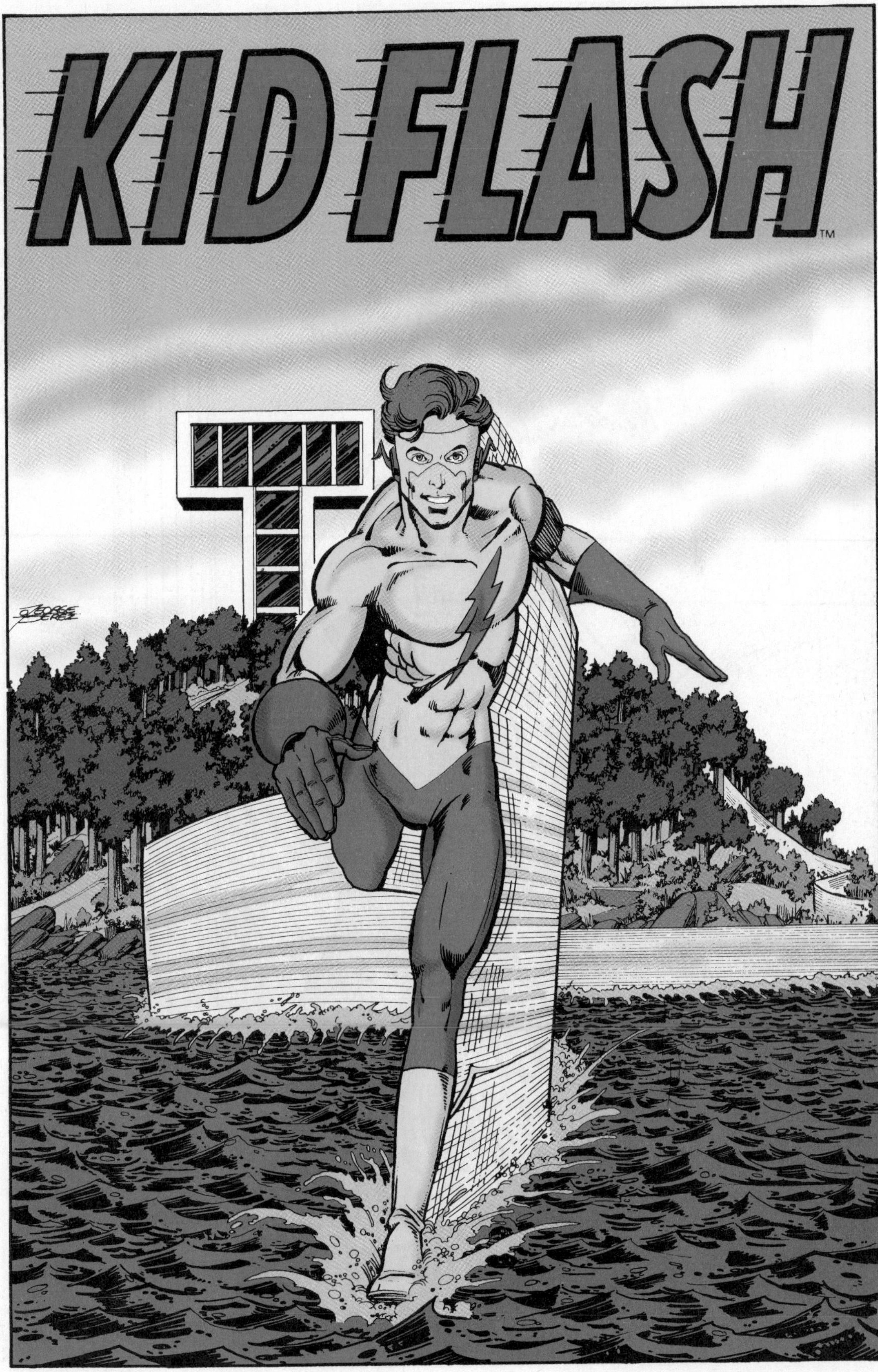
KID FLASH™

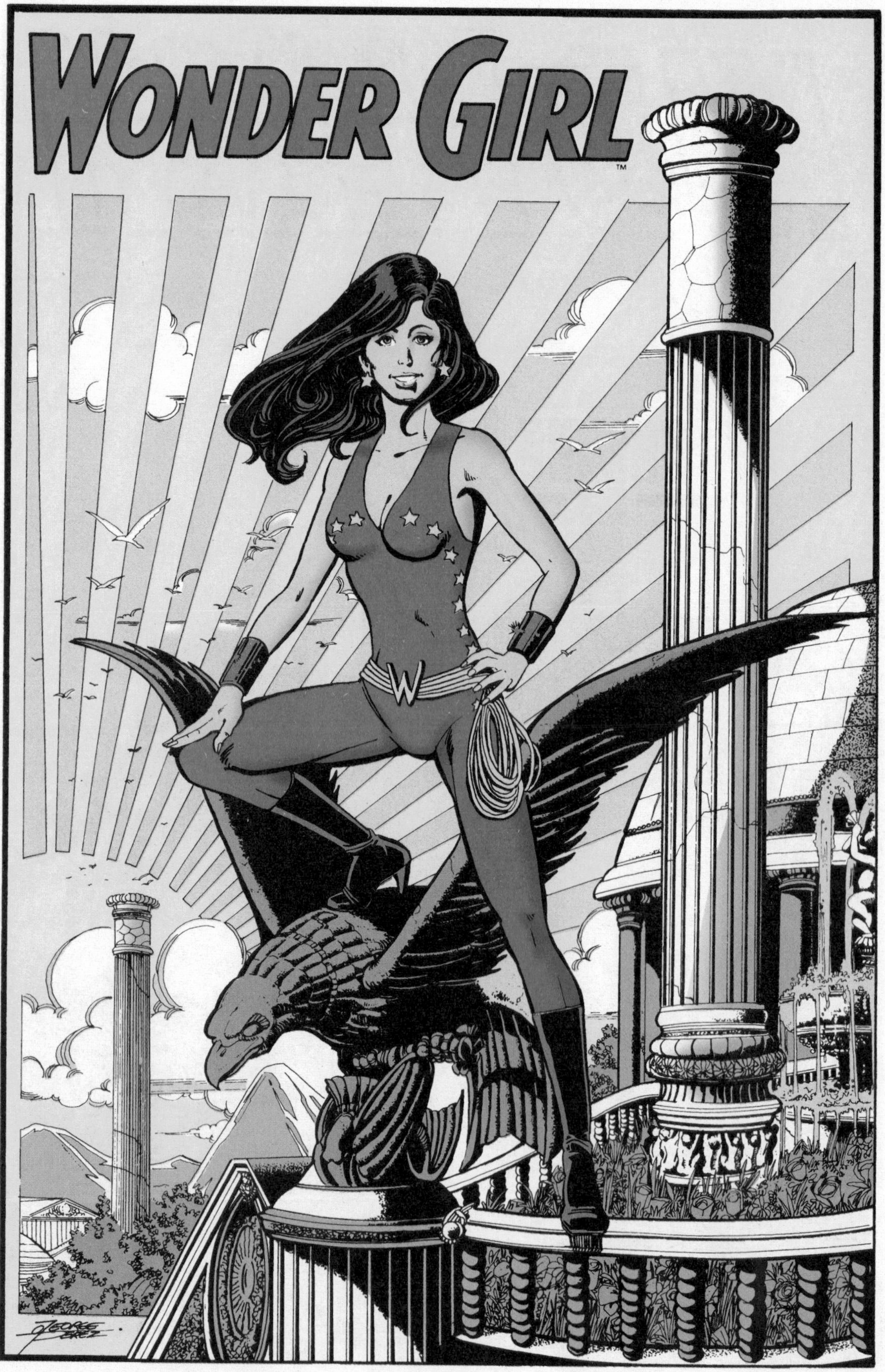
WONDER GIRL
™

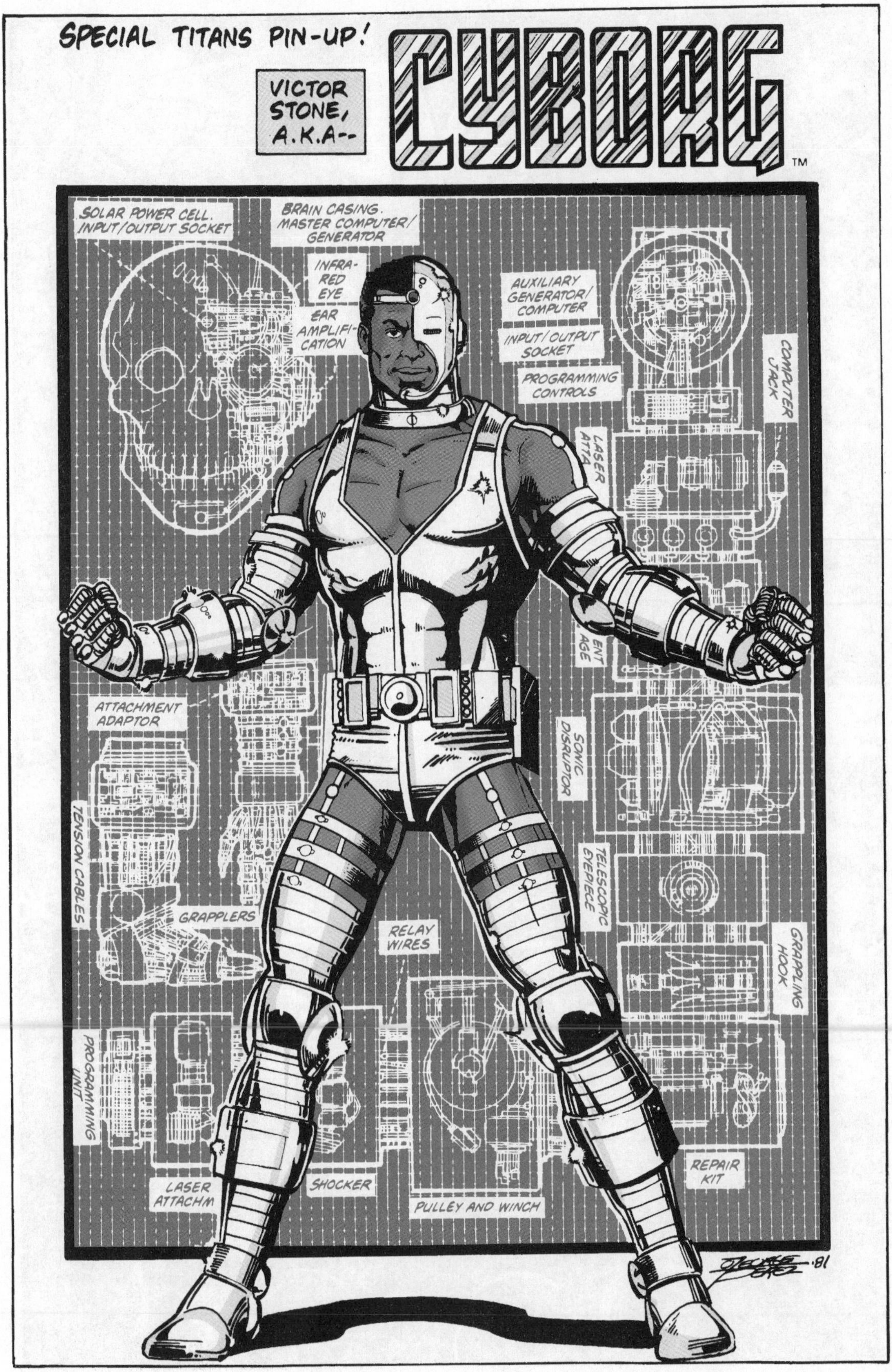

SPECIAL TITANS PIN-UP!
VICTOR STONE, A.K.A--
CYBORG™
SOLAR POWER CELL. INPUT/OUTPUT SOCKET
BRAIN CASING. MASTER COMPUTER/ GENERATOR
INFRA-RED EYE
EAR AMPLIFI-CATION
AUXILIARY GENERATOR/ COMPUTER
INPUT/OUTPUT SOCKET
PROGRAMMING CONTROLS
COMPUTER JACK
LASER ATTA
ENT AGE
ATTACHMENT ADAPTOR
SONIC DISRUPTOR
TENSION CABLES
TELESCOPIC EYEPIECE
GRAPPLERS
RELAY WIRES
GRAPPLING HOOK
PROGRAMMING UNIT
REPAIR KIT
LASER ATTACHM
SHOCKER
PULLEY AND WINCH

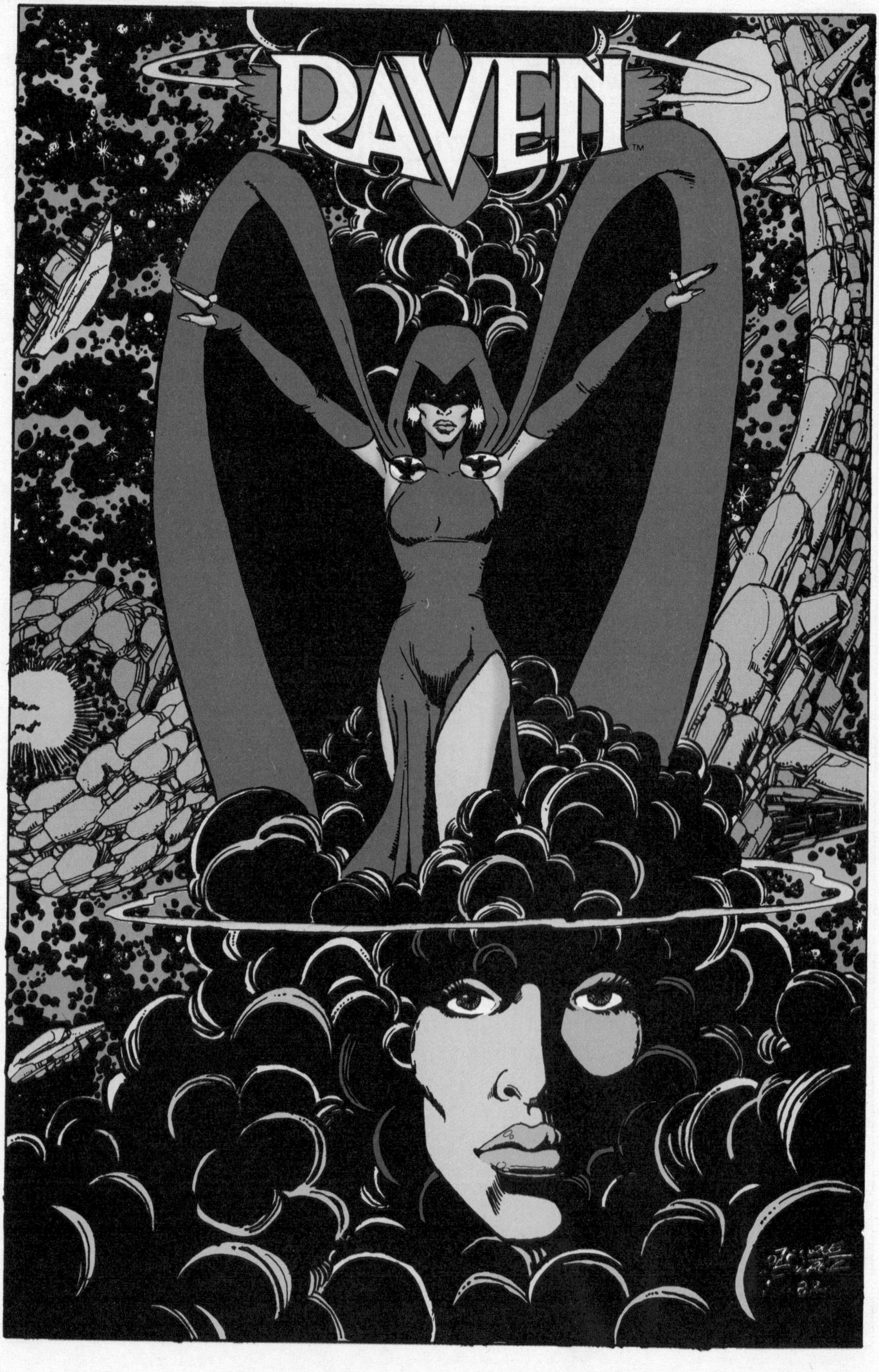
RAVEN™

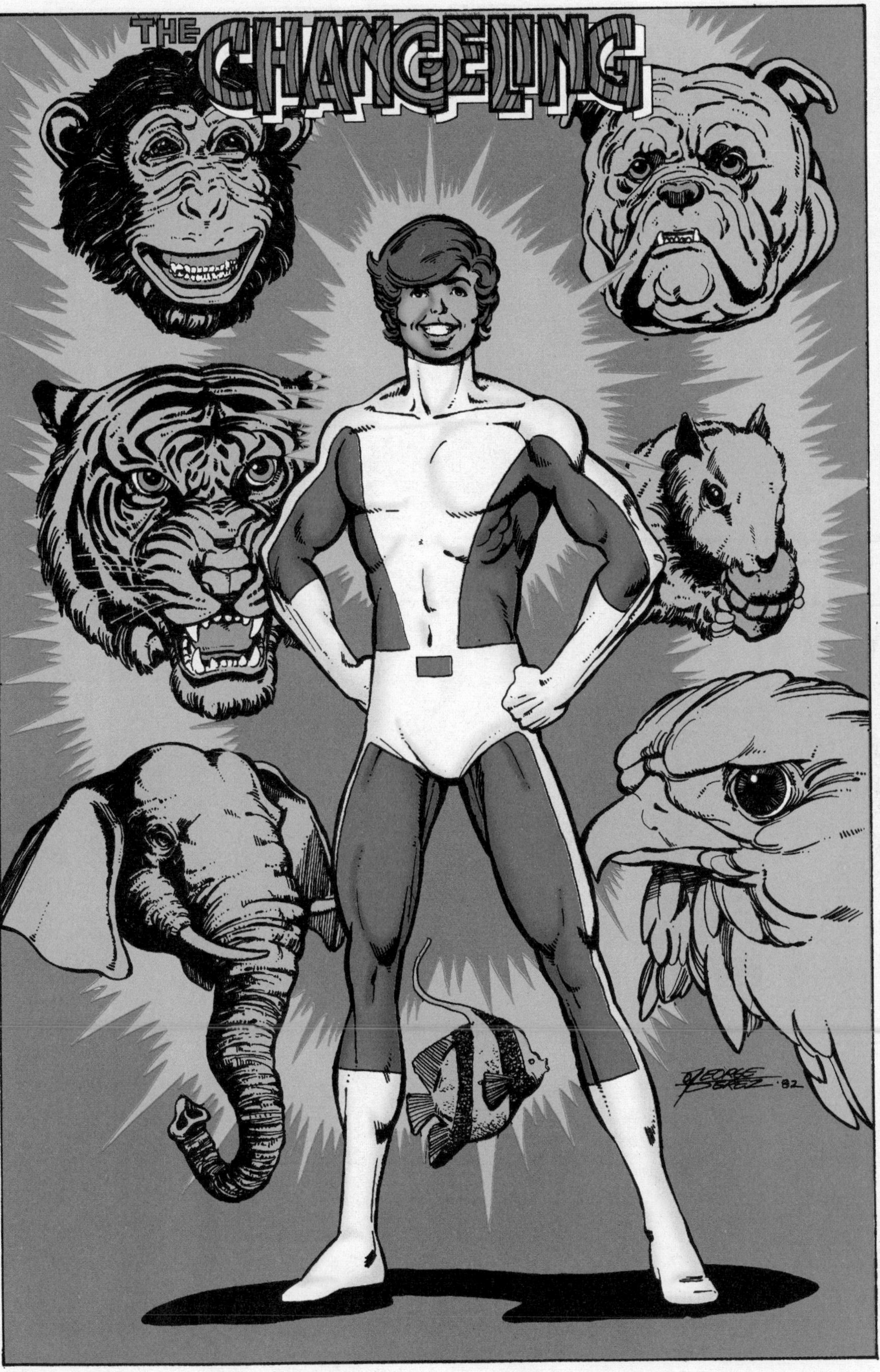
THE CHANGELING
GEORGE PEREZ '82

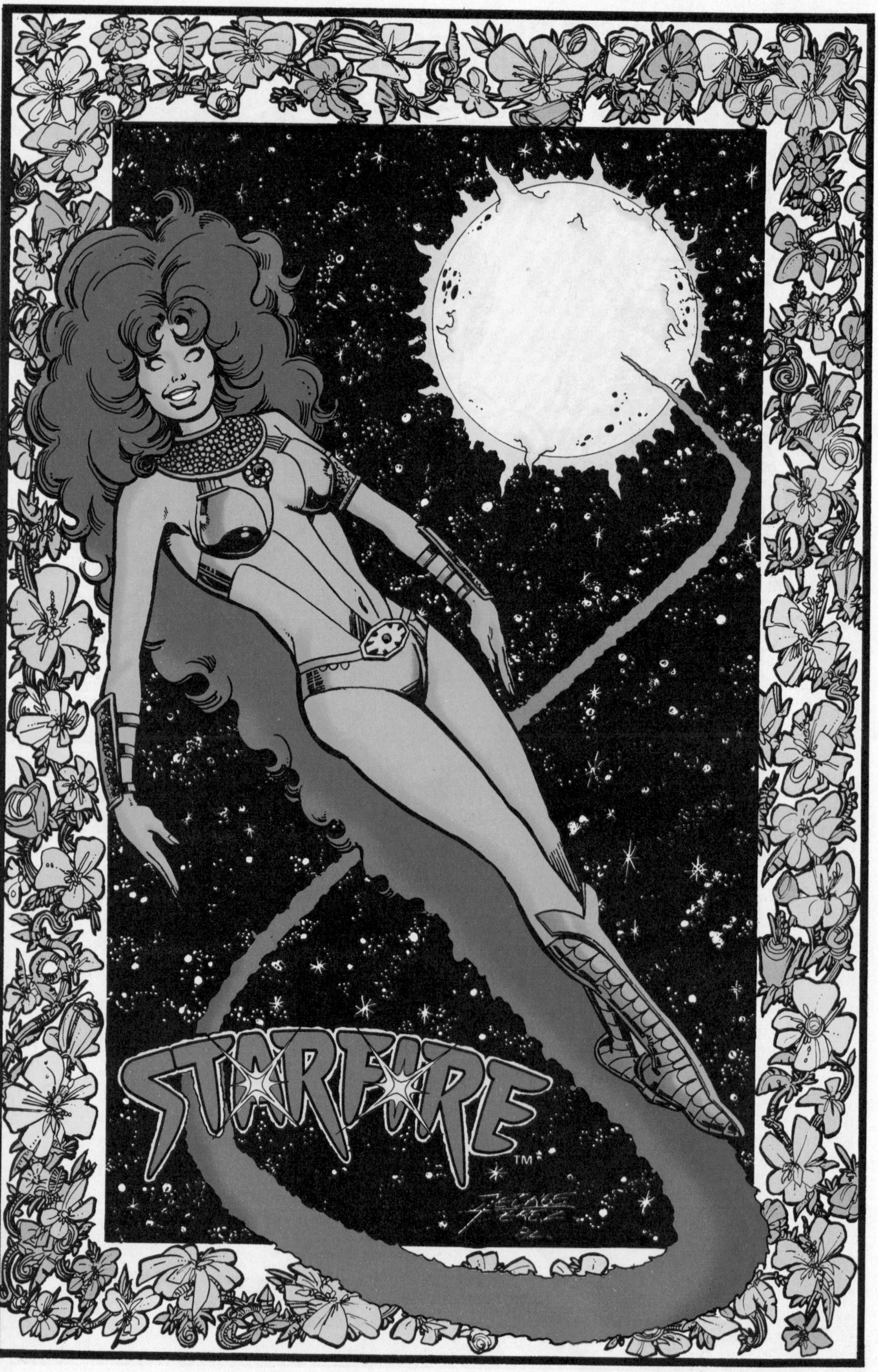
STARFIRE
TM

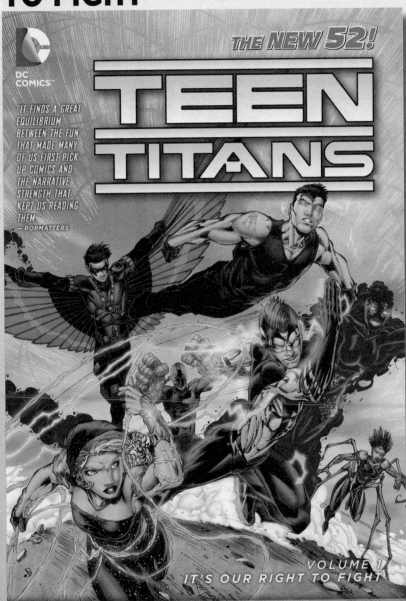

DC COMICS™

START AT THE BEGINNING!

NIGHTWING
VOLUME 1: TRAPS AND TRAPEZES

**NIGHTWING VOL. 2:
NIGHT OF THE OWLS**

**NIGHTWING VOL. 3:
DEATH OF THE FAMILY**

**BATMAN:
NIGHT OF THE OWLS**

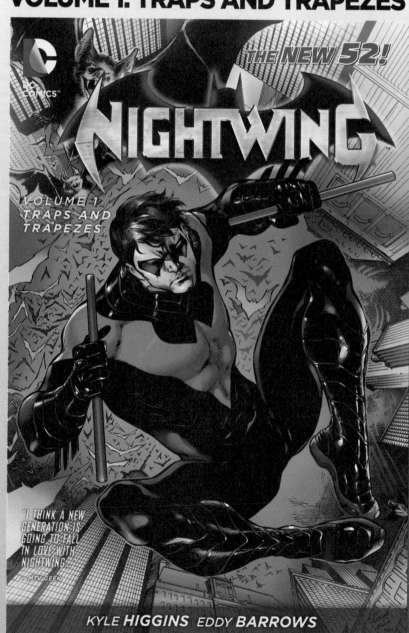

KYLE **HIGGINS** EDDY **BARROWS**